CONGO STORIES

CONGO STORIES

*Battling Five Centuries
of Exploitation and Greed*

JOHN PRENDERGAST AND FIDEL BAFILEMBA

Foreword by Soraya Aziz Souleymane
Postscript by Dave Eggers
Afterword by Chouchou Namegabe
Illustrations by Sam Ilus
Photographs by Ryan Gosling

GRAND
CENTRAL
PUBLISHING

NEW YORK BOSTON

Grand Central Publishing
Hachette Book Group
1290 Avenue of the Americas, New York, NY 10104
grandcentralpublishing.com
twitter.com/grandcentralpub

First Edition: December 2018

Grand Central Publishing is a division of Hachette Book Group, Inc. The Grand Central Publishing name and logo is a trademark of Hachette Book Group, Inc.

The website www.congostories.org and the other websites referred to in this book are independent entities not affiliated with the Hachette Book Group.

The publisher is not responsible for websites (or their content) that are not owned by the publisher.

"Map: The Congo in 1990" from *King Leopold's Ghost* by Adam Hochschild. Copyright © 1998 by Adam Hochschild. Reprinted by permission of Houghton Mifflin Harcourt Publishing Company. All rights reserved.

Print book interior design by Faceout Studio, Paul Nielsen

Library of Congress Cataloging-in-Publication Data
Names: Prendergast, John, author. | Bafilemba, Fidel, author. |
Souleymane, Soraya Aziz, writer of foreword. | Eggers, Dave, writer of
postface. | Namegabe, Chouchou, writer of afterword. | Ilus, Sam,
illustrator. | Gosling, Ryan, photographer.
Title: Congo stories : battling five centuries of exploitation and greed /
text by John Prendergast and Fidel Bafilemba ; foreword by Soraya Aziz
Souleymane ; postscript by Dave Eggers ; afterword by Chouchou Namegabe ;
illustrations by Sam Ilus ; photographs by Ryan Gosling.
Description: First edition. | New York, NY : Grand Central Publishing, a
division of Hachette Book Group, 2018.
Identifiers: LCCN 2018021726| ISBN 9781455584642 (hardcover) | ISBN
9781549194788 (audio download) | ISBN 9781455584611 (ebook)
Subjects: LCSH: Congo (Democratic Republic)—History. | Congo (Democratic
Republic)—Politics and government. | Congo (Democratic
Republic)—Economic conditions—1960- | Resource curse—Congo (Democratic
Republic) | Mines and mineral resources—Political aspects—Congo
(Democratic Republic)
Classification: LCC DT658 .P74 2018 | DDC 967.5103—dc23
LC record available at https://lccn.loc.gov/2018021726

ISBN: 978-1-4555-8464-2 (hardcover), 978-1-4555-8461-1 (ebook)

Printed in the United States of America

WORZALLA

10 9 8 7 6 5 4 3 2 1

Contents

"To be hopeful in bad times is not just foolishly romantic.

It is based on the fact that human history is a history not only of cruelty,

but also of compassion, sacrifice, courage, kindness.

What we choose to emphasize in this complex history will determine our lives.

If we see only the worst, it destroys our capacity to do something.

If we remember those times and places—and there are so many—where people

have behaved magnificently, this gives us the energy to act, and at

least the possibility of sending this spinning top of a world in a different direction. And if we do act,

in however small a way, we don't have to wait for

some grand utopian future. The future is an infinite succession of presents,

and to live now as we think human beings should live,

in defiance of all that is bad around us, is itself a marvelous victory."

—HOWARD ZINN[1]

Congo under Belgium's King Leopold II, circa 1900

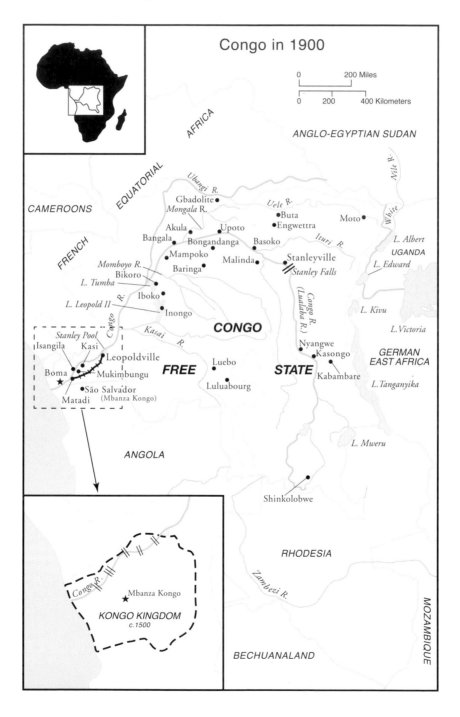

Foreword by Soraya Aziz Souleymane, Congolese Development and Mining Expert

When I was asked to write a foreword for a book about the Democratic Republic of the Congo (hereafter "Congo"), I was very excited because I knew it would have a lot to do with natural resources, my field of expertise. To me, it was about time that a book with this potential audience would give an echo to the Congolese people talking about their struggle. Anyone writing about the conflicts in Congo knows Fidel and his passion for our country. That is why this book doesn't come as a surprise. I became acquainted with his work in 2009, when I started pointing out the connection between natural resources exploitation and the violent conflicts that were (and still are) devastating my country. As for John, I met him in Washington, DC, at a Senate hearing in 2011. John has been working on raising awareness on African conflicts for many years.

When I talk about Congo in the United States, most people first just want to know where the country is located. In Europe, however, people know well where Congo is. This is probably because of the colonial past linking Europe and Africa. You see, colonization was not just about bringing religion and civilization to the "barbaric" indigenous people of Africa. In Congo, colonization was about controlling and exploiting the strategic natural resources of a country that could not defend itself from these outside forces. To some extent, especially for ordinary Congolese people who are deeply impacted by the violent exploitation of our natural resources, this is still the case.

For five centuries, Congo's institutions and infrastructure have been designed to strip the country of its natural resources. When I say "natural resources," I mean human beings through the slave trade as well as timber, precious metals and stones, wildlife, and recently oil. Congo has a very poor road network, but all sites of natural resource exploitation are accessible via road and connected to the country's rivers as well as to the Atlantic or Indian Oceans in order to facilitate exporting these resources. After the Belgian colonial period ended, Congo, like most African countries, went through a brutal dictatorship and the plundering mentality continued, this time with the complicity of some of Congo's leading politicians as well as local and international businessmen.

Congo is a vast country (larger than Europe and about a quarter the size of the United States) endowed with many natural resources. In 2000 the United Nations estimated its mining potential to be upward of $24 trillion. But besides mining, Congo has the world's second-largest equatorial forest providing oxygen to the world, the second-largest river in Africa, which could potentially provide electricity to the whole African continent, and a wide range of bird and mammal species endemic to the Congo Basin or Albertine Rift.

This abundance of wealth has made Congo a net creditor to the rest of the world. Many countries from all over the world have benefited from Congo's natural resources even while the Congolese people rank among the poorest in the world, with more than 80 percent of Congolese earning under $500 per year. Every person or network of people ruling Congo since 1885 has done so with the aim of enriching themselves (with the exception of Joseph Kasa-Vubu and Patrice Lumumba, who were respectively the first Congolese president—from 1960 to 1965—and the first prime minister, for three months before the latter was assassinated in 1961). The plundering of Congo has been engineered and maintained to benefit a few people for more than five hundred years, and that is what this book is about.

The army calls all civilians "*monguna*," which can be translated to "the enemy." This is the result of a long tradition of protecting the oppressive masters in power against any uprising by the people. First the army protected the Belgian masters against the indigenous people, then the *Forces Armées Zaïroises* (FAZ) protected former president Mobutu Sese Seko against the Zairians, then a Rwandan occupying force protected the elder President Laurent-Désiré Kabila against the Congolese, and as I write this today the army protects Joseph Kabila (Laurent-Désiré Kabila's son), Congo's president since 2001, against the Congolese people.

There has never been an army in Congo that actually protects the people. This predatory mentality can also be observed at the local level. Army officers will occupy a village, exploit its natural resources, and oppress the local population. The multiplication of army chains of command is another way the masters have deliberately sabotaged the army, preventing it from fulfilling its natural mission: protecting the people, assets, and territory of Congo.

The lust for Congolese resources has brought out the worst in humanity. Brutal killings, torture, mutilations, dispersed communities, torched villages, people being buried alive…And the horror has gone beyond Congo. As you'll read in this book, the uranium used in the atomic bombs dropped on Japan was mined in Congo. Today, terrorists are still trying to access Congolese minerals, with whatever consequences this could have for the world.

Fortunately, as much as there are some Congolese participating in the plunder of their own country, there are many more working tirelessly to raise awareness, educate the masses on their rights, and organize resistance and ultimately transformation. This book is about them too—their struggles, their efforts, and their successes.

In addition to providing a solid background to the situation in Congo, this book will inform the reader about success stories and incredible initiatives from Congolese men and women working on the ground and making a positive impact.

Finally, this book is about you, the reader, as well. Many want to help but don't know where to start. The book will link you to a vast network of Congolese and friends of Congo who unite to build awareness, change policy, and support local initiatives. Be part of the story, be part of the change.

CONGO STORIES

CHAPTER ONE

Why Congo?

Honorata's Story

Honorata Kizende—her real name, which she insists on using
because she wants her story told—has a hard smile and the kind
of faraway eyes that have seen too much. She has a very expres-
sive face and wears a leopard-print dress.

A few years before we met, Honorata was married with seven
children, living in Shabunda in the eastern part of the Democratic Republic of the Congo (hereafter "Congo," as distinct
from the Republic of Congo, or Congo-Brazzaville, a neighboring country separated by the Congo River). She was a teacher at
the time, and like teachers everywhere she was grossly under-
paid. To supplement her income, she would go to the mines on
weekends to sell salt.

On one fateful day, she reached the mine at around four p.m.
A militia unit originally from Rwanda[2] had appeared at the
mine earlier that day and was engaged in looting. Honorata was
abducted along with other women and girls. They were made
to walk a circuitous route through the forest for hours, to make

them lose their bearings—to prevent escape. Eventually they were taken to a militia camp in the forest, and when the soldiers in the camp saw the women, Honorata heard them say, "We are happy, the food has arrived."

Shortly after their arrival, the soldiers began beating Honorata so ferociously that they knocked her bottom front teeth out. After this, four men spread her out, holding her arms and legs down while a fifth man raped her. This was repeated by the other four soldiers.

One of the soldiers noticed her wedding ring and cut it off, damaging her finger. He said, "Now you are not married: you are the wife of everyone; you are the food of everyone."

Honorata was held captive for fifteen months. During her captivity, she and the other women and girls were taken to a new location every few months to meet new soldiers belonging to that same militia, and raped again. She lost count after a while.

"I was a wife and a teacher, and now I was being called 'food.'"

Honorata could not resist because they had guns. The militia often fought over the control of different lucrative mines, which is why Honorata and the other women were moved around so much. One day during heavy fighting, twenty of the women and girls decided to try to escape. The villagers they encountered when they fled were afraid to help them because they feared the militia would come for them next.

However, despite the danger, a Congolese nurse decided to protect Honorata and the other escapees. He hid them in his small farmhouse in the forest. Honorata learned about the passwords that allowed people to go safely from one area to another. If they didn't know the passwords, they were killed. The nurse always had them go with people who knew the passwords. Sometimes they had to wait a week until they could move safely to the next district. Battling heat, rain, and wind, Honorata estimated they walked 350 kilometers (nearly 220 miles) in the forest to reach the relative sanctuary of the main border town, Bukavu. Honorata sent word to her family that she was safe and finally liberated from the militia. But to her horror, her husband refused to allow her to come home, rejecting her because she had had sex "with those who cannot be called human."

Fortunately, she and four of the other women who had escaped from the militia met a Congolese sailor who had a house in Bukavu but was often away. He had mercy on them, allowing them to stay in the house—another in a long list of Congolese Good Samaritans who helped keep Honorata and her companions alive. In order to survive, Honorata worked as a porter for merchants in town. Two of the other four women were pregnant from the repeated rapes. She cared for them at the house.

One morning, Rwandan government soldiers who had invaded Congo came to the house and broke down the door. Two of the soldiers stayed outside. Five entered the house. They asked the women where their husbands were. Though the women said they had no husbands, the soldiers accused them of being the wives of Congolese militia members. They told the women that now they would have many husbands. The women were forced to take their clothes off and lay down. The soldiers said there are no old women in Congo.

All seven men raped all five women. Honorata didn't know how they had the stamina for that. She begged them not to rape the two younger and smaller women who were pregnant. They raped them anyway. Neither fetus survived the attacks.

Honorata spent two weeks bleeding after the rapes. A nun took her to a health center to be treated, and then she was transferred to Panzi Hospital in Bukavu, where the heroic and world-renowned Dr. Denis Mukwege is the chief surgeon. She was diagnosed with five infectious diseases and spent three months in treatment.

After her treatment, Honorata was enrolled in a small crafts course. She was physically present but was not really there. As strong as she was, the severe trauma of her experiences had taken its toll.

Eventually, Honorata was sponsored by the American non-profit organization Women for Women International (www.womenforwomen.org), and with the first support she received, she started selling bananas and avocados. This changed her life.

She reconnected with her older son and sent money for him to go to school. Her other six children remained in Shabunda with their father.

Honorata returned to being a teacher with Women for Women International's Congo program, this time teaching other rape survivors. She has taught health, rights awareness, decision-making, and nutrition. Her oldest son is now a state agent in the mining sector and a father of four. Her second son is an engineer agronomist with two daughters, one of whom is named after Honorata. Her third son has a license in public health. She never returned home to Shabunda, 290 miles (470 kilometers) away. "They are still in the forest," she said in a hushed voice, referring to the militia that initially took her captive.

Honorata became an inspiration and mentor to countless Congolese women who have experienced physical and emotional trauma. She believes she should help other survivors, using her training to change their lives, just as it changed hers.

When Honorata was asked what gives her hope, she replied, "The work I do gives me hope, and the exchange of ideas with women gives me hope."

When she was asked about her dreams for Congo, she demanded that "Rape and war should end in Congo. They are the diseases that are devastating Congo, a calamity. I dream of peace in Congo."

———

Honorata's experience is reflective of two coexisting realities we repeatedly came across in Congo. On the one hand: tremendous human suffering as a result of centuries-long, greed-fueled exploitation. On the other hand: resilience, resistance, movement-building, and hope for change, laying the groundwork for an altered future.

Real peace requires confronting and addressing the core interests that drive war, the "greed and grievance"[3] that has fueled conflicts all over the world throughout human history. The peace Honorata seeks for Congo requires an understanding of what drives Congo's cycles of war and suffering, and how America and Europe particularly have benefited extraordinarily and directly from the results of that suffering. We should look directly at this fraught history of unchecked greed and exploitation, acknowledge our own role in its perpetuation, and learn what we can—and must—do differently to help bring about real change.

It's complicated and messy, and there isn't just one answer. But there are things we can do to support the people and actions in Congo and globally that can alter the negative trajectories that have led to so much suffering in that embattled country.

To be sure, the history of the world's progress has a gruesome underbelly, consisting of racism, slavery, appalling exploitation, war, and genocide. But our contention is that the case of Congo's suffering over the last five centuries stands out in so many different ways. In fact, we considered naming the book *A Monstrous Greed*, from the words of a sixteenth-century Congolese king who had the foresight to summarize the next five hundred years of his country's destiny as he watched his people being kidnapped en masse by European slave raiders and shipped across the Atlantic Ocean.

———

For these past five centuries, Congo has been the earthly equivalent of a Vampires' Ball. Wealthy commercial interests from outside the country—including human traffickers, kings, colonists, presidents, tycoons, bankers, mining magnates, arms dealers, mineral smugglers, elephant poachers, and military leaders—have colluded with Congolese leaders to loot the country of its greatest resources. Congo is a country that has one of the richest natural resource bases in the world, one that a Belgian geologist in the 1890s described, apparently without irony, as a "veritable geological scandal."

Over the last five centuries and right up to the present moment, the United States and Europe have been inextricably connected to this complicated country in the very heart of Africa. The nation now known as the Democratic Republic of the Congo (formerly Zaire, before that the Belgian Congo, before that the Congo Free State, before that the Kongo Kingdom and other neighboring kingdoms) has provided massive benefits to the people of Europe and the US, largely without public recognition or acknowledgment. Major advances in the development of Europe's and America's economies were fueled by what has been taken from Congo, from captured human beings to stolen minerals to ransacked wildlife.

By following the money and greed over five centuries, we tell the story of how major global events have driven huge surges in demand for Congo's riches—from colonial plantation agriculture to the advent of the automobile, from the Industrial Revolution to World Wars I and II and the Cold War, to the dramatic expansion of the global weapons trade, the rise of cell phones and laptops, and the mass marketing of electric and hybrid cars. The exploitation of the Congolese people who provided the labor to deliver the goods to satisfy world demand has been shocking. Even after the formal end of the transatlantic slave trade, at certain junctures the treatment of Congolese workers rivaled conditions during the major slave-raiding period. Forced recruitment, beatings, extreme poverty, hunger, segregation, and the continuing sale of human beings occurred, at different times, in Congo. The exploitation of rubber, copper, gold, tin, uranium, cobalt, tantalum, diamonds, oil, forests, and elephants have each produced unique forms of suffering for Congolese people and wildlife.

The causal link between Western convenience and opportunity and Congo's suffering is direct and devastating. Product by product, Western innovations have driven demand for ingredients from Congo.

The negative impact this massive extraction has had on Congo may have no parallel in human history. At one point, roughly a third of the Congo region's population had been sold into the transatlantic slave trade. Not long thereafter, as the Europeans descended in perhaps the ugliest chapter in all of Africa's colonial history, some ten million Congolese people lost their lives in the context of a greedy European king's brutal approach to extracting Congo's natural resource riches. Congo's mineral wealth was key to supporting World War I, ending World War II, and intensifying the Cold War.

And in its latest chapter, Congo has experienced the deadliest war since World War II, with more than five million deaths. As the philosopher and revolutionary Frantz Fanon is said to have posited, "Africa is shaped like a gun, and Congo is its trigger. If that explosive trigger bursts, it's the whole of Africa that will explode."

Instead of protecting its people and developing its economy, successive Congolese regimes, from the Belgian king Leopold and the subsequent colonial era right up through the regime of Joseph Kabila (who at the time of this writing had just indicated he would not seek a third term, and he had named Emmanuel Ramazani Shadary as the candidate to be his successor), have operated more like a mafia than a government, organizing the state to cooperate with all manner of foreign vultures in looting the natural resources and privatizing the considerable wealth of the country. All the money that should have been taxed and used for social services and infrastructure ended up in the pockets of wealthy Congolese and foreign business interests. Today's corruption in Congo cannot be separated from the kleptocratic system, the roots of which go back to colonial-era depredations, as well as more than a century of massive bribery and kickback schemes by multinational corporations.

But this book isn't just about that history of exploitation and how America and Europe benefited. It is also full of stories of Congolese people who have decided to take matters into their own hands and change the equation, the narrative, and the status quo. They are devising new and creative forms of resistance and transformation that are changing the terms of the relationship between Congo's rulers and its people from the inside out, as well as altering Congo's relationship with the world. In solidarity, there are activists in North America and Europe who are building a movement to change the terms of that exploitative relationship from the outside in, aiming for a fair, equitable, and respectful partnership between Congo and the rest of the world.

Unless consumers and voters act, insatiable American, European, Asian, and neighboring African companies and governments will not stop taking whatever they want or need from Congo, because the undeniable truth is that the world desperately needs the natural resources that Congo has. Therefore, if unchecked, companies, governments—and through them, indirectly and usually unwittingly, we as consumers—will do what is necessary to get access to those natural resources that end up in products that make our lives better, more convenient, and less expensive.

But the destructive pillaging of Congo need not continue. It is heartening and remarkable to see what a global grassroots people's movement—led by Congolese people risking their lives on the front lines—has been able to achieve in bringing an element of fairness and justice to the relationship between Congo and the rest of the world. The situation is complicated, yes, but there are solutions, and there is a multitude of activists in Congo—and many in solidarity with them all over the world—standing up for change.

The hopeful signs of progress that have emerged in Congo during the past decade are in large part because of the efforts of Congolese "upstanders"—as Samantha Power calls those who stand up in the face of injustice; the opposite of bystanders[4]—working heroically to make a difference in their communities. But it is also in part because of a people's movement half a world away in the US and in Europe, led by students who care about their direct connections to the pain of the Congolese people.

———

The primary elements of the book will be Ryan's photographs, Fidel's interviews with and profiles of Congolese upstanders, and John's research into the history, commerce, and interests linking Congo with the US and Europe, as well as the efforts of Congolese and good-willed people around the world to alter the trajectory of Congo's history of exploitation. Though you may not know it from its portrayal in the news media and movies, Congo is not just a story of war, poverty, disease, and dependence. Through Ryan's photos and the accompanying stories, some of the beauty of the country and its people will be featured. And illustrations by a Congolese artist, Sam Ilus, highlight the vibrant and creative artistic community in Kinshasa.

This is not the definitive history of Congo, and we are not posing as experts. We are, however, aspiring to understand how the United States and Europe have benefited from Congo for centuries, what the impact has been on the Congolese people, how those people have reacted and resisted, and what Americans and Europeans can do to right the imbalance. After all, simply looking at corrupt African leaders today doesn't take into account the centuries of international exploitation and mass extraction that have required deeply corrupt multinational relationships and networks in order for the banks, mining companies, neighboring countries, and others to carry out this mass looting.

Congo is a case study in globalization and fighting for fairness. There is a growing movement of Americans and Europeans, especially young people, who want to know that their clothes, food, and technology are ethically sourced and want to understand how to be good global citizens. In that vein, Congo is a perfect case study of:

- the causes of global inequality (why some countries are so much richer than others)
- America's and Europe's role in perpetuating inequality; i.e., how European invasions and colonial domination initiated some of these problems and the US later enforced the status quo or prevented positive evolution while exploiting the situation for America's and Europe's benefit, and
- what can be done about these systemic injustices, rooted in addressing the history that created inequality and reforming the structures that sustain inequality, which taps into many of the forces that are animating young activists now across Congo, Africa, America, and Europe.

Three distinct themes will be highlighted:

First, Congo's cyclical crises are a direct result of its connections to America and Europe. The world was "interdependent" with Congo long before interdependence was even a concept. The timing of inventions, innovations, and peak demand in America and Europe has had profound impacts on Congo as the latter supplied personnel or material for Western progress for five centuries.

Second, Congolese are fighting back against these forces of inequality and injustice. Congolese from many different backgrounds will tell their stories, demonstrating why there is so much hope for Congo's future. We believe this small sampling of courageous narratives will strike imaginations and inspire readers around the world.

Third, because the causes are in part global, the solutions must not be left to the Congolese alone. By themselves, they cannot address the actions of multinational corporations, global and local banks, arms dealers, mineral smugglers, predatory neighboring armies, and governments in the US, Europe, Asia, and Africa that have inflamed and profited from the crisis in Congo. The good news is that as part of the international response and resistance to these globalized root causes, multinational activism has played a significant role, especially the activism of American and European students in solidarity with Congolese human rights movements and against the rapacious behavior of war profiteers.

It's not an exaggeration to say that millions of precious human lives are at stake in Congo.

When you use your laptop, remember that minerals from Congo have made it more affordable and make it work more efficiently.

When you pick up your cell phone, remember Honorata and all the other Congolese who have suffered or died as a byproduct of the technological convenience you hold in your hand.

We're supporting the building of a movement that tells the politicians we elect and the companies from which we purchase that we cannot allow such heinous human rights crimes to continue. We must speak out as loudly and creatively and innovatively as we can and say…*not on our watch*.

CHAPTER TWO

The Story of the Kongo Kingdom

Before and After the Europeans Landed

Instead of starting with the European invasion that instigated the global scramble for Congo's resources, we want to begin the story with what Congo was like *before* the Portuguese explorers landed in the late 1400s. Things were very different then, which begs the question of what would have happened to Congo and, more broadly, to Africa if the European explorers, missionaries, merchants, slave traders, and colonial armies had never shown up.

Before Congo, there was Kongo, otherwise known as the Kongo Kingdom.

"Kongo civilization and the formidable artistic legacy it engendered—without doubt among the world's greatest—developed across a vast swath of Central Africa over a period of two and a half millennia. Its diverse populace gave rise to a series of distinct polities that have been engaged with the West for a third of that time," writes art historian Alisa LaGamma.[5]

Origins

The name Kongo descends from *nkongo*, "hunter," a hero, an adventurer, in the Kikongo language people spoke along the Congo River. The people there told stories of the kingdom built by its founder, Lukeni lua Nimi, stories already generations old when Portuguese explorers, the first modern Europeans to visit, heard them in the late 1400s and Jesuit missionaries wrote them down.[6]

The earliest known periods of the Kongo Kingdom are marked by stories of innovating technology and expanding territory. Although archaeology in this region is still at an embryonic stage and will likely yield much more information as efforts increase over time, there is already plenty of evidence that the territory that became the Kongo Kingdom was characterized by a complex society. There were iron and steel workers by 350 BC—as, elsewhere in Africa, Carthage was challenging Rome—and social classes and a political authority appear to have existed by AD 100.[7]

By the 1300s, the first formal states emerged in present-day Congo, led by the Kongo, Lunda, Luba, and Kuba kings. One of the chief reasons for the development of these states, some of which were as big as modern-day Indiana or Ireland, was the advent of agricultural surpluses, which allowed them to more easily weather hard times. The states had feudal and hierarchical characteristics. The king was the indisputable leader who protected and supported his subjects, resolved disputes, consulted the elders, and took care of those in need. Not unlike today, each kingdom was broadly dependent on the distinct personality of its king. There were wide swings from progress to decline and back again, depending on the quality of the leadership and the intensity of the civil wars that often accompanied succession from one king to the next.[8]

———

In Kongo, each week of four days started with a holiday. The people farmed bananas and other fruits and crops, and raised cattle, pigs, and goats. The unit for distance was a day's walk; they marked time with the phases of the moon. They paid the king taxes, with egg-shaped cowry shells serving as money.[9]

Although there was no written language in the Kongo Kingdom, they used another way to communicate: their *langage tambouriné* (drummed language). New developments were drummed through-out the kingdom, traveling up to 600 kilometers (370 miles) a day. European explorers called it the *télégraphe de brousse* (bush tele-graph). This mode of communication was developed 1,500 years before Morse code.[10]

At peace, men collected materials for building and for cloth, utensils, medicines, and palm wine. Women fed their families by farming.[11]

The Kongo peoples had a unique and elaborate belief system. The universe was separated into the realm of the living and the realm of the dead, which existed parallel to each other. One's life consisted of a progression through one realm and then the other, crossing the threshold that divides the two realms, which was believed to be a large body of water. The midpoint along the path was when one would transition to the afterlife. The living realm was marked by blackness, while the ancestors were full of color. Symbols drawn with chalk made from riverbed clay were connected to concepts of virtue, purity, and ancestral contact. The spirits of ancestors were regularly invoked. Power or weakness was seen in part as stemming from the ability to tap into these mystical connections. For exam-ple, a village chief, those with many children, those who lived long lives, and those who attained wealth were seen to have the ability to connect to ancestral spirits and their energies.[12]

———

The Kongo Kingdom produced luxury cloth and fabric, which was used also as a currency, although when more intricately woven it was considered priceless. Sixteenth-century Kongolese art was on the radar of the world's art elite. Kongolese textiles were consid-ered by some explorers to be on par with those from Italy at that time.[13] When trade with the outside world began to accelerate,

Alisa LaGamma elaborates, "Exquisitely crafted decorative arti-facts produced by local artists as diplomatic gifts began to circulate outside the region. A very limited number of these presentation pieces survives in the form of carved ivory oliphants[14] and finely woven raffia textiles and basketry."[15] A *New Yorker* article about a recent museum exhibit of Kongolese art concluded, "There are no other sculptures in the world so fierce and sorrowing."[16]

The Kongo Kingdom's diverse artwork consisted of copper and iron works, wood carvings, baskets, mats, and pottery, influencing artists such as Matisse and Picasso. Cubism was in part derived from pieces of art from Congo.[17]

———

Most European histories of the Kongo written before the 1960s, when serious and impartial research began to be conducted, assumed that the Portuguese created the Kongo Kingdom. But this historical inaccuracy has been rectified through more recent studies. As Congolese historian Didier Gondola observes, "Most colonial researchers were prejudiced regarding African history. Because the kingdom was so well organized, these research-ers quickly dismissed the possibility that indigenous initiative might have played a role in Kongo's development. But Kongo emerged as the major state in equatorial Africa at least two cen-turies before the arrival of the Portuguese."[18] Foreshadowing later developments, the most important variable in why the kingdom developed when and how it did seems to have been the natural resources afforded by its location. The population expanded in the fourteenth century primarily because of the development of agriculture as well as copper smelting.[19]

The Kongo Kingdom was marked by healthy political struc-tures. Not unlike other African governing structures before the colonial invasion, the lowest political level was the village, com-posed of closely connected families—often led by women—called *kanda*. A group of villages was administered by districts led by roy-ally appointed officials. Provincial governors were the next level of leadership, answerable directly to the king. Women were the backbone of families in the kingdom, and they controlled who could be members of the *kanda*. Referred to as a matrilineal system, the mother and her sons were part of the *kanda*, whereas the father was not, even though he might be the household head. The mother's brothers possessed legal authority over the mother's children, while the father remained their guardian.[20] Seniority dictated power, wealth, and privilege in each *kanda*.[21]

By the late 1400s, the Kongo Kingdom was prosperous and growing. There were six main provinces governing some three million people. Supported by a council of elders, the king was considered the supreme ruler, and gave the governors of each province significant military, economic, and political powers. The governors and their provincial armies would join the king in war. At its height, the Kongo Kingdom's army grew to 80,000 men. The governors taxed their subjects and delivered a significant percentage of the revenue to the king while paying themselves through those same taxes. The governors also oversaw judicial mechanisms and maintained roads.[22] The king had nearly absolute authority over his appointed officials, who often came from his own family to ensure loyalty.[23] The provinces paid tribute to the king in the form of cloth, ivory, hides, slaves, and food, which he used to grant gifts and favors to cement his authority and build alliances. The king also used these gifts to maintain a large number of officials, soldiers, musicians, pages, and advisers in his court.[24] In the 1500s, the kingdom sent diplomats to reside in Portugal, Spain, and the Vatican.[25]

By the time the Portuguese arrived in the late 1400s, the Kongo Kingdom was already led by an evolved and highly centralized government. One Italian ambassador who visited opined that the houses in Kongo were the finest in all of that part of Africa, drew comparisons between the capitals in Kongo and Portugal, and complimented the kingdom's judicial system.[26]

The Europeans Land, and Everything Changes

Historian David Van Reybrouck uniquely imagines the scene of the Kongo's first contact with the Portuguese: "In 1482 the coastal inhabitants of that empire had seen something extremely remarkable: huge huts looming up out of the sea, huts with flapping cloths. When those sailing ships anchored off the coast, the people along the shore saw that there were white people in them. These had to be ancestors who lived at the bottom of the sea, a kind of water spirit. The whites wore clothes, lots more clothes than they did, which seemed to be made from the skins of strange sea creatures. All highly peculiar. The inexhaustible quantities of cloth the strangers had with them made the people think they probably spent most of their time weaving, there below the ocean."[27]

Many aspects of European life were quickly copied in Kongo. In 1491, less than ten years after the Portuguese first landed, the Kongolese king was baptized. He took on the name of the Portuguese king, João.[28]

Some of the early European writings about Kongo focused on allegations of cannibalism that were more about feeding the fascination and prejudices of European audiences than rooted in any empirical reality experienced by any of the writers, who made up stories they claimed were eyewitness accounts. The images and words fed stereotypes by depicting "the new and the exotic that clearly attracted the fascination of a European readership."[29]

———

Civil wars within the Kongo Kingdom were frequent in the aftermath—and partly as a result—of the arrival of the Europeans, picking up in intensity after the mid-1600s. These conflicts were driven in part by the impact of the transatlantic slave trade, which created warped financial incentives for some Kongolese to participate in the trade. And the wars also accelerated the European penetration of the Kongo Kingdom as one of the major sources for enslaving human beings for export to the Americas.[30]

It is likely that slavery was legal in the Kongo Kingdom before the arrival of the Europeans. As the European slave traders expanded their operations in the region, the number of people captured and sold out of Kongo spiraled upward, reaching thousands per year by the early 1500s. The king at the time, Afonso I, was not opposed to slavery conceptually, but he tried to stop "illegal" enslavement and the expansion of the abduction of people within his territory for export abroad.[31]

The Kongo Kingdom's enslaved people were those abducted in war, criminals, and debtors.[32] Although the practice was cruel and vicious in many ways, there were differences between slavery in the Kongo Kingdom and the European transatlantic pipeline that funneled Africans to the New World. For example, in the Kongo Kingdom enslaved people could eventually earn or be granted their freedom, and there was intermarriage between free and enslaved people.[33] But slavery's very existence in the Kongo Kingdom and other parts of Africa proved to be a slippery slope that contributed to the cascade that would supply the New World colonies with slave labor.

More than twenty million Africans were subjected to the most egregious mass kidnapping in human history, with half of those people sent across the Atlantic to the New World, and this region was at its epicenter. European raiders attacked the kingdom with the intention of removing Kongolese authority figures in order to destroy the indigenous symbols of community leadership and thus undermine any resistance to Europe's expansion of human trafficking.[34]

As the European human traders descended on the region, it was only a matter of time before the central authority of the Kongo Kingdom began to unravel. Local chiefs were enriching themselves by kidnapping and selling people to the Europeans, and they had no reason to remain loyal to the king. Finally, in 1665, the

Portuguese defeated the diminished Kongo Kingdom's army and beheaded the king. By the late 1800s, European powers had colonized the entire territory of the kingdom.[35]

◇◇

FOR MORE ON THE KONGO KINGDOM, VISIT OUR BOOK WEBSITE AT
www.congostories.org

◇◇

CHAPTER THREE

How Congo Helped Build America and Europe

*Following the Money and Greed
for Five Centuries*

Time and time again, when the US and Europe needed some ingredient to help advance Western progress or interests, they turned to Congo to provide it. But the vast majority of Congolese people had no say in the arrangements made, and they have suffered on a scale that has very few historical or global parallels.

This is the five-century story of an absolutely breathtaking relationship in which nearly all the benefits accrued to European and American companies and consumers, while all the costs were borne by the Congolese people. The Western world has literally taken whatever it needed from Congo, with catastrophic consequences. Rather than terms of trade, these were terms of pillage and plunder.

Thus, for the Congolese, the country's wealth of natural resources has proven to be more of a curse than the blessing it should have been.

Rather than presenting a purely chronological history of Congo, we explore its last five centuries through the lens of a series of stories that follow the money, revealing the unchecked greed that has been the gasoline fueling this looting frenzy. Each discrete historical section focuses on something Europe and/or America has needed from Congo for their advancement, and how the outsiders came and took what they needed, usually with extreme violence, further impoverishing the Congolese people.

- The need for labor on the plantations of the New World drove the dramatic expansion of the transatlantic slave trade, with Congo's territory as one of its main sources for enslaved people.
- Meeting the demand for ivory for a variety of consumer products as well as rubber for tires in a growing automobile industry led a Belgian king to take personal ownership of Congo's territory, killing millions through forced labor.
- When World War I caused a spike in the demand for copper, a key ingredient in many weapons, the West turned to Congo's massive deposits, again using harsh tactics to extract the needed resources.
- In World War II, the US outmaneuvered Nazi Germany for access to the world's most important uranium deposit, in Congo, which facilitated the development of the atomic bomb while ignoring the impacts on the health of the Congolese forced to work in the mines.
- During the Cold War, the competition over uranium, copper, and other minerals between the United States and the Soviet Union led the US and Belgium to conspire to assassinate the first elected prime minister in newly independent Congo and then support a coup that installed a kleptocratic dictator for three decades.

- When diamonds began to be used for industrial purposes, global demand for Congo's diamonds spiked, with negative impacts on exploited mining communities.
- The rapid spread of cell phones, laptops, and video games sparked a spectacular increase in the price of the key raw materials in these gadgets—tin, tantalum, tungsten, and gold—and provided the fuel for what became known as Africa's First World War, in which over five million people perished.
- The discovery of oil in one of Congo's national parks and the growing demand for ivory (globally) and charcoal (regionally) contributed to increased elephant poaching and deforestation in the parks.
- And today, as the electric car industry accelerates, the global demand for cobalt, the main ingredient in the lithium battery, has led to a spike in child labor in Congo's cobalt mines, which provide up to 60 percent of the world's supply.

This chapter will elaborate on each of these historical phases, following the money and the greed from resource to resource, documenting the benefits to the United States and Europe while Congo was devastated time and again.

"A Monstrous Greed"
European and American Demand:
Enslaved Labor for New World Plantations

During the period of British colonialism and for decades thereafter in an independent United States, agricultural development in America's southern states fueled massive economic growth and wealth for a subset of white British and American landowners and businessmen. This extraordinary agricultural production was built on the backs of enslaved men, women, and children, kidnapped from Kongo and other African territories, who were forced to labor in the plantation economy of the New World of North and South America. In fact, the very first group of enslaved people from Africa who were sold in North America came in part from the Kongo Kingdom.[36]

In Britain's colonies in North America, the plantations were concentrated in the American South. Because indentured laborers were more expensive and Native Americans perished in large numbers due to genocidal assaults and European diseases, the British decided to prioritize a "free" source of labor via the transatlantic slave trade from Africa. By 1750, Africans composed roughly 40 percent of the American South's population.[37] The system was geared to feed Europe's voracious appetite for plantation produce. The British used Africans for free labor and used the American colonies for the raw materials needed for Europe's progress and eventual Industrial Revolution.[38]

Treating people as commodities was a new concept in Africa, according to Congolese historian Didier Gondola. "The slave trade transformed preexisting notions about humanity and disrupted social hierarchies. African states came to rely on the income generated by selling captives to European traders on the coast and not on their agriculture-based economies. Ultimately, this contributed to their own downfalls. Kongo…virtually disintegrated as a result of intense demand for slaves on the Atlantic."[39]

The transatlantic slave trade—and the concept of humans as property as well as slavery as a permanent, hereditary status tied to race—would forever change the territory comprising modern-day Congo, and Africa more broadly. This international crime devastated Congo in so many ways: disrupting communities and culture; robbing society of vibrant young men and women; and transforming African trade from a multifaceted, self-sustaining set of practices into one that disproportionately relied on slave trafficking. The short- and long-term effects were devastating.

The best estimates conclude that approximately four million people were captured in the Congo Basin and transshipped to the Americas, representing roughly a third of the people enslaved and sent across the Atlantic and a quarter of the enslaved people working on cotton and tobacco plantations in the American South.[40] As the slave trade expanded, rival kingdoms fought major battles over which African chiefs would control the incredibly profitable trade with the Europeans.[41] The historian Martin Meredith concludes, "Kongo's domestic slavery thus became part of an international traffic in slaves."[42]

Kongo's concept and practice of slavery was not the same as the transatlantic slave trade. Kongo's system of slavery did not involve selling people into a permanent, hereditary status based on race. It is commonly assumed that those Kongolese participating in enslaving people knew what they were selling enslaved people into—a race-based permanent status—and actively engaged in that, when in fact there was little understanding that this was the case.

"Slaving fever" drove the Portuguese in their contact with the Kongo Kingdom by the early 1500s. Kongolese and other Africans "were force-marched to the coast, their necks locked into wooden yokes" so that they could be shipped to the New World.[43] The profits were enormous, and many succumbed to the greed, including priests, teachers, and professionals who had set out from Portugal with far different motivations. By the 1600s, some fifteen thousand people a year were being exported from the Kongo Kingdom to America. In the late 1700s, the demand for slaves in the US started to grow, which fueled the market further, and the numbers kept expanding. Untold numbers perished as they were abducted, forced to march to the coast, and then piled into impossibly stuffed boats across the Atlantic in what became known as the "middle passage." After the 1700s, the slavers began shipping enslaved people alongside ivory.[44] The Portuguese and British were the most active in facilitating this commerce.

Kongo's King Afonso I ruled for four decades during the first half of the sixteenth century. Although a slave owner himself, King Afonso wrote letters to his counterpart in Portugal, King João III, pleading for mercy: "My Lord, a monstrous greed pushes our subjects, even Christians, to seize members of their own families, and of ours, to do business by selling them as captives."[45]

———————

Portuguese encroachments over time undermined the Kongo Kingdom. Various Portuguese Catholic missionary groups competed for influence, which led to further disunity in Kongo.[46] The historian Lamin Sanneh concludes, "The tripartite alliance of commerce, civilization, and Christianity in premodern Africa was turning out to be a deadly combination."[47]

Kongo's King Afonso I initially tried to ban the slave trade but was the target of an attempted assassination by Portuguese merchants in 1540, and eventually he gave up his efforts in order to sustain the Kongolese economy.[48] After King Afonso died, Portuguese machinations and the devastation wrought by the transatlantic slave trade accelerated the deterioration of the kingdom, which was ravaged by continuing cycles of war and conquest while the region was depopulated by the slave raiders.

"The Horror, the Horror"
European and American Demand:
Ivory for Consumer Products

Historian Adam Hochschild describes the trigger for the first great global rush on Congo's extensive natural resources: "Because it could be easily carved, ivory in the nineteenth century was a more rare and expensive version of what plastic is today, with the added cachet of having an exotic origin—a cachet that grew greater with the public idolization of African explorers. Ivory from elephant tusks was shaped into knife handles, billiard balls, combs, fans, napkin rings, piano and organ keys, chess pieces, crucifixes, snuff-boxes, brooches, and statuettes.... The hundred pounds of ivory in an average pair of African elephant tusks could make hundreds of piano keys or thousands of false teeth."[49]

Americans and Europeans couldn't get enough of ivory's finished products. With ivory, size matters, and the elephants of 1800s Congo had some of the largest tusks in the world.

From the 1870s, a transition occurred in how that ivory was secured in Congo for its destinations abroad. Instead of European colonists and merchants fairly trading for a few tusks, it became much more cost-effective for European-backed forces to simply raid, loot, and pillage entire Congolese villages for their ivory stocks and other valued items. This phenomenon was memorialized in Joseph Conrad's novella *Heart of Darkness*, wherein he wrote, "The word 'ivory' rang in the air, was whispered, was sighed. You would think they were praying to it." As David Van Reybrouck concluded, "Raiding became more important than trading; fire-arms tipped the scales."[50] Conrad later wrote about his experience in Congo, which informed his writing of *Heart of Darkness*, calling it "the vilest scramble for loot that ever disfigured the history of human conscience and geographical exploration."[51]

Belgium's King Leopold II, who reigned from 1865 to 1909, first began paying attention to Congo because of what he saw as ivory's extraordinary potential for profit. As Leopold's grip on Congo slowly expanded, his agents there were expected to maximize the acquisition of ivory. Leopold's officials and their African militias undertook violent ivory raids, killing elephants and taking ivory stocks from villagers. Eventually, Leopold banned the Congolese from selling ivory to anyone other than his own authorities.[52]

Ivory was part of a larger shift sweeping through Africa. As slavery was being abolished throughout Europe in the first half of the 1800s, Africa's raw materials became the favored import to Europe, led by ivory. Ivory poaching and other forms of resource exploitation were as ruinous to Congo's economy as the transatlantic slave trade, leading to a reduction in subsistence agriculture, and in turn to famine and unrest.[53]

KING LEOPOLD'S STORY:
His "Magnificent African Cake"

Listen to the yell of Leopold's ghost
Burning in Hell for his hand-maimed host.
Hear how the demons chuckle and yell
Cutting his hands off down in Hell.
—**Vachel Lindsay**, *"The Congo" (1914)*

From an early age, King Leopold II of Belgium wanted his own colony. "From 1875 he fell under the spell of Central Africa," David Van Reybrouck asserted. Leopold wanted a piece of what he called "this magnificent African cake."[54] In the mad "scramble for Africa" among European colonial powers, Belgium was a latecomer to the party. But Leopold drove ahead of his country's ambitions and made his own arrangements.

King Leopold's quest was to enrich himself and Belgium. Hochschild observed, "The man whose future empire would be intertwined with the twentieth-century multinational corporation began by studying the records of the conquistadors."[55] Leopold once told one of his advisers, "Belgium doesn't exploit the world. It's a taste we have got to make her learn."[56]

Leopold wrapped up his commercial intentions in humanitarian rhetoric. His professed objectives were to focus on ending the slave trade and to advance science and morality.[57]

In the early 1880s, King Leopold deployed Lord Henry Morton Stanley (see our book website at www.congostories.org for a profile of Lord Stanley's depredations) to contract with local chiefs to buy up the rights to large swaths of Central Africa on incredibly unfair terms. In 1884–85, behind an impressive diplomatic campaign, Leopold persuaded the United States to become the first country to recognize his personal ownership of Congo, and then had it concretized during the Berlin Conference, which carved up Africa among the European powers, formally creating the Congo Free State with Leopold as its sovereign authority. Though Leopold owned the area personally, he never went there.[58] The borders of his new property were roughly what they are today: it was the size of the United States east of the Mississippi River, or if Europe is the measuring stick, it is larger than Italy, England, Spain, and Germany combined—seventy-five times the size of Belgium.[59]

There was no other colony in the world owned privately by one man.[60]

Leopold created his own private occupying army in Congo, called the *Force Publique*, which at its peak had 19,000 officers and soldiers. One of their favorite instruments of terror was the *chicotte*, a whip made from hippo or rhino hide. To be only scarred by a whipping was fortunate, as the *chicotte* often killed the victim. The *Force Publique* was a busy army, as insurgencies sprang up frequently against the terrible conditions created under Leopold's rule. There were uprisings by the Yaka, the Chokwe, the Boa, and the Budja peoples, among others. One rebellion led by a sergeant named Kandolo, who dressed in white and rode on a bull, ended up controlling the Kasai region for half a year. The rebellions foreshadowed the turbulence that would come to most of the colonies in central and southern Africa, which culminated in the guerrilla wars that ended colonialism decades later.[61]

Leopold's workforce in his colony was largely composed of slave labor, from porters to soldiers, while back in Europe he was making grand statements against slavery. The depth of his hypocrisy was demonstrated by his 1887 appointment as governor of the eastern province of a notorious slave dealer from Zanzibar, Tippo Tip. His partnership with one of the world's most infamous slave traders began to generate opposition to his commercial plans and ambitions.[62]

In the 1890s, Leopold began establishing "children's colonies" in Congo, which he claimed were for educational purposes, but in reality they became a recruiting pool for his army. The colonies were often established by Catholic missionaries working closely with Leopold's regime. Discipline in these colonies was enforced by the *chicotte*, and malnutrition and disease were rampant, killing half of the children.[63]

Hochschild explains what attracted Europeans to Congo: "For a white man, the Congo was also a place to get rich and to wield power. . . . The Congo offered a chance for a great rise in status. Someone fated for a life as a small-town bank clerk or plumber in Europe could instead become a warlord, ivory merchant, big game hunter, and possessor of a harem."[64]

Leopold spent some of the profits from Congo on massive vanity projects throughout Belgium.[65] But many of his expenditures were personal, and many of his purchases were abroad. He was a major landholder on the French Riviera, with beautiful homes and boats.[66]

Leopold's use of slave labor and the brutal tactics used to fulfill rubber quotas produced millions of casualties. But the Belgian authorities didn't think that the Congolese who perished were worthy of having their deaths recorded in any kind of official statistics, so historians can only estimate. Most studies conclude that Congo's population was cut in half between 1880 and 1920. A 1924 census found the population to be ten million, so the likelihood is that ten million people died at the hands of the regime,[67] a number corroborated by the Congolese historian Isidore Ndaywel è Nziem.[68]

Once a global human rights campaign (see chapter 11) created enough pressure that Leopold knew his days as owner of his own colony were numbered, he decided that he would sell the territory to the Belgian government. He dragged out negotiations to give himself time to hide his enormous Congo-related wealth. In the end, the Belgian government agreed to take over all of Congo's massive debts, which Leopold had recklessly accumulated, finish the renovations on a number of the king's homes and other projects, and pay him a handsome yearly fee "as a mark of gratitude for his great sacrifices made for the Congo."[69]

In trying to estimate how much Leopold profited from his colony, Belgian historian Jules Marchal estimates conservatively that his ill-gotten gains totaled approximately $1.1 billion in today's dollars.[70]

When Leopold finally turned over Congo to the Belgian government, he burned the state archives, which took over a week and filled the Brussels sky with ash. "I will give them my Congo, but they have no right to know what I did there," Leopold told his aide.[71]

Leopold's monument in central Brussels is listed as a Point of Interest on Trip Advisor. When we checked the reviews, the first one said this: "Leopold was a good guy and a real leader, despite all the propaganda that tries to ruin his name."

"The Rubber Terror"
US and European Demand: Rubber Tires for an Expanding Auto Industry

In 1887 the inflatable rubber tire was invented, and the subsequent expansion of the automobile and bicycle industries set off a global rubber boom. Demand escalated beyond tires to rubber hoses, tubing, gaskets, and insulation for wiring. Global rubber prices spiked. Most of the world's rubber was being produced in the Amazon Basin, accompanied by the region's own horrific human rights abuses,[72] but an enormous impact was almost immediately felt in Congo, where half of the territory was covered in rubber vines. By the late 1890s the elephant herds had thinned and rubber exceeded ivory as the main Congolese export.[73] Congo exported over eleven million pounds of rubber per year by 1900, and the extraordinary reserves of wild rubber became the crown jewel of King Leopold's commercial empire.[74] By 1900, Congo was by far the most profitable African colony.[75]

Using the profits from rubber and other commodities from Congo, Leopold remade Brussels.[76] He commissioned numerous buildings, city projects, and public works, which resulted in the nickname the "Builder King."

This pattern of profits being violently earned and externalized for the benefit of another country has been replicated numerous times throughout the world's history. In a modern example, one of the elite neighborhoods of Kigali in Rwanda is nicknamed "*Merci Congo*" (thank you, Congo) in a nod to the money made off Congo's minerals that has enriched Rwanda.[77]

"[T]he Congo Free State," wrote W. E. B. Du Bois, "with all its magniloquent heralding of Peace, Christianity, and Commerce, degenerating into murder, mutilation, and downright robbery, differed only in degree and concentration from the tale of all

Africa in this rape of the continent already furiously mangled by the slave trade."[78]

As with the plantation economy in America, the key to Congo's profitability was the use of forced and slave labor to meet Leopold's production requirements. The work of harvesting the rubber trees was physically challenging and time-consuming, and very few Congolese were willing to do it. In response, Leopold's authorities settled upon a strategy: they would invade villages, round up the women (or in some cases children or elders), and hold them as hostages until the village chief brought the required rubber quota. Any male resisting the order would result in his wife being killed. Men were whipped with the *chicotte* if they didn't meet the quota. And King Leopold's army, the *Force Publique*, oversaw this entire operation with extreme violence. The Congolese were "paid" for the rubber in cloth, beads, or salt.[79] Virtually the entire male population of Congo was subject to forced labor.

Hostage-taking wasn't the only barbarity practiced by the Belgians. If a village rejected the imposition of their rubber quota, the troops of the king or the rubber company would shoot everyone in the village to send a message to neighboring areas. Each bullet had to be accounted for and proven to have been used to kill someone, and the proof required by the Belgian state was the severed right hand of the executed.[80] One bullet, one hand. According to Hochschild, "'Sometimes,' said one officer to a missionary, 'soldiers shot a cartridge at an animal in hunting; they then cut off a hand from a living man.' In some military units, there was even a 'keeper of the hands.'"[81]

———

Rubber quotas were collected by armed guards who were themselves paid depending on how much rubber they collected. The Belgian administrator who had the highest volume of rubber in Congo would go on bloody looting expeditions, killing thousands of people and burning hundreds of villages. Leopold had succeeded in replacing slavery with another terrifying system. The policy destroyed Congo's indigenous agriculture and internal trade, while malnutrition skyrocketed and diseases spread.[82]

American president Theodore Roosevelt was pressed to respond to the rubber terror, but he claimed that "it was a literal physical impossibility to interfere" and dismissed proposals for intervention as "imbecile."[83]

Keep in mind the context of how little African lives mattered to the European colonialists at that time. Testing and experimentation with drugs were carried out on Congolese people without their permission to advance certain medical discoveries. For example, at the end of the 1800s field hospitals were set up in Goma in eastern Congo. Patients who had sleeping sickness were quarantined and "served as guinea pigs for all sorts of new medicines.... Doctors could decide where people could live or go, could force treatment, and could move villages for health reasons."[84]

Depot for Western Armies
US and European Demand:
Copper for a Century-Long Arms Race

Nearly every weapon used in the many wars of the twentieth century was in part made of copper, due to its ability to conduct electricity, resist oxidation, and transmit heat. Armored tanks, fighter jets, submarines, machine guns, and rifles all were more effective because of copper.[85] During World War I, the American Institute of Metals trade journal left nothing to the imagination: "It is almost impossible to kill a man in an up-to-date and scientific way without using copper."[86]

The United States and Great Britain used millions of artillery shells in World War I that had brass casings made primarily from Congolese copper. Cannons, bombs, bullets, torpedoes, and naval instruments also utilized copper from Congo.[87] Copper deposits in Congo, discovered in the late 1800s, eventually became some of the richest in the world,[88] and by 1929, Congo had temporarily become the world's third-largest copper producer.

It was still legal to use the *chicotte* whip in the colony's mines, and in general the colonial authorities used forced labor strategies that differed little from when King Leopold II owned the territory. Mine safety was a constant issue—five thousand miners perished in copper mines and smelters in Katanga between 1911 and 1918.[89]

Congolese copper continued to evolve as an essential ingredient for warfare. During World War II, Congo was a crucial raw materials depot for the Allied powers fighting the Germans, Italians, and Japanese, and copper was critical in that regard. During the Vietnam War, American demand for copper increased as a result of a surge in weapons production and arms deals, and copper prices again soared on the world market because of that and a large copper strike at the time.[90]

A History-Changing Mineral
US and European Demand: Uranium for the Atomic Bomb

In a mid-1939 letter, Albert Einstein dramatically warned President Franklin D. Roosevelt that the Nazi regime could potentially develop an atomic bomb. He informed Roosevelt that uranium was the key, and "the most important source of uranium is Belgian Congo." Historian Susan Williams, who has written the definitive book on this issue, states that Einstein's "letter fired the starting pistol for America to enter a kind of race that the world had never known before: the race to develop the atomic bomb before Germany."[91]

In order to beat Hitler to the punch, the US needed high-quality uranium ore. The largest source was in the Shinkolobwe mine in the Katanga province in Congo. The mine was owned by a major Belgian mining company and contained over 90 percent of the global reserves of uranium. The uranium ore there was by far the highest quality in the world. Susan Williams explains: "The unique richness of the Katanga ore was essential at that time for any physicist hoping to build an atomic weapon."[92]

The US resolved to control global uranium supplies at all costs. This meant focusing in large part on controlling supplies from that Congolese mine.

Once Nazi Germany invaded and occupied Belgium, 1,200 tons of Congolese uranium ore were shipped to New York in 1940 to be stored for safekeeping, leaving 1,000 tons of mined ore still stockpiled in the mine. Great concern followed Germany's Western European march about which side the Belgian Congo would take in the war after Belgium itself was conquered, and in whose hands the remaining 1,000 tons of uranium would end up. Incredibly, despite Hitler's conquest of Belgium, the governor-general of the Belgian Congo decided to side with the British, and he was supported by the Belgian colonial army. He committed to providing the anti-Nazi Allies with strategic minerals and other products, such as rubber, vital to the war effort.

In response to fears that the Germans could acquire some of Congo's uranium, the US wartime intelligence service, the Office of Strategic Services, deployed personnel to the Congo to oversee efforts to ensure that the balance of the uranium—all of it—made it safely to the US.[93]

For the remainder of the uranium in the Congolese mine, the options for removing it and exporting it to the US were fraught with challenges. The closest port was in Lobito Bay in Angola, but Nazi spies were well ensconced there. The United States decided instead to ship it out through Congo's port of Matadi, which required traveling fifteen hundred miles by two different train lines and in a barge on the Congo River but would allow the ore to stay within Congo's borders. Then it had to cross the Atlantic, where German submarines were patrolling, leading to the sinking of 200 tons of ore.[94] Using a massive trove of recently unclassified documents that reveal previously top-secret motivations for and actions involving US efforts around the atomic program and the essential and extraordinary role Congo played in it, Susan Williams's book *Spies in the Congo* provides an exhaustive account of how the uranium's perilous journey to the US was accomplished against stunning odds.

On August 6, 1945, the United States dropped an atomic bomb on Hiroshima. One hundred forty thousand people perished. Three days later, they dropped another on Nagasaki. Six days later, World War II was over.

Subsequent studies concluded that one of the reasons Germany and Japan did not create an atomic bomb before the US was that they could not gain access to the kind of high-quality uranium the US acquired from the Congolese mine.[95] The key was ensuring that no significant amount of Congolese uranium was smuggled from Africa to Germany between 1943 and 1945.[96]

Susan Williams concludes that Congolese uranium was "a mineral that had the power to change history."[97]

However, that wasn't all that was changed. The lives of the Congolese workers in the uranium mine also were dramatically impacted. The miners did not know what they were extracting and were exposed to huge amounts of radiation. They were never told by the mine owners that the entire area was polluted, including the water, and they were never informed about the grave risks associated with being exposed to uranium. No company or government kept any health or scientific records. "This was a process for which the US, the UK, and Belgium bear a heavy responsibility," Susan Williams concludes.[98]

No statistical data were ever kept about radioactivity or its impact on local communities in Congo, so there isn't a scientific study to quantify the damage. In 2004, following a mine collapse, a limited investigation was undertaken by the International Atomic Energy Agency, which established that miners who had been digging for cobalt and uranium in the area were likely exposed to higher levels of radiation. Congolese professor Nda Bar Tung noted that such levels could lead to cancer or birth defects.[99]

Today, the town surrounding Shinkolobwe mine "is dead and is haunted by the ghost of Hiroshima."[100]

When Elephants Fight, the Grass Suffers
US and European Demand: Compliant Cold War and Commercial Clients

With the end of World War II, the new looming threat to the West was posed by the Soviet Union and its desire to build its own nuclear arsenal. To accomplish this, the Soviet Union was also searching for uranium ore.[101]

The Congolese uranium mine in Katanga was reopened in March 1945, providing high-quality uranium to the US. It remained America's primary source into the 1950s. For this and other reasons, Congolese historian and political scientist Georges Nzongola-Ntalaja notes that Congo was "an important element of Washington's geopolitical strategy in the context of the Cold War."[102] Congo was the first African country to become part of a "tug of war" between the two superpowers. "To leave Congo to the [Soviet Union] would seriously compromise America militarily," according to David Van Reybrouck.[103]

Throughout the Cold War, the potential for the Soviet Union to acquire Congolese uranium was a major concern for the US, just as it had been regarding Germany during World War II. The Pentagon created plans for an occupation of key territories in Congo in the event of a Soviet advance into Western Europe and sent CIA agents to the region as well as arms to Belgian troops in Congo to head off any chance of rebellion. Because of growing American demand as its atomic project expanded, additional protection of the Shinkolobwe mine was required, and eventually a massive NATO military station was built near the mine.[104]

American writer John Gunther, who visited Katanga in the mid-1950s, concluded, "Rock mined from this remote area in the Belgian Congo is capable of burning up the world."[105]

After years of tremendous Congolese resistance to Belgian colonial rule, Congo was finally due to receive its independence

in 1960. The Belgians set an independent Congo up for failure, supporting secessionist movements and ensuring that there were few experienced people to run the government. There were only a couple dozen Congolese college graduates by 1960, and no Congolese army officers, engineers, agronomists, or doctors. At the time of independence, the colonial Belgian Congo administration had approximately five thousand management positions within the civil service. A grand total of three of them were filled by Africans.[106]

The first-ever election in Congo resulted in the victory as prime minister of a charismatic thirty-four-year-old leftist named Patrice Lumumba. He was a strong proponent of economic as well as political freedom for Africa, an extremely popular message in Congo but one that alarmed American, British, and Belgian governments and companies, which had huge investments in Congo, especially in the mining sector. His economic nationalist message resonated throughout Africa, and he was impervious to Western bribes.[107]

In the year before Congo became independent and Lumumba was elected prime minister, he was asked whether the US would maintain access to the uranium in Congo. Lumumba responded, "Belgium doesn't produce any uranium, and it would be to the advantage of both our countries if the Congo and the US worked out their own agreements in the future," implying that things would be much different than under Belgian rule. However, the Belgian company that owned the mine decided to seal it up with concrete before the country became independent.[108]

Uranium and other Congolese minerals already placed Congo at the center of Cold War interests, but the post-independence stakes soon spiked. Eleven days into Congo's independence, the mineral-rich region of Katanga seceded, backed by Belgium. In response, Lumumba asked the Soviet Union for assistance in responding to this challenge. The United States was deeply alarmed. The US ambassador to Belgium, William Burden, sent a cable to the State Department that said, "Only prudent, therefore, to plan on basis that Lumumba Government threatens our vital interests in

Congo and Africa generally. A principal objective of our political and diplomatic action must therefore be to destroy Lumumba government as now constituted."[109] With the reported backing of President Eisenhower, Allen Dulles, the CIA director in Washington, telegrammed the CIA station chief in Congo that the removal of Lumumba "must be an urgent and prime objective and…this should be a high priority of our covert action."[110] Soon thereafter, the CIA dispatched deadly poisons to its station chief, Larry Devlin, who later wrote, "One was concealed in a tube of toothpaste. If Lumumba used it, he would appear to die from polio."[111] Devlin said President Eisenhower viewed Lumumba as a "mad dog."[112]

Not coincidentally, both Ambassador Burden and CIA Director Dulles had financial interests in Congo.[113]

The United States and Belgium were supporting anti-Lumumba factions, hoping they would carry out his assassination. And they did. A Belgian pilot flew the plane that brought the kidnapped and tortured Lumumba to Elizabethville in January 1961, where he was shot by a Katangan firing squad overseen by a Belgian officer.[114] His killing, ironically, occurred just seventy-five miles from the uranium mine. As Adam Hochschild notes, "Two Belgians then cut up his body and dissolved it in acid, to leave no martyr's grave. We cannot know whether, had he survived, Lumumba would have stayed true to the visionary hopes he embodied for so many people in Africa, but the United States and Belgium saw to it that he had no chance to try."[115]

In the aftermath of Lumumba's assassination, the US backed Congolese army officer Joseph Mobutu, who had helped arrange the assassination and had earlier worked for the Belgian colonial army. For a half decade, Congo was torn apart by secessionist struggles, rebellions, and divided government. During that time, Mobutu met with President John F. Kennedy in the White House in 1963, further cementing ties with the US. Two and a half years later, backed by President Lyndon Johnson's administration, Mobutu successfully orchestrated a coup and took power for the next three decades. In 1967 he nationalized assets owned by the main Belgian mining company, which controlled the uranium mine. The mining profits then went to Mobutu personally and the mining companies with which he made arrangements.

Five years into his reign, Joseph Mobutu renamed himself Mobutu Sese Seko, with nicknames ranging from "The Guide" to "The Helmsman" and "Father of the Nation." He also renamed Congo itself, calling it Zaire.[116]

The United States gave Mobutu over a billion dollars in economic and military aid during his time in power, with France and other European countries along with the World Bank and International Monetary Fund contributing heavily as well. Mobutu was a reliable ally against the Soviet Union and provided a staging base for CIA and French military operations. And he protected American and European investments as if they were his own. He visited President Ronald Reagan at the White House a number of times, and Reagan called him "a voice of good sense and good will."[117] He was President George H. W. Bush's first African head of state official visitor, with Bush calling Mobutu "one of our most valued friends."[118]

Mobutu began with some promise over his first few years in office, when he sought to build up the Congolese state and economy. He took the country down a destructive path, however, as he continued to consolidate his rule. He was able to solidify a dictatorship and loot massive wealth from the country, allegedly becoming the eighth-richest man in the world in the process.[119] In the 1970s and '80s, Mobutu personally amassed up to $4 billion in wealth while Congo's economy shrank by 60 percent.[120] In Europe, Mobutu owned a dozen castles as well as houses in wealthy neighborhoods in Belgium, France, and Switzerland. He also owned a palace in Venice, a villa on the French Riviera, and hotels and estates in Portugal. In the Congolese city of Gbadolite, he created a Chinese village and imported people from China to inhabit it. The city also boasted a 158,000-square-foot palace with marble, mahogany, and crystal throughout, and an airport designed for the Concorde supersonic plane. His wife had a 160-foot-long walk-in closet. He would fly in the great chefs of Europe for huge parties for thousands of guests.[121]

Deep Cuts
US and European Demand:
Cheap, Industrial, Blood Diamonds

A company founded by King Leopold and controlled by him and the Guggenheim family, the *Société Internationale Forestière et Minière du Congo*, or *Forminière* for short, controlled diamond production in the early part of the 1900s.[122] Within two decades of the first discoveries of diamonds in Congo, it was the second-largest diamond producer in the world. Most of the diamonds were not gem quality but rather were suitable only for industrial use in cutting tools. However, by the 1930s, the German corporate giant Krupp had developed a tungsten alloy that was stronger than steel, and the only thing hard enough to cut and shape that alloy was a diamond, ideal for industrial-strength saws, drill bits, and other tools.[123]

This suddenly created new demand for the massive deposits of industrial diamonds in Congo. Sir Ernest Oppenheimer of De Beers fame moved in on Congolese mines, buying up all production from the Belgians who controlled Congo and the mines.

After years of studying the issues, diamond expert and development professional Ian Smillie concludes: "Diamonds, the foundation on which a modern-day Congo might have been constructed, were instead a curse. They were at the center of the country's problems, almost from the day they were discovered in 1907. It is possible, in fact, that Leopold II would never have relinquished control of his 'free state' had he understood the extent to which diamonds were spread—not far below the surface—across vast swathes of territory."[124]

During World War II, the Belgian Congo produced 65 percent of the Allies' industrial diamonds, which had recently become indispensable for the production of military hardware. This was a major advantage over the Axis Powers, who had to rely on lesser sources, including French colonies in West Africa.[125]

By the 1950s, the Belgian Congo was producing 70 percent of the world's industrial diamonds. And as with other resources, forced labor was a major part of the equation in Congolese diamond mining.[126] It also contributed greatly to the kleptocracy, as Mobutu looted up to $2 million a month from diamond revenues, using them as bribes in Europe and around the world.[127]

In the aftermath of Mobutu's fall and in the context of Rwanda's and Uganda's occupation of large swaths of eastern Congo in the late 1990s (see chapter 5), both Rwandan and Ugandan official exports of diamonds increased dramatically, with an estimated $20 million a month in diamonds being smuggled out of Congo through its two neighbors.[128] The smuggling networks inevitably became divisive, and the two governments had a falling-out on Congolese soil.

Smillie elaborates: "Uganda and Rwanda both appointed 'governors' of the territories they occupied, and a welter of small air cargo companies emerged to ferry loot back to Kigali and Entebbe. Many of these companies, and the banks that sprang up in Kigali and Kisangani, had owners or shareholders closely related by blood or politics to the Presidents of Uganda and Rwanda.... The diamond records, like all records in the Congo, represent only the tip of an iceberg, with the most realistic 1999 estimates of stones moving through Kisangani pegged at $70 million."[129] Zimbabwe was also feeding off Congo's diamond industry, making deals with President Kabila to help him stay in power in exchange for diamond concessions.

The competition between Rwanda and Uganda over the diamond smuggling networks inside Congo eventually exploded into open war. The Congolese city of Kisangani, Congo's third largest, was the main diamond trading center, and Rwanda and Uganda fought three major battles on Congolese soil—within Kisangani—in 1999 and 2000. In June 2000, they fought for six days, firing six thousand shells at each other that often ended up falling in neighborhoods adjacent to the target, killing 760 civilians.[130]

Loot to Kill
US and European Demand: Raw Materials for Cell Phones, Laptops, and Video Games

Few things in our modern era are as ubiquitous as the stable of electronics products that existed only in science fiction a few decades ago: cell phones, laptops, smart televisions, tablets, video games, etc. Global demand for these products began really generating steam in the 1990s, and that matters to Congo for two reasons. First, some of the raw materials needed to power these electronics products are sourced from Congo. Second, increases in global minerals prices have been connected to conflict in eastern Congo. For example, the biggest surge in demand for one mineral, tantalum, occurred just as Rwanda and Uganda were settling in for a long military occupation of much of the eastern third of Congo, which is where these minerals happen to be concentrated. Later in the 2000s, the steady increase in the price of tin and gold helped drive conflict in tin- and gold-producing areas.[131]

Congo's "conflict minerals" are primarily tin, tantalum, tungsten (the 3Ts), and gold. The 3Ts are indispensable to modern electronic devices. Tin functions as a solder on circuit boards in every electronic device we use. Tantalum stores electricity and is essential to portable electronics and high-speed processing devices. Every time you send a text message or open an app, tantalum is used. Tungsten enables cell phone vibration alerts.[132]

Rwanda and Uganda reinvaded Congo in 1998 and ended up controlling large areas of eastern Congo, either directly through the deployment of their own troops or indirectly through their support for violent militias. Originally Rwanda and Uganda overran Congo in 1996 in order to confront the remnants of the Rwandan force that committed the 1994 genocide and that had escaped across the border into Congo when a Rwandan rebel group led by Paul Kagame chased them away and took power. Kagame later

became Rwanda's president. For a few years, Rwanda and Uganda fulfilled some of their initial stated objectives, which included finding the Rwandan Hutu militias and defeating them while bringing their leaders to justice. The militias were not defeated but were seriously weakened.

Two things happened during this period to alter Congo's history. First, the Rwandan and Ugandan forces committed massive war crimes in their pursuit of the Rwandan insurgents. The Rwandan government army chased the Hutu militias—who protected themselves with human shields of Rwandan civilian refugees—through the Congolese forces, killing what is estimated to be hundreds of thousands of those refugees in the process. This had a profound impact on political and military groupings and alliances in eastern Congo, and led to a complete militarization of the region, turning crimes against humanity such as mass rape, child soldier recruitment, and village burnings into routine practices.

Second, the motivations of the Rwandan and Ugandan occupying forces began to morph as the global prices of the minerals they were sitting on—the 3Ts and gold—rose in the late 1990s and into the 2000s. Over time, commercial opportunities opened up through their control of thousands of square miles of territory when the price of the materials that were being mined there was exploding on the world market, a development that was too lucrative to ignore. The Rwandan and Ugandan armies began to invest heavily in highly illegal and violent mineral extraction and smuggling operations. Rwanda focused on tin and tantalum (the latter popularly called "coltan"—for columbite-tantalite—in eastern Congo), the prices of which were surging in international markets.

In some cases, resource theft in eastern Congo has been highly orchestrated, spanning multiple countries and involving indicted war criminals, militias, smugglers, merchants, military officers, and government officials. Beyond the war zones, the networks involved mining corporations, front companies, traffickers, banks, arms dealers, and others in the international system that benefit from theft and money laundering.

"The scramble for Africa was now being organized by the Africans themselves," concluded David Van Reybrouck. Tantalum became Rwanda's biggest earner from eastern Congo. Van Reybrouck continued, "What rubber had been in 1900, [tantalum] was in 2000: a raw material…that was suddenly in acute demand around the world." In 2000 there was a global tantalum rush against the backdrop of a perceived supply shortage. Nokia and Ericsson had produced a new generation of cell phones, and Sony had released PlayStation 2 across the world during the Christmas season. Tantalum prices rose almost 1,000 percent in one year, from $30 to $300 per pound, and eastern Congo was the world's leading supplier. The amount of money Rwanda made from the war reportedly outstripped its financial costs by a three to one margin. The real money was made by the arms dealers, multinational mining companies, and businessmen operating in the shadows.[133]

Tantalum wasn't the only mineral whose price was increasing. The price of tin steadily rose throughout the 2000s. That was due to electronics sales increases and a new European regulation, called Restrictions of Hazardous Substances, banning lead solder, which led to the rapid development of tin as the primary replacement for lead as a solder—the main use of tin in electronics. And the price of gold skyrocketed in the 2000s as well, going from less than $300 per ounce in 2000 to $1,800 per ounce in 2012.[134]

Rwanda had to pay 60,000 soldiers and deal with a restive political situation at home, which required an expensive security and patronage system.[135] In 2000 and in subsequent years, the Rwandans earned an estimated quarter of a billion dollars annually as they oversaw the smuggling operation and armed the militias. Individual commanders enriched themselves, resulting in a luxury housing boom in Kigali and Goma during the war.

Rwandan commanders were in charge of loading tin and tantalum into planes. The occupying Rwandan forces controlled "all stages of mineral production, from the digging to air transport to the export company in Kigali," Congo expert Jason Stearns noted. Rwanda sent hundreds of Hutu prisoners to work in the mines.[136]

Human rights groups and the UN Group of Experts have documented significant illicit mining and related violence by dozens of armed groups and Congolese army commanders. As recently as 2010, the UN Group of Experts found that in the Kivus "almost every mining deposit [was] controlled by an armed group," and they were committing such brutalities as sex slavery, child soldier recruitment, and murder.[137]

In July 2015, Goma-based Congolese activist and head of the organization Women's Synergy for Victims of Sexual Violence (SFVS) Justine Masika Bihamba, told Fidel and The Sentry's Holly Dranginis, "Ten years ago, we were under de facto control of armed groups. . . . We hardly slept, death could come at any time. The country was ungoverned."[138] Justine's organization provides medical and legal services to survivors of sexual violence. That work has led her to also lead grassroots initiatives against the conflict minerals trade. In South Kivu, Lubula Igomokelo, an assistant director at the Panzi Foundation, also works with survivors of sexual violence. He has seen scores of patients come to Panzi Hospital in Bukavu seeking help for life-threatening war-related injuries, including brutal rape. He told Holly and Fidel, "The link between minerals and violence was something that became obvious, in a sense. The [sexual violence] victims were all coming in for treatment from areas with very active mining."[139]

All that Glitters
US and European Demand:
Gold for Jewelry and Electronics Products

In the United States alone, the gold jewelry industry is worth approximately five billion dollars annually.[140] Halfway around the world, however, the extraction and smuggling of gold serve as important means of funding for armed groups and army commanders in Congo, where violent armed groups mine, tax, and smuggle gold and perpetrate widespread atrocities.

Gold has many uses beyond jewelry. It is the highest-value mineral used in most electronics products, and roughly 10 percent of gold is used in electronic products worldwide.[141] It is an ingredient in high-tech medical devices, it is traded by investors and banks, it can be melted into gold bars, and it is sometimes used to move money illicitly without using cash to evade the global financial system.[142]

In Congo, gold was discovered by Australian prospectors near the border of Uganda in 1903, and northeastern Congo soon evolved into the most important gold mining area in Central Africa.[143] Few consumers knew that many of the gold miners in the 1920s in Congo were press-ganged and "bound together at the neck by a wooden yoke or a noosed rope."[144] Over time, industrial mining produced large exports.

By the late 1990s, in the context of Rwanda's and Uganda's invasions of Congo, the situation had devolved into a blood-filled Wild West scenario. There were teenage "CEOs" of gold mines. All of the gold mining in the eastern war zone at the time was done by hand with hoes, pickaxes, or rudimentary equipment. By then industrial mining was a thing of the distant past. Colonial-era machines were rusting in the sun and rain. According to the UN Panel of Experts on Congo, natural resources from gold to diamonds to tantalum were being smuggled to Uganda, the operation run in part by a Ugandan general, Salim Saleh, who is the half brother of Ugandan president Yoweri Museveni. Many bigger mines were controlled directly by the Ugandan army. Competition between Rwanda and Uganda over these mines and smuggling opportunities, along with their rivalry over diamonds, led the two countries to go to war on Congolese soil, as described in the previous section. Uganda and Rwanda were both exporting gold officially from their countries even though neither of them had significant known deposits of the metal.[145]

In the early 2000s, the Mongbwalu gold mining concession in Congo was gained and lost by Congolese proxy militias backed by Rwanda and Uganda five times over the course of eighteen violent months. An estimated two thousand civilians were killed. Militias oversaw the mining, and in some places miners were not paid and were regularly beaten.[146]

Sexual and gender-based violence (SGBV) has been widespread in mining areas in eastern Congo. UN experts have documented high rates of SGBV by armed groups and army commanders.[147] The Sentry's Holly Dranginis notes, "Minerals and other resources fund and motivate armed groups to use rape, sexual torture, and enslavement to gain control over territory and trading routes."[148] Studies conducted in mining areas have documented increased rates of prostitution, rape, and forced marriage—including that of young girls—as well as a lack of access to employment in the mines.[149]

Furthermore, children form a significant part of the labor force at some gold mines, where they work mainly as surface miners, rock crushers, transporters, or gold washers.[150] Although these tasks are less rigorous than those of adults, child miners are more prone to severe injuries.[151] For many gold miners, a large portion of their income goes to servicing debts,[152] driving some miners into debt slavery.[153]

Gold remains a major driver of violence and funder of armed groups and abusive Congolese army units in eastern Congo today.

The UN estimated that almost all of Congo's artisanally produced gold, or roughly $400 million per year, is smuggled out of the country.[154] Gold is easy to hide because of its high value in small quantities—half a million dollars' worth can fit in a briefcase—and a smuggling system has been in place for decades. The illicit conflict-gold supply chain moves mainly to Uganda and Rwanda, where it is refined by smugglers, or to Burundi. Then much of the gold arrives in Dubai, a major global gold trading and refining hub that has its own smuggling loopholes, and is then traded to North America, Europe, or India.[155]

Official export figures for gold from eastern Congo are a mere fraction of real annual production. Meanwhile, countries neighboring Congo are dramatically increasing their official gold exports, and much of that gold is likely to have originated in eastern Congo, given the relatively low gold production in these neighboring countries. Rwanda's official exports surged tenfold between 2014 and 2016, and Uganda's increased by 85,000 percent from 2014 to 2017.[156]

Rwanda is now exporting one ton of gold per month, according to the UN Experts Group, quite a feat for a country that has very little gold of its own.[157]

Rwandan-backed Congolese militia commander Bosco "The Terminator" Ntaganda ran a large-scale conflict-gold smuggling ring in Congo[158] before surrendering in 2013 and being handed over to the International Criminal Court. Ntaganda's trial at the ICC, which is ongoing, began in September 2015. He is facing eighteen counts of war crimes and crimes against humanity allegedly committed in northeastern Congo between 2002 and 2003.[159]

Not to be outdone, a major regional gold refinery was built in Entebbe, Uganda, in 2016, and the country slashed its tax rate on gold exports to zero, which will increasingly draw gold smugglers from Congo and the surrounding region looking to avoid paying taxes. The value of Uganda's gold exports had already seen an extraordinary surge, from $240,000 in 2014 to $377 million in 2017. Uganda now has the lowest tax rate for artisanal gold in the entire world.[160]

Conflict gold remains a major obstacle to peace and a driver of the black market economy in eastern Congo. While significant progress has been made on reducing armed groups' profits from three out of four conflict minerals in Congo—tin, tantalum, and tungsten—gold continues to finance armed groups and corrupt army officers and officials in Congo and the region.[161]

Mafias in the Game Parks
Global Demand: Oil, Ivory, Cooking Fuel, and Pet Gorillas from Sacred Lands

Congo's two vast game reserves, Virunga and Garamba National Parks, contain extraordinary wildlife and natural wonders such as volcanoes and tropical forests. The beautiful animals and natural resources draw intrepid tourists but predictably also draw predatory companies and armed groups out to exploit the elephants, gorillas, oil, and natural forests, often violently and illegally.

Covering roughly 3,000 square miles in northeastern Congo, Virunga is Africa's oldest national park and a UNESCO World Heritage site.[162] Virunga's biodiversity is unmatched by any other protected place in Africa and includes rare bird species, some of the last mountain gorillas on earth, and endangered forest elephants. The park gained renewed attention as the subject of the 2014 Academy Award–nominated documentary *Virunga*.[163]

In the mid-1990s, foreigners came into the area, this time from just over the Rwandan border in the wake of Rwanda's genocide. When the current director of Virunga, Emmanuel de Merode, a Belgian prince and career conservationist, took over in 2008, the park was under the de facto control of Rwandan government–backed rebels.[164]

Elephant Poachers

After ivory's heyday in the late 1800s and early 1900s, ivory poaching spiked again in the late 1990s in response to increased demand, this time mainly from China and other Asian destinations. Since then, poachers have been killing the elephants of Garamba National Park in Congo at an unprecedentedly rapid pace. Unlike in the past, many of the poachers are heavily armed groups and use professional techniques. Some of the poachers have been involved in Central Africa's many conflicts and have carried out multiple atrocities against civilians, creating misery and suffering for years.[165]

Joseph Kony's Lord's Resistance Army, elements of the Congolese national army, and armed poachers from South Sudan and Sudan have led the surge in poaching in Congo,[166] using their revenues in part to fund their continuing military activities through weapons and ammunition purchases.[167]

This increase in poaching and ivory trafficking is both qualitatively and quantitatively different from previous experience. In the past, poachers have relied on relatively low technology tools and have tended to kill one or two elephants at a time. Now elephants are being shot from helicopters,[168] and according to the organization African Parks, whose rangers manage Garamba on behalf of the Congolese government, recent attacks have resulted in up to eight elephants being killed at a time, with the tusks often being removed by chainsaws. Since the 1980s, the Garamba elephant population has fallen to about 1,300 from approximately 20,000, largely due to poaching.[169]

Global prices for smuggled ivory set new records in the mid-2010s based on high demand in East and Southeast Asia, especially China. By 2014, at the peak of the surging demand, elephant tusks were sold at up to $950 per pound in China.[170] This led to a surge in poaching in Congo and other areas of Central Africa, particularly in Garamba National Park.[171] However, as Enough's Sasha Lezhnev points out, high-profile campaigns to reduce global demand for ivory, aimed especially at China, and China's new domestic ban on trading ivory has reduced the price significantly. By early 2017 the Chinese price for ivory had fallen by nearly two-thirds to $330 per pound,[172] leading to a decrease in price in Congo.[173]

Oil Wildcatters

With improving technology unearthing more and more oil deposits in East and Central Africa, it was only a matter of time before exploration reached the Congolese forests. Finally, a major oil discovery was made underneath Virunga National Park, setting up a dramatic showdown between environmentalists and a multinational oil corporation.

When the British oil company SOCO International began prospecting for oil, it engendered a great deal of resistance both locally and internationally. Government soldiers reportedly beat villagers who protested the company's efforts. When SOCO attempted to build a cell phone tower in Virunga, a park warden tried to stop them and was kidnapped and tortured. The park director, Emmanuel de Merode, opposed the project as well and was ambushed, shot multiple times, and nearly assassinated.[174]

The oil is located under Lake Edward, adjacent to Virunga, and thus if an oil spill were to occur, it would contaminate water used by millions of people. "Any toxins from here could flow up to the Mediterranean," said de Merode, who despite his royal descent back in Europe lives in a tent in the park and earns $800 a month. "It could reach all the way to Spain."[175]

Global Witness found evidence that SOCO paid tens of thousands of dollars to a Congolese army officer—the equivalent of roughly thirty years of his salary—who allegedly was spearheading violent attacks against those opposed to the oil project.[176]

Numerous international and Congolese conservation groups have supported campaigns to protect Virunga, in particular from oil drilling by SOCO or other companies. De Merode and his colleagues in the national park service have fought what de Merode has called "a long battle" to prevent drilling.[177] Bolstered by attention garnered from the documentary *Virunga* and essential investigations by Congolese groups like Innovation for the Development and Protection of Environment (IDPE) and international organizations like Global Witness, they seem to have won for the moment.

SOCO ended its exploration activities in Virunga in 2014 after significant public pressure resulting from the documentary, and the company let its license lapse in 2015 after performing seismic testing. However, in 2018 the Congolese government announced that it would open parts of Virunga and Salonga national parks to oil drilling. International and Congolese NGOs are campaigning to protect the parks and block the drilling in them.

Gorilla Killers

Kahuzi-Biega National Park, south of the Virunga National Park, is considered a critical habitat for the world's largest ape, the Grauer's gorilla, which has suffered a staggering 77 percent decline in just one generation according to a recent report by the Wildlife Conservation Society.[178] Grauer's gorilla is only found in eastern Congo. Some gorilla nests have been completely wiped out. A 2016 study estimates that only 3,800 Grauer's gorillas have survived in the forest, which justifies their ascension to the status of Critically Endangered on the IUCN Red List of Threatened Species.[179]

"Bushmeat" is popular throughout Congo, especially in areas adjacent to the national parks, so the demand for gorilla meat is constant. Baby gorillas are also stolen from the forest and sold as pets, with a large export market in Southeast Asia.

Over 140 park rangers have died protecting the gorillas in Virunga National Park.[180] Because of the enhanced efforts of the park rangers, the mountain gorilla population has slowly been increasing, providing hope for future conservation efforts related to the species.[181]

Forest Destroyers[182]

The ongoing presence of armed groups, combined with extensive illegal poaching and mining, make Virunga the least secure national park in the world, according to park and UN officials.[183] Virunga is also affected by an unprecedented rate of human encroachment, with four million people—many of whom pursue livelihoods like farming, fishing, and charcoal production in violation of national and international regulations—living within a day's walk.[184] Nearly all of these nearby residents, including the city of Goma with a population of one million, rely on wood or charcoal for cooking. Virunga hosts some of the only remaining old-growth forest in the region, making it increasingly threatened.[185]

An illegal charcoal cartel is helping to finance one of the most prominent militias in Central Africa and destroying parts of Africa's oldest national park. Nursing alliances with Congolese army and police units and operating remote trafficking rings in the sanctuaries of Congo's protected forests, the Rwandan militia FDLR is a kingpin in Africa's Great Lakes region's organized crime networks and a continuing threat to human security. For years the group has helped sustain its activities by exploiting valuable natural resources, including minerals, ivory, fish, and marijuana. But one of the FDLR's most successful revenue-generating businesses is the illicit charcoal trade in Virunga National Park.[186]

Headquartered deep in the remote southwestern sector of Virunga, the illegal charcoal trade is lucrative. Some have estimated it has an annual value of up to $35 million.[187] The FDLR and its collaborators have developed tremendous business acumen, increasingly motivated by profit incentives and enabled by high-level Congolese state cover. As one park ranger told Fidel and Holly, "Armed groups have turned Virunga into their sanctuary."[188] The FDLR is under sanctions by both the United States and the United Nations, and its charcoal trafficking activities constitute ongoing violations of both sanctions regimes. In the regular course of business, the FDLR also commits a range of domestic and international crimes, including forced labor and illegal taxation. Yet impunity for charcoal trafficking crimes remains absolute for high-level perpetrators. The FDLR's business elements are distinct from its traditional combat structure and "have become the main modus operandi for FDLR survival," according to a 2014 UN study.[189] Even the most effective efforts to address the FDLR's military and political interests will fail if its profit incentives are left untended.

The success of the illegal charcoal trade relies on the widespread deforestation of parts of Virunga and the perpetration of human rights abuses, including reprisal murders and sexual slavery. These acts stoke one another and accelerate cycles of insecurity, poverty, fear, and environmental destruction. As activist Jeredy Malonga told Fidel and Holly about the FDLR, "They use violence directly to make the [charcoal] business work."[190]

The FDLR does not work alone. Some Congolese national police and military commanders are involved in the illegal charcoal trade. They draw significant revenues from profit sharing with the FDLR,[191] as well as from their own production, trafficking, and taxation of illegal charcoal. Some state officials also provide critical protection to the FDLR's commanders and officers in Virunga.

Illegal charcoal trafficking is an extremely violent business. The trade itself involves a range of crimes and human rights violations, including extortion, forced labor, murder, and sexual slavery. It is a mafia-like enterprise with profit as its primary objective and violence as a crucial means for achieving that objective. The FDLR's charcoal cartels resemble a South American drug trafficking network more closely than a traditional rebel army, given the group's strategic use of human rights violations, diverse alliances, and capitalization on the extreme poverty and weak governance that permeate many rural civilian communities.[192]

FIDEL'S
UPSTANDER STORY

◇◇

*Through a series of interviews conducted by Fidel,
Congolese Upstanders tell their life stories. All of them are risking
their lives to defend human rights, press for peace,
resist dictatorship, provide education, and prepare a better
future for their fellow Congolese.*

Dominique Bikaba

My name is Dominique Bikaba. I was born in 1972 in Chombo, a village located about 1.5 kilometers (one mile) from the Kahuzi-Biega National Park, a forest which nourished my childhood and the conservation work I am doing today. Chombo village is surrounded by abandoned tea plantations and facilities from colonial times, a situation which provided my childhood with a huge cultural mixture and exposure to different peoples from across the country and the region.

In the 1970s, the land on which we relied for subsistence was established as a national park, the current Kahuzi-Biega National Park. My grandparents, my community, and all indigenous peoples (pygmies) who lived in its boundaries were forced to leave without compensation. The evacuation happened when the dictator Mobutu was ruling the country. My grandparents and a bunch of expelled indigenous people settled together at the edge of the forest, where my grandparents accessed different land from their relatives who already lived there.

I'm now executive director of Strong Roots Congo, which is a nongovernmental organization based here in Bukavu, in eastern Congo. We work in conservation, actually focused on the conservation of great apes, and our mission is to save great apes from extinction. The eastern lowland gorillas are an endemic sub-species of gorillas, which means that they only live here in Congo, in the forest. They've dramatically declined from 17,000 to about 3,800 in the last twenty years.

So we—including the global community—have a responsibility to really do something to reverse this equation, to ensure that we can save the eastern lowland gorillas from extinction. The main threats come from armed conflict, illegal mining, poaching, hab-itat loss...all those kinds of things. We're working with all key stakeholders to ensure that we can preserve this gorilla, which is the largest primate on earth and it lives only here. You don't see any of them in zoos or anywhere else. So if we lose them in their nat-ural habitat, then they are gone forever. It's our responsibility, and friends outside and inside Congo can help ensure that we preserve this subspecies of gorillas.

When people talk about Congo, they only know that Congo has forever been in armed conflicts, with human rights violations and violence against women. But I think there are also good things in Congo. We've been facing these challenges of armed conflict, been targeted by militias, by rebels. We've had Congolese rebels, we've had foreign rebels, all of them acting like animals, so this animos-ity has been a big challenge for our conservation work in Congo.

But looking at species in the forest, the biggest problem is illegal mining. And illegal mining has fueled conflict by bringing money for warlords to buy guns to kill people. When you look at species, illegal mining has decimated our richness in terms of species: goril-las, elephants, and chimpanzees. More than 450 elephants have been slaughtered.

You have the good intention, the commitment, but there are things you cannot stop. Like how do you rebuild peace in the region? I'm not talking just about Congo, but the entire region. People think it's a communal conflict, one community against another community. That's wrong. It's not that. It's a regional problem. It's a regional problem where you have other nations coming and fighting in Congo, directly killing gorillas, directly killing elephants, promoting the illegal wildlife trade across the region. These are disputes among nations. Regional organizations have to intervene to ensure Congo is at peace. It's not something we can just build by ourselves from Bukavu, inside Congo.

Talking about illegal mining, we don't eat minerals in Congo. Even the people who are involved at the local level, like in artisanal mining, they can sell minerals, but at the end of the day, minerals are used somewhere outside Congo. With this demand from outside, the challenge is increasing. So normally in the region where we work, they mine coltan [tantalum], they mine cassiterite [tin], they mine gold. And protected areas are not protected against this challenge, because we've counted many miners, illegal miners, inside Kahuzi-Biega National Park. At one time we counted about eighty thousand miners inside Kahuzi-Biega National Park, mining, killing, and poaching. These minerals have been exploited, brought outside, to make cell phones, to make computers. Everybody knows that. What do we do to stop that?

In 2010 I testified on conflict minerals before the US Congress, supporting the Dodd-Frank Act. It had a great impact on mining in Congo. And I think the progress we are seeing in terms of illegal mining and traceability is thanks to this law. If this law hadn't passed in the US, I don't know where we would be today. Not just for people but also for wildlife and forests.

We've lost more than five million people killed here in Congo. Everybody knows about the genocide in Rwanda in 1994, but very few people talk about the five million Congolese people who have perished in Congo. For me, that's not fair.

———

Conservation is dying in Africa, and particularly here in Congo. I appreciate and am very grateful for all the support we've been getting for conservation in Congo, but we are looking at new approaches to conservation. We never succeed with conservation without involving local communities and indigenous people. We love gorillas, we love chimpanzees, but it's tricky: it's stupid to think that we can love gorillas and chimpanzees and hate people living around the forests, people who have been conserving the species even before conservation came into the picture. That's why our approach is to involve local and indigenous communities in every conservation effort we make here. That has shown the biggest success we've had in conservation work. For me, the big success I see is the number of people who now know about conservation, who know about Grauer's gorillas, who know what they can do to protect the earth. I'm talking about local community members in the region where we are working, because I'm doing conservation today and I come from this community. All the poachers, they come from this community. So if this community is well prepared, well educated, then conservation is going to succeed.

Sometimes people say they understand conservation—"We understand that we have to protect everything, we are not killing gorillas." They say they are hunting or trapping antelopes and so on, and unfortunately it's gorillas who fall into the traps, who lose hands, legs, and die. They say, "We don't have a choice, we don't have another option. We are starving. We are hungry." The socioeconomic situation is very challenging. People are obliged to look out for themselves because the government is not providing services to them. We've been able to make people understand that these species are a part of Congo, part of themselves. This is a meaningful existence to their forest. This information, this knowledge, is in communities today, and people who want to continue this work have been trained to continue the battle to ensure that Congo's natural resources are protected.

We've been intensifying our efforts around the Kahuzi-Biega National Park. And even though we have this dramatic decline of Grauer's gorillas in the region—actually, 77 percent of the gorillas have disappeared in less than twenty years—the part where we've been intensifying our activities, the highland part of the park of

Kahuzi-Biega, is the only habitat where the gorilla population has been stable for this period. It's even increased slightly. This means that if we could really intensify activities in other areas around the forest, the population could be protected.

We're working with several communities who say they love conservation: "This is our land. We depend on this land for subsistence. We can make gorillas come back again to our region because we feel proud of that. Even if we don't get anything in terms of governmental services, our children will see this. Our children will learn about this. It would be a big shame for us if we had gorillas and our grandchildren could not see them anymore and they see them just in books." Those are people who've never been to school but who are willing to put their land in conservation to ensure gorillas come back again.

The international community, the government of Congo, civil society, and the private sector set up a committee to monitor mining activities. They are ensuring that mining is allowed only in areas where it should be done. And they've set up a fund in which a small percentage of all mining transactions goes to support local development in communities where there has been mining. For me, that's very important. And that's a step which has been taken to ensure that when the government is not able to do something, where the Congolese wildlife authority is not able to do something, there is this committee working to ensure that the mining system is regulated.

I'm hoping we'll have sustainable peace in Congo. When we have a sustainable peace, things can work on their own. We need a leader who has a vision, a leader who can just open a little light for our country so people can follow. Everything you see here in Bukavu, none of it is done with the government. Everything is done by the people themselves. So what would happen if they had just a little help from the government? It could be very different. So these people are looking forward, are moving forward, and really want to see things changing. That's a big hope. They are not saying,

"Ahh, we are tired." No, they are moving moving moving, saying "We need something to change, we need a big movement."

I'm running an NGO now, a nonprofit for conservation and sustainable development. Someone else is protecting human rights. Someone else is in the media. Someone else is in education. And others are really pushing the government. They are activists. We need to shake up our government a little bit. We are members of the African Union and the UN. They can help Congo by shaking our government leaders, saying, "Hey, this is wrong, it shouldn't be like that." We're fighting internally to ensure that things go right, but we need a little hand from outside.

Congo has about one million square kilometers of forest, which represents 50 percent of the African forest. Half of the African forests are located in one country. So if we decimated our forests in Congo, it's not just Congo's forests, it's Africa's forests, it's the world's forests. It's not regulating climate just for the Congolese people. It's a global issue. That's just an example. I can cite hydrology. I can cite support for mining.

People outside Congo shouldn't keep quiet. They should say something about what is happening in Congo. They should urge their government. They should urge their funders. People writing books should write something about Congo.

We need to understand that Congo is another part of the same earth, the same world we share. It's not like a separate world and others are in another world, no. Imagine if you cut out Congo. It would be a world where we're missing something. We are on the same globe, and we should unite together. We need to be together to build this partnership.

◇◇

CONTACT INFORMATION FOR STRONG ROOTS CONGO:

strongrootscongo.org

◇◇

Powering the Auto Industry's Future
Global Demand: Cobalt for Electric Car Batteries

The electric car is quickly moving from an oddity to the automobile of the future, and car companies are investing heavily in advancing the technology. Tesla, Renault, Nissan, BMW, GM, Volkswagen, Volvo, Daimler, Fiat Chrysler, Hyundai, Honda, Ford, and Toyota have all publicly committed to increasing electric car production,[193] in part as a response to the damage that emissions have done to the climate. At the heart of electric and hybrid cars is the rechargeable lithium-ion battery, which also powers laptops and cell phones, and most lithium batteries require cobalt. And over half of the world's cobalt is located in Congo—50 to 60 percent of the world's estimated reserves.[194] In 2017, 58 percent of the world's cobalt supply came from Congo, though its share of the market could exceed 70 percent by 2025.[195] Predictions run as high as a thirtyfold increase in the demand for cobalt by 2030.[196]

The *Washington Post*'s Todd Frankel describes the context: "Lithium-ion batteries were supposed to be different from the dirty, toxic technologies of the past. Lighter and packing more energy than conventional lead-acid batteries, these cobalt-rich batteries are seen as 'green.' They are essential to plans for one day moving beyond smog-belching gasoline engines. Already these batteries have defined the world's tech devices. Smartphones would not fit in pockets without them. Laptops would not fit on laps. Electric vehicles would be impractical. In many ways, the current Silicon Valley gold rush—from mobile devices to driverless cars—is built on the power of lithium-ion batteries."[197]

Cobalt also has important military uses. The Pentagon has identified cobalt and copper as "strategic and critical minerals" for the production of military planes, missile guidance systems, electronics, and other hardware. Cobalt is a critical material in military and commercial jet engines as a superalloy, and it is very difficult to substitute for that use because of cobalt's very high heat resistance, according to the Defense Department. As of 2014, 16 percent of the cobalt supply was used in superalloys, 5 percent in magnets, and 42 percent in batteries, all of which are used in military hardware.

With the electric car market taking off, and demand for smaller, high-performance batteries in many products increasing, the demand for cobalt is exploding. Global demand for cobalt tripled in the first half of the 2010s, doubled in 2016, and the projections keep increasing for future growth. Bloomberg New Energy Finance thinks cobalt demand could increase thirtyfold by 2030.[198] Goldman Sachs projects that the electric car industry will be worth $244 billion by 2025.[199]

The world's largest producer of the mineral is, of course, Congo. "There will be no lithium-ion battery industry without [Congolese] cobalt," mineral industry analyst Caspar Rawles maintains. "We expect cobalt supply from [Congo] to become more dominant in the market."[200] Another industry analyst, Andries Gerbens, warns: "The cobalt-supply dependency on the Congo is a risky situation."[201] This dependence has sparked multiple research efforts at finding an alternative to cobalt to utilize in efforts to improve the life and cost-effectiveness of batteries.

Most cobalt production comes from industrial mines in Katanga, but there is also a large artisanal trade. Up to 150,000 Congolese artisanal miners search for cobalt and copper, which are mainly mined together, with little more than hand tools, lacking proper safety measures and leading to frequent deaths and injuries. Mines in many cases are simply hand-dug holes in the ground, with tunnels probing dozens of feet into the earth. There is little to no safety equipment or support structures to protect the miners from cave-ins.[202] Surrounding communities are exposed to toxic metals—including lead, cobalt, and uranium—and water pollution that cause numerous health problems, with one study around Lubumbashi, the biggest city in the Katanga region, concluding that the area was one of the ten most polluted in the world.[203]

One very damaging impact has been in the numbers of children employed in the mines in the main cobalt- and copper-producing region of Congo. The exact number remains unknown. UNICEF estimated the number at forty thousand boys and girls in 2014, but organizations on the ground think it is higher.[204] Anecdotal evidence from one investigation dramatically concluded, "There were children digging in trenches and laboring in lakes—hunting for treasure in a playground from hell."[205]

It turns out that cobalt mined by hand, especially by children, is less expensive than industrially mined cobalt. Companies don't have to pay salaries or fund a huge mining operation.[206] As one study found, "In addition to the health concerns, coercive forms of labor (forced or exploitative), can have adverse long-term consequences, not just for the children themselves, but also for societies as a whole."[207]

The cobalt and copper industry in Congo has also been linked to extensive corruption and lack of transparency. Corruption occurs in several ways, including direct bribery by outsiders; opaque contracting and subcontracting in which senior officials and/or Kabila family members profit; nontransparent dealings by the state-owned mining company Gecamines; flipping of mining assets that are deliberately undervalued and then sold for immense profits; and smuggling of artisanally mined cobalt. For example, per a US Justice Department indictment, Israeli businessman Dan Gertler, according to sources familiar with the case, reportedly paid millions of dollars in bribes to senior Congolese officials in exchange for copper and cobalt mining assets that he sold for immense profits, a charge he denies.[208] Also, $750 million went missing from Gecamines between 2011 and 2014.[209]

The profits from the global cobalt boom have certainly not trickled down to Congolese mining communities. Over 65 percent of families in one study say they do not have enough to eat.[210]

Some companies, like Apple, are working hard to address the problems in their supply chain. Other companies' efforts are more questionable. Tesla promised the *Washington Post* they would send a representative to Congo to develop strategies to clean up their supply chain. When the *Post* followed up a half year later, Tesla still hadn't sent anyone.[211] Tesla then commented in March 2018 that it conducted audits of suppliers on their risk management policies, but it was unclear what concrete steps the company was taking to reduce child labor or corruption in cobalt mining in its supply chain.

Fidel's Upstander Story

⬨⬨⬨⬨⬨⬨⬨⬨⬨⬨⬨⬨⬨⬨⬨⬨⬨⬨⬨⬨⬨⬨⬨⬨⬨⬨⬨⬨⬨⬨⬨⬨⬨

Through a series of interviews conducted by Fidel, Congolese Upstanders tell their life stories. All of them are risking their lives to defend human rights, press for peace, resist dictatorship, provide education, and prepare a better future for their fellow Congolese.

Petna Ndaliko

I was born in Goma, and the hospital that saw me born is now buried under lava. Growing up, I remember having a sense of stability and possibility. Life was ordered and people lived according to their values. The social structure was clearly defined, and there was a feeling that everybody in the community was looking after each other, and that made conflict management possible.

I had a pretty idyllic childhood up to a point. I was born into an upper-class family, so the biggest challenges I faced were how to escape from the neighbors after raiding their pomegranate trees. But then, as the political and economic fabric crumbled, more and more my world turned upside down. I witnessed and confronted many challenges. On a personal level, our family experienced a sudden economic downturn, which catapulted me into a position of responsibility for my eight younger siblings.

At the same time, I witnessed the structures that had brought so much security to daily life disintegrate as Mobutu's regime was collapsing and people were forced to fight for their survival. So in many ways I experienced the shift from stability to chaos on the level of the family and of the nation simultaneously.

One event that had a very decisive impact on me as a young person was the 1994 genocide in Rwanda, which forced hundreds of thousands of people to seek refuge in Congo (then Zaire). Most of them were women and children and most of them came to Goma. After a few weeks a lethal cholera epidemic broke out. My mother sent the children in my family to stay with relatives outside the city, but I insisted on staying with her in Goma. As we saw so many people dying from cholera, she and I did what we could to help by feeding and giving medicine to people who were hungry, sick, and suffering. We didn't have enough supplies to attend to everyone, but my mom just kept finding more and more things to give away and use for bandages. For me it was shocking when we would set out to feed people again the next day, only to discover some of the ones we were helping had died. There is the image stuck in my mind of a baby still sucking on her dead mother. That was the breaking point for me. So I asked my mother what was the point of helping people who are going to die anyway. And she told me never to turn away from responsibility no matter how dire the situation is, because it is not my place to judge or give in to despair, it is my place to take action when and how I can. "Because you never know," she added, "if the extra hour we give someone with our humble food might open up a possibility we could never predict."

The lessons my mother taught me about community responsibility and perseverance are the foundation of my work as a filmmaker, activist, and educator. Simply put, I believe stories are the pillars of critical thinking and the lynchpin of action, or, as I say to my students, if you want to change the world, change the story. I put this principle into practice in my own films and in my role as founder and artistic director of the Yole!Africa cultural center in Goma.

As a filmmaker, I address issues of human rights and social justice by emphasizing optimism and humanity despite crippling circumstances. Through my films I aim to change the stories being told not only about Congolese but about marginalized and exploited people everywhere. This commitment to social justice also shapes my work with Yole!Africa, where I have created a physical space for young people to gain practical skills in many forms of storytelling (media production, filmmaking, journalism, photography, music, dance) as well as a mental space for students to learn the tools of critical thinking and begin to apply them to the problems of our region, our nation, and our world. In this way Yole!Africa simultaneously contributes to improving the lives of young people materially, through education and employment opportunities, as well as psychologically, through empowerment and imagination.

The greatest success story is the transformation I have seen in Goma. What was, at the founding of Yole!Africa in 2002, a city completely devoid of cultural institutions is now, in 2017, among Congo's most creative and culturally vibrant locations. Further, when Yole!Africa started, civic engagement was not on the menu in youth circles, but now there are a number of nonviolent youth movements tackling social and political issues in our city, so much so that today Goma is the symbol of civic engagement in Congo. That for me is a story of success, because when I started Yole!Africa young people had hardly any options. Between the devastation wrought by the eruption of the Nyiragongo volcano, the political unrest, the humanitarian disasters triggered by the Rwanda genocide, and other problems, there simply were not many options for young people, let alone possibilities to gain the vital benefits of arts and cultural work.

In fact, when I first started Yole!Africa, people told me I was crazy to think of art and civic engagement in times of actual war. But I believed then—and still do—that creativity, imagination, education, and nonviolent expression are essential human rights and that fostering these capacities in youth contributes as directly to conflict resolution (whether on a small or large scale) as fulfilling material and physical needs. Seeing this manifest in Goma's thriving cultural life and record of civic engagement is, to me, proof of the power of art.

The biggest challenge we face now is, somewhat ironically, the stories that circulate globally about Congo and the interventions they spark. The more the world hears about unending chaos, savagery, and hopelessness, the more the world looks for those things and overlooks the rest. In turn, "activism" becomes a race to put Band-Aids on emergencies, most of which are misrepresented and thus misunderstood.

This launches a vicious cycle in which donors have more and more power to dictate the shape and methods of interventions, yet their decisions are often based on stories that don't represent the reality that we actually live. As you might imagine, funding for arts centers is not often prioritized when stories of disease and carnage dominate the media. For me, both as a filmmaker and as artistic director of Yole!Africa, this means I either have to compromise my integrity and appeal to funders with stories of chaos, savagery, and hopelessness, or act with integrity and operate with severely insufficient funding. The issue for me is not the money. Money is not the motivating factor for my work. The problem is that our capacity to change the story and thereby influence the interventions we receive is directly linked to our ability to raise funds for updated equipment, technologies, and facilities, and to pay operating costs and salaries (none of which appeal to funders responding to chaos, savagery, and hopelessness). So, in some ways, we are stuck in the very story we are trying to change.

My dream is to build a state-of-the-art media education center in Goma that allows youth to meet international standards in storytelling, then to replicate the Yole!Africa model across Congo and beyond. I envision this as a curriculum of critical arts intervention that brings arts, education, critical thinking, practical professional skills, employment opportunities, empowerment, and imagination to young people in conditions of crisis everywhere in Africa.

As I tell my students, Congo's problems are problems of wealth, not of poverty. Thus my hope and dream for Congo's future is that [Congo's first prime minister Patrice] Lumumba's vision for our country be realized. That means that Congo takes ownership of and responsibility for its many resources, that the nation prospers, and that it supports positive development across Africa. To my mind, this is at once an economic and a mental shift: it is a matter of political and economic autonomy but equally a matter of education, imagination, and the implementation of a new vision based on the rich human resources of our nation. For my part, this dream is best achieved through telling alternative stories and through educating future generations with the tools of self-representation that allow them to change both the stories being told and the solutions being sought to our problems.

For those people committed to Congo specifically, it is essential to go beyond the mainstream media stories and find avenues for understanding what is actually happening on the ground. More importantly, it is essential to support local organizations that are addressing the real needs of local communities. Sometimes this means being flexible about—or changing—funding structures, sometimes this requires adapting perceptions of "needs" to include the priorities of local communities even when they contradict international media reports. And one more thing: hearing the "local perspective" is not simply a matter of talking to anyone from Congo. What I mean is talking—over a long period of time—to those of us who have global and local perspectives and can speak honestly without fear of recriminations. It is only then that the true voices of empowered Congolese will inform the development of our nation.

Like all conflict zones, Congo should be represented as a place of complexity, not simply a place of disaster and need. Ours is a nation with a very complicated history—from its brutal colonization as the private personal property of Belgian King Leopold II to its current exploitation for coltan [tantalum] and other natural resources. This history continues to shape the political, economic, and social fabric of Congo, which affects our daily lives. But this history is too often ignored or omitted in representations of Congo. Instead, Congo's "story" is typically reduced to rape, cannibalism, and other unimaginable atrocities. Or else it is about the s/heroes from the West who come to save us. Both of these versions are harmful because they distort reality and justify international interventions that do not effectively address the issues we are facing. In my opinion, Congo's story should be told through the eyes, ears, lenses, and microphones of the many talented, capable, and competent people—both Congolese nationals and others who understand Congo's history and culture—who want to share and contextualize the actual realities we experience, from the traumas and injustices to the triumphs and joys. What I see is the world telling a specific story of Congo—over more than a century—that enables foreign nations to benefit from Congo's resources while absolving themselves of guilt for plundering a space inhabited by respectworthy human beings.

◇◇

CONTACT INFORMATION FOR YOLE!AFRICA:
https://yoleafrica.org

◇◇

CHAPTER FOUR

A Den of Highly Armed Thieves[212]

With such a historical backdrop, it's not surprising that Congo evolved into a true looting machine.[213] A rotating den of highly armed thieves at the top has used extreme violence to privatize the wealth of the country, going back to the mid-to-late 1800s. International commercial collaborators use associations with senior Congolese officials to plunder the country's resources. Congo is one of the wealthiest countries in Africa as a result of its natural endowments, but its people are some of the poorest in the world. Billions of dollars are being siphoned out of the country while billions in humanitarian and peacekeeping assistance are coming in to tidy up the mess.

The Business Model of Violent Kleptocracy

Governments are supposed to provide security and respond to the needs of their people, but it hasn't ever worked that way in Congo. Going back to King Leopold's administration and then the Belgian colonial era, successive Congolese governments have been controlled or hijacked by small groups of politicians, businessmen, and military commanders, working closely with international bankers, arms dealers, and governments around the world. Their aim? To steal from the treasury, violently extract natural resources, and privatize all the considerable wealth of the country. This has left the government bankrupt and the people repressed, pitted against each other, and in extreme poverty.

King Leopold may have been the most egregious example, but there have been many contemporary Leopolds since then, seeking to make Congo's riches their own. In fact, Mobutu Sese Seko, who ruled Congo from 1965 to 1997, is seen as the "inventor of the modern kleptocracy, or government by theft."[214] At the time of our writing in mid-2018, President Joseph Kabila is perfecting the kleptocratic arts. Like his predecessors, he has subverted democratic processes and violently repressed independent and opposition voices in order to retain power indefinitely. There is a business model of violent kleptocracy, where a few looters at the top of the pyramid inside and outside the country score massive profits, and the vast majority of people are left impoverished and repressed.

Multiple levels of exploitation occur. The army and rebel or militia leaders control or tax the mines and have used rape as a means of social control, intimidating local populations and punishing those perceived as disloyal.

The middlemen based in neighboring countries arrange for the purchase and resale of Congo's resources to international business interests run by people who are often accomplices. They acquire minerals to satisfy the insatiable demand of upstream vampires in the form of multinational corporations, which utilize the minerals in their products. Until they were forced to, they asked no questions about how the minerals ended up in their hands at such unbelievably low prices. Shady bankers and accountants help facilitate the theft, money laundering, and hiding of the ill-gotten wealth in shell companies, real estate, and bank accounts in other people's names.

Finally, there are consumers around the world, who are usually completely unaware that our purchases of cell phones, computers, jewelry, video games, cameras, cars, and so many other products are helping fuel violence halfway around the world, not comprehending or appreciating the fact that our standard of living and modern conveniences arc in some ways made possible and less expensive by the suffering of others.

This is not incompetence or state failure; the very purpose of the captured government in Congo is to make money for those in charge and their international facilitators and enablers. Sarah Chayes's writings about hijacked states in Afghanistan and elsewhere helped us understand this much more clearly.[215]

Congo expert Jason Stearns sums it up nicely: "[There is a saying in Kinshasa:] Mobutu used to steal with a fork—at least some crumbs would fall between the cracks, enough to trickle down to the rest of us. But Kabila, he steals with a spoon. He scoops the plate clean. . . . The Congo of today is in some ways more similar to the sixteenth-century Italy of Machiavelli…than to any modern twenty-first-century state."[216]

Fidel's Upstander Story

◇◇◇◇◇◇◇◇◇◇◇◇◇◇◇◇◇◇◇◇◇◇◇◇◇◇◇◇◇◇◇◇◇◇

Through a series of interviews conducted by Fidel, Congolese Upstanders tell their life stories. All of them are risking their lives to defend human rights, press for peace, resist dictatorship, provide education, and prepare a better future for their fellow Congolese.

Rebecca Kabugho

My name is Rebecca Kabugho. I was born in Goma on the first of September 1993. I grew up in Goma. I live in Goma. So I'm a Gomatrician.

I was born into gunfire all over Goma, as the Rwandan war was raging until it led to the Rwanda genocide in 1994. So I am kind of a result of that war. I was born amid bullets, grew up amid bullets.

I grew up with my mom, who was mostly alone. She was taking care of us herself because Dad was away. I only met my dad when I turned four or five years of age. It's a big challenge growing up like that without the love of both of your parents. I'm the fourth of five children—four daughters and one son, so all of us daughters were sharing the love of our brother.

The eruption of the Nyiragongo volcano in Goma—I think when I was still in fourth grade in elementary school—was another challenge, as we had to flee Goma and find refuge elsewhere.

My mom had to choose which among her daughters and her only son she would pay the school fees for. I always told my mom that we should share the money equally. If she had ten dollars, then we should get two dollars each to make sure none of us was treated unfairly, regardless of age or sex.

I've been a Lucha member since 2013, but I really became committed to the struggle in 2014. Lucha stands for "Struggle for Change" [*Lutte pour le changement*] and we fight for change in Congo. Lucha is a movement of young people who came together to do something different from the many NGOs and political parties in Congo. Structurally, those NGOs and parties are headed by coordinators and chairmen who make all the decisions. With Lucha, we decided to do something differently, with a parallel leadership where every member can give their opinion and then we decide collectively. There's no boss who wakes up in the morning and makes decisions.

At Lucha there's no chairman who sanctions members. We are led by values and principles, and it's been that way since Lucha was created five years ago. We are here. We're working for the country. We believe that hope for Congo's future lies within its youth. The fight for freedom is our contribution for the country to pull out of this crisis. Congo doesn't give us the choice. We have no time to waste going to the beaches, going shopping, etc. We are here to work, because our parents failed.

I'm not ashamed to say it: our parents failed. Because if we're living in a country torn apart, a Congo where its citizens are not happy to live but want rather to run away from it and go abroad, that is a testament to the failure of our parents. However, we think that to make a change in this country, we must live in it and go through all the challenges it is home to. That's the essence of our fight for change.

The situation in the country doesn't give us the choice between enjoying life partying at home and the fight. It's a big responsibility, as you wonder, What shall I do after five years of university when there's no job opportunity in the country? Am I just going to stay at home or keep studying endlessly? Joining in the struggle for change has become a mandatory choice, because if it is successful, at least tomorrow you can enjoy having access to running water and electricity. Even today, students are going to school without washing, and they're studying without light because there's no electricity. So we fight not just for ourselves, because we don't see actual results yet. But we're fighting for generations to come! We're aware that the struggle is a long process, but it's upon me to fight for those generations to come.

We fought really hard in 2016. I have even been jailed for six months for promoting democracy, but we have failed. However, I'm proud of what I did because we have at least tried. I can't stay in my corner complaining that we failed to promote a peaceful presidential transition; but at least I stood up and said, "Kabila must step down, we want an alternative, we need democracy in Congo!" So, personally, I don't see that as a failure, because I have at least tried.

Besides, there's running water in some parts of the city of Goma today following a big campaign we led. We had people sign a petition for the provision of running water in the city of Goma because it just didn't make any sense that we were so close to Lake Kivu but we had no running water in our compounds and faucets. Why was that? So Lucha ran a big campaign in 2013, and today there's an alternative water provision system in the city.

Another success is the worldwide echo our struggle has had. In 2017 I was honored with the International Women of Courage Award by the US State Department. Once again I say thank you, because such recognition consolidates our struggle; it really encourages us. It was a big surprise! I was not expecting such recognition. And it's even more astonishing that it's the US that organized something like that: it should have been up to the Congolese government to thank its brave ones.

In addition, Lucha militants share actively in world forums on democracy, and that is a sign that the world is paying attention to what we're doing. We're sharing in global efforts with high-profile political leaders from all over the world to talk about democracy in Africa and in our country in particular.

We're facing a lot of challenges with this struggle. One of them is repression. We have been arrested, detained, and sentenced illegally by the Congolese justice system. There's no freedom of expression. People need to realize that the future of this country lies in their hands. There's a group of leaders who have taken the entire nation hostage. If we take our responsibility in hand as a nation, we can cause things to change.

Most people in positions of power send their children to school abroad. How can they think of rebuilding this country if their children are not attending school here? How will they think of paying the teachers decently while their children are not studying here? How will they think of paying medical staff while they don't get treated here in Congo? How can they think of building better roads while they're driving expensive cars and trucks? How will they think of developing the country while they have all they need at home?

It's our money they're stealing. People are sweating every day with skyrocketing taxes. There is nearly 100 percent inflation in the local markets. People are being impoverished by their own government. Such an economic situation in the country is a challenge.

It was around four a.m., February 16, 2016, that we got taken away. On the eve of our arrest, the North Kivu governor had invited all the people of Goma to mobilize and welcome our national football [soccer] team following its African Nations Championship victory against the national team from Mali. The Congolese national team had been massively supported by the people of both Goma and Bukavu during the African Nations competition in Kigali. We had therefore planned to take advantage of the situation to get our message out, as people would be assembling following the governor's call. We had hand-written our message on pieces of paper, but we didn't finish doing it the day before, so six of us decided to stay up all night in order to finish the job. Our message was simple: "In 2016 we have won the African Nations cup; in 2016 we will win the democratic transfer of power. There will be democracy and liberty!" That was the message.

We don't know who reported us to the police when we got taken away. The prosecution accused us of being an insurgent group and a group of bandits. The tribunal first gave us a two-year sentence. We appealed and got the sentence down to six months. But a few days before we finished serving the sentence, we learned that President Kabila had granted us a presidential amnesty. But I reject that amnesty even today. We all rejected it, because we never asked for it and never accepted the charges brought against us. We demanded that the charges against us be dropped. That, in short, is how we got arrested. There were six of us and I was the only female.

In December 2016 I was jailed for the second time, following my claim that Kabila should step down. I was put in prison twice but arrested four times. I was arrested the first time by ANR [the Congo government's National Intelligence Agency]. I was detained, beaten up, tortured, and they even subjected me to a simulated drowning. We got beaten up seriously for trying to press for the liberation of political detainees in Kinshasa in 2015.

We dream of a new Congo! A new Congo where justice, freedom of expression, and good education will reign. A new Congo where the efforts of the Congolese will benefit the majority! We can do so much on our own, but unfortunately, some are giving up by fleeing the country that was left to us by our ancestors, a Congo that Lumumba paid for with his life. Liberty is our hope, our dream, and with our strength and our commitment, we know this country will be pulled out of the crisis. And we stand ready to keep on fighting!

We are really encouraged by things like what the US State Department did when they recognized our work. It's something that really incentivized us to move forward with the struggle, because now the entire world knows of the courage of our movement. And I think we need now to show what we're really capable of doing.

I think any part of the world that is facing similar challenges can learn from us, because bad governance and lack of access to running water and electricity are common in many places. I have seen, for instance, homeless people in Los Angeles, and I'd be happy to see people in the United States stand up for the homeless. That's the essence of our struggle —hopefully inspiring upstanders in other countries making demands of their governments for the change that is needed there. Apart from that, I don't know what else I could ask for, because Congo has got everything, all kinds of wealth. I'm not going to ask for money, because Congo has got everything except good governance and a citizenry demanding accountability from its authorities.

I hope our struggle inspires everybody. That's the ideal. We'd like to see people standing up in the United States, in France, etc. It's not always rosy over there. There are thorns in their political, economic, and cultural systems too, and it's upon citizens of those countries to take up their responsibilities and stand up for their rights.

I think I'd ask anyone wishing to talk about Congo to talk not only about negative things but also about what's positive in Congo. And among the positive things I'm seeing are the young people, who are the hope of this country. Chaos, massacres, etc. are what people hear about most in the press. But that is not the only thing that's going on in Congo, which is a big country with an informed youth population who are holding out hope for a bright future for Congo, and that's worth highlighting.

People simplify the history of Congo. It's our duty as Congolese people to talk about the true history of Congo.

◇◇

CONTACT INFORMATION FOR LUCHA:
www.luchacongo.org

◇◇

CHAPTER FIVE

Africa's First World War

Reverberations from Rwanda's Genocide

One of the great cataclysms of the twentieth century, the 1994 genocide in Rwanda took approximately 800,000 lives in 100 days, the fastest rate of mass murder in recorded history. As the Rwandan government and its associated Hutu militias were carrying out the genocide, rebel leader Paul Kagame's primarily Tutsi force fought against the genocidal government, quickly captured the Rwandan capital of Kigali, and eventually drove that regime and its allied militia forces out of Rwanda. Along with those forces, nearly two million Rwandan refugees, mostly Hutu, went across borders into neighboring countries, primarily Congo (then called Zaire). Diseases like cholera killed some 40,000 refugees in the camps. Over 100,000 former Rwandan soldiers and militias—the perpetrators of the genocide—hid themselves among the refugees.

The Aftermath of Genocide

The aftermath of the Rwandan genocide spilled over into Congo in the mid-1990s, acting like gasoline on the fire of preexisting intercommunal tensions and conflict. The situation was made worse by the rapacious divide-and-conquer strategy of the Congolese government in its eastern provinces bordering Rwanda. The Rwandan Hutu soldiers and militias hiding in Congolese refugee camps resumed their attacks on Rwandans from across the border, continuing the Rwandan Civil War on Congolese soil. They maintained their genocidal ideology aimed at destroying the Tutsi "cockroaches," as the militias' propagandists called them. Illustratively, one of their leaders, Colonel Théoneste Bagasora, pledged to "wage a war that will be long and full of dead people until the minority Tutsi are finished and completely out of the country."[217]

Congolese president Mobutu began to provide support to some of the Rwandan Hutu insurgents in the camps, which deeply alarmed former rebel leader Paul Kagame, who was setting up a new government in Rwanda amid the ashes. Kagame and his colleagues knew that if a neighboring government provided sustained support to the genocidal rebels in the refugee camps, the possibility existed that those rebels, using the refugees as human shields, could invade Rwanda and try to finish the genocide.

In 1996 Kagame went to Washington to warn President Clinton that if the international community didn't do something to counter the threat to Rwanda's embryonic post-genocide government, then Rwanda's army would be forced to take matters into its own hands.

The First Congo War

And that is just what Rwanda did later in 1996, given that the international community did nothing to counter the cross-border attacks into Rwanda from the refugee camps in Congo. With Uganda's help, Rwanda invaded Congo, targeting the rebels and scattering the refugees. Rwanda first attacked the biggest refugee camp in Congo, driving half a million Rwandans home in three days. Another half million dispersed into eastern Congo's forests.[218] At the same time, Rwanda created and armed a Zairian rebel group—the AFDL, led by gold and ivory trafficker Laurent Kabila—to provide some kind of local cover to Rwanda's invasion, which was supported by Uganda, Angola, Burundi, Tanzania, Ethiopia, Eritrea, and Zimbabwe.[219]

Kagame's army pushed through the refugee camps all the way to the capital, Kinshasa—over twelve hundred miles—justifying the move to overthrow Mobutu by pointing to his support for and protection of the Rwandan Hutu militias. Parenthetically, this was Kagame's third successful regime change, as he had previously helped lead the takedown of a dictator in Uganda and captured power in Rwanda from the genocidal regime, and now had engineered the removal of Mobutu. Eyewitnesses said Rwandan troops killed huge numbers of Rwandan Hutu refugees who had fled the camps into the interior of Congo. Rwandan army troops and columns of Congolese child soldiers affiliated with Laurent Kabila's AFDL rebel group committed a number of massacres of refugees; in Tingi Tingi camp, for example, tens of thousands of Hutus were slain.[220] In the Congolese region bordering Rwanda, Rwandan government forces "systematically rounded up and killed thousands of Hutu villagers, accusing them of supporting the *génocidaires* [the Rwandan Hutu militias]."[221] A UN investigation found that tens of thousands of refugees were deliberately killed, the majority of whom were children, women, the elderly, and the sick.[222] The UN report concluded that there may have been "acts of genocide" committed, as the killing was done in such a systematic way.[223]

The Tutsi populations—both Rwandan and Congolese—have been at the center of the conflict in eastern Congo, just as they have been in Rwanda and Burundi. Jason Stearns asserts that "No other sentiment has justified as much violence in the Congo as anti-Tutsi ideology." Tutsi have been both "victims and killers" on a massive scale, the violence "fueled by struggles over land tenure, citizenship, and access to resources."[224]

The US and UK supported Kagame and by extension his intervention in Congo, deeply embarrassed by their non-response to the Rwandan genocide just a few years earlier. About that American and British support for Rwanda's invasion, historian David Van Reybrouck concludes, "The backing for Rwanda and the rebels would unleash years of misery."[225]

Kabila Turns on Rwanda

Laurent Kabila was installed as president in May 1997, and he changed the name of the country back to Congo from Zaire. He spent a lot of time signing all kinds of shady deals with mining companies and immediately began displaying authoritarian tendencies. Within a year, he had turned on his former patrons in Rwanda and Uganda. He whipped up sentiment against Rwandan Tutsis, playing on preexisting prejudices, as a wide swath of Congolese people thought (and continue to believe) that the Rwandans want Congo's raw materials and land.

Most damagingly, Laurent Kabila's government began supplying arms to some of the Rwandan Hutu militias. Shortly thereafter, according to political scientists Philip Roessler and Harry Verhoeven, "Paul Kagame gave the green light to proceed with a regime change strategy in Congo."[226]

The Second Congo War

In July 1998 Kabila announced that all Rwandan and foreign soldiers had to leave Congo. Within a week, Rwanda invaded Congo again, and the Second Congo War was on. This time the invading Rwandan army went straight for Kinshasa, commandeering planes all over East and Central Africa and flying soldiers directly to the outskirts of Congo's capital city. However, unlike the first time, the Rwandans didn't seek Angola's approval in advance. Angola had its own strategic calculations, and neighboring Zimbabwe had economic motives. Angola attacked Rwanda's forces when they were about to take Kinshasa, and Zimbabwe deployed forces to Kinshasa to defend Kabila's government.

Eventually, ten African countries and thirty local militias became embroiled in the conflict,[227] which came to be known as

Africa's First World War. Congo, Angola, Zimbabwe, Namibia, Sudan, Chad, and Libya were allied against Rwanda, Uganda, and Burundi, producing a bloody military stalemate. At the time, Kabila continued to support the Rwandan militias responsible for the genocide in eastern Congo against the Rwandan government's army and Rwandan government-backed militias, adding a further layer of explosive complexity.

An African Scramble for Congo's Resources

A free-for-all for Congo and its resources ensued. The Rwandan government army fought against Rwanda's genocidal anti-government militias on Congolese soil, as did Ugandan government soldiers and rebel groups backed by Rwanda and Uganda. Eastern Congo was literally on fire.

From 1999 to 2002, Rwanda and Uganda militarily occupied and controlled nearly half of Congo, and Zimbabwe and Angola benefited with commercial partnerships with Kabila in the other half. David Van Reybrouck observes, they "[helped] themselves on a massive scale to the raw materials present there.... Booty had taken precedence over power.... All wars are dirty, but when the political motive makes way for a pecuniary one, things go completely sour. War became a worthwhile economic alternative...a lucrative business."[228] As discussed in chapter 3, competition was violent and fierce over copper, cobalt, gold, diamonds, and the 3Ts, as well as ivory, charcoal, and the prospect of oil.

Jason Stearns concludes about this period, "The Rwandan, Ugandan, and Congolese proxies eventually ran amok, wreaking havoc." [229] Two million Congolese were displaced into the forests, some without even any clothes—"*les nudistes*," they were called—searching for food in the forest.[230]

Congo's natural resources were behind nearly every move. President Kabila began selling off many of Congo's valuable assets to his foreign allies in exchange for their help in protecting his regime. He created important military and commercial partnerships with Zimbabwe and Angola, two fellow violent kleptocracies, in an array of industries that included oil, diamonds, other minerals, banking, agriculture, and timber. Zimbabwean generals set up businesses in Congo to deal diamonds and provide services to the Congolese government and army. As Zimbabwe's own governance crisis intensified in the late 1990s and early 2000s, Congo provided a way to keep Mugabe's generals happy by allowing and facilitating them to make money there. At the peak of Zimbabwe's intervention, over 12,000 Zimbabwean troops were stationed in Congo.[231] In return, Kabila's regime was saved from the Rwandans and Ugandans.[232]

PHOEBE'S STORY, 2010

My name is Phoebe Mapendo. I am the head of a women's group called Mama Amkeni. I came here to this IDP [internally displaced persons] camp because I was fleeing the war.

How I got here is a long story. If these armed groups discover that you have any kind of mineral in the ground on your farm, you get kicked out or killed. It was during the night that they came. There was shooting everywhere. All of a sudden there was a break in the fighting. When the shooting stopped, we heard people screaming everywhere, and suddenly these men came with weapons to try to force in doors and kill people with knives.

Men especially got killed, and women were pulled out of their homes and raped in the open air. It was very tough because everybody was fleeing in different directions. I remember I was just stepping and jumping over dead bodies, but I can't tell you the exact number. I walked seven hours to reach this place of refuge, this camp. When everyone fled I was separated from my husband and my children. I have found two of them in the past months, but not the others. And I found my husband a few months ago as well. I don't know where our other children are.

Aid agencies have been providing food, though not enough, but at least we're getting something. What we're lacking most is clothing. Because we had nothing when we came here, in the camp we were given some cooking utensils and blankets, but they get worn out. The situation has been so tough in this camp because I'm trying to raise children while I'm now displaced from my home. Providing clothing for all the children is a big pressure for me, but worse than that I can't afford their education. To make a little money, we often work on the local farms near here, but sometimes they don't have work for us.

All these children here are supposed to be the future of this country, but given that they are not attending any school because they can't afford it, we don't know what their future will be. So it has been quite tough. We would ask if you could help bring us peace so we could go home and live normal lives.

I dream of having my own house again. I had a farm, I had livestock, I had everything. I could provide for my children. I could provide for their education. But today, it's like prison where I am in the camp, because these things are no longer normal. We have been displaced several times and we're living like beasts. So if it was only up to me, if I was in a position of power, I would have stopped this greedy business.

For Congo, I dream of just one word: peace.

Postscript:

At the beginning of 2017, Phoebe passed away in labor following the closure of the health center in the area where she was living. She gave birth to a healthy daughter.

OTHER VOICES
WE COULDN'T IGNORE[233]

We have spent much of our time in Congo talking with survivors of the relatively unknown conflicts that have torn their country apart. Here are snippets from conversations with a few of them in an internally displaced persons camp we visited in 2010 at the height of the violence in eastern Congo and the messages they asked us to carry back from them.

Marie is a rape survivor twice over. She overcame her trauma to found a women's organization that helps others who have survived sexual crimes. "Please stop this bloody business," she pleaded to the companies profiting from the minerals mined in her area. "You are fueling conflict. Families are being torn apart. Women are being raped. Communities are being destroyed so armed groups can profit from mines. Companies should stop supporting this and do ethical business."

The conflict in Congo has left millions homeless, fleeing from their villages after they were burned to the ground or looted by armed groups. In an internal refugee camp, we met Mapendo, a young woman who survived an attack on her village in which members of an armed militia went door to door raping women and killing men. In reply to our questions, she said starkly, "There is no difference between the companies [who profit from Congo] and the people doing the killing here in Congo."

The leader of one internal refugee camp we visited told us, "The problem in Congo is greed. They should prosecute the greedy people—wherever they come from—who benefit from illegal minerals."

A young man named Innocent who was living in the camp after being driven from his home by an armed group taking over a nearby mine concluded, "The people that are doing this to me are the people who are making the products that use these minerals."

Esther, another displaced camp resident, challenged us in a unique way: "I want the users of these minerals to come live in these camps with us so they can understand what we are going through."

Finally, a fourteen-year-old girl whom we befriended spoke with a level of clarity well beyond her years when she told us, "Anyone who buys a cell phone should question their conscience and insist on fair trade."

CHAPTER SIX

Road to Congo

by Ryan Gosling

My first memory of our trip nearly eight years ago is of crossing from Rwanda to Congo. We passed immediately from paved roads to those of ruin and hardship. I came to understand that the roads were that way by design. Someone we were traveling with said, "If you want to keep people from organizing and rising up, don't pave the roads."

For the most part, the roads leading to and from the mines were kept in good repair. But all the rest of the roads used by the Congolese people to travel, do business, and live their lives were not. They were a constant reminder of the struggle of the people we met and the individual stories that you'll read about in this book.

My personal road to Congo began when I went to a screening of *Hotel Rwanda* almost fifteen years ago. I was very affected by the film and had an opportunity to talk with Don Cheadle afterward. We talked about some of his experiences in Africa and his commitment to the goals of those whom he had met there. He introduced me to John Prendergast and that sparked an immediate friendship. I was inspired by the work of the Enough Project and wanted to understand more.

I was incredibly fortunate to be invited by John and Fidel to go along on the trip. I brought my camera as a way of remembering some of the people and experiences.

Once we arrived, one thing was clear from those who were inviting us into their homes to hear their stories of survival and their efforts to create change: there was a legitimate expectation and hope that we would find a way to share their stories with others.

We were told many personal stories by many people, but a central theme emerged. It was one of an unwavering refusal to be silenced or broken. It's hard for me to imagine being able to move on after the horrors many of them have experienced. However, they have gone beyond moving on. To have the strength to take those nightmares and use them as fuel to make the hopes and dreams of their families and country a reality is the definition of heroic.

In the postscript to this book, Chouchou Namegabe says, "Women in particular pay the heaviest price" in the cycle of war and violence. I echo her praise of the Congolese women who have fought for their own survival and that of their communities. The remarkable women I was so privileged to meet had endured and used their strength to support and lift others. They were caring for their families; going to school; running support and advocacy groups; and organizing in their communities.

I'm extremely grateful to Fidel and John for assembling this powerful group of Congolese activists, professionals, and artists to tell their stories and stories of Congo. I'm also grateful to be asked to share some of these images so that I might be able to deliver on the expectation of those I photographed.

The Congolese are fighting for their freedom and for their future. It meant more to me than words can express to have met every person I photographed, along with all of the people who are supporting them in their efforts to achieve justice and to live the lives to which they are entitled.

Fidel's Upstander Story

◇◇◇◇◇◇◇◇◇◇◇◇◇◇◇◇◇◇◇◇◇◇◇◇◇◇◇◇◇◇◇◇◇◇◇◇◇

Through a series of interviews conducted by Fidel, Congolese Upstanders tell their life stories. All of them are risking their lives to defend human rights, press for peace, resist dictatorship, provide education, and prepare a better future for their fellow Congolese.

Justine Masika

I am Justine Masika Bihamba, and I was born in 1965 in Butembo but moved to Goma when I was four months old. So, I'm in Goma, I grew up in Goma, I'm getting old in Goma and will die in Goma! I'm the eldest of a big family of thirteen siblings. And our father was a businessman. Thus I grew up in good conditions. At that time it was not common for children to be driven to school, but we were. So my dad was a renowned businessman, and I had a happy childhood. And I was lucky enough to have a good education, because paying for my schooling was not a problem for my parents.

I was sickly, such that I had to interrupt my schooling from the third year of high school. I was forced to rest because I had atrocious headaches. Thank goodness I had parents who could afford to take me to hospitals outside Congo. I spent six months in a Rwandan hospital, and once back home, I had to stay out of school for that year. But apart from that, everything else was fine. I'm from a Christian family that is obedient to God and that prayed a lot.

After my education, I found a job at a local NGO that was promoting peasant women's rights. And thanks to my job, I understood the hardships women were facing, but also the potential they were endowed with. I came to the conclusion that those women needed to be supported, and that's how I became an upstander for women's rights.

Women's main problem is often a lack of education. So we do sensitization campaigns raising women's awareness about their rights that they should be claiming. Raising awareness also includes showing women that they are endowed with much more potential than men but they ignore it.

Our job consists first of helping women to discover their self-potential, their strengths, their weaknesses, and their limits. That's the job we do on a daily basis. In addition to that, and in light of SGBV [sexual and gender-based violence], rejection, and marginalization, we have been focusing on sexual violence survivors to help them recover their self-confidence and dignity. We show them that no matter what they've gone through, they remain integral human beings. We empower them politically by consolidating their leadership within their communities after we have assisted them medically and psychologically. Their communities need to witness their transformation.

Successes that stick with me are those we achieve when a woman comes to us crying and saying she no longer wants to live. "I must die. I'm nothing. I've been abused." But after we have attended to her, she realizes that she is an integral woman and feels confident and decides to fight for herself. That is our success!

I would be happy to see women become free and enjoy their full rights. When we talk about women's rights, they're always wrongly interpreted by our communities. So our communities need to come to the realization that men and women are equal: they have equal chances and equal rights.

The general belief in many communities is that a man is superior to a woman, and unfortunately women have internalized that. They believe that they're inferior and their place is to stay at home making babies, whereas the woman is man's companion according to the Bible. So her place should be to be a partner to her husband,

and both must help each other, together making Congo a dream country.

The most difficult challenge we face is insecurity all over our country. There is no peace. In addition to that and bad governance, we face cultural and traditional stereotypes. So while it's vital that we work for a sustainable security-sector reform and total peace, we need to win over traditional leaders toward the abrogation of degrading customs so that women can be more promoted.

Drawing on the history of other nations, my hope is that Congo will change one day. But that requires that we educate our youth, because when they understand, then we can be sure of a better future. We must work on the youth because when you see the Congolese political class from both sides—the opposition and the ruling majority—none of them has internalized the general well-being of the people.

All I can ask of those who want to support Congo is that they should demand that the Congolese constitution be respected and help us prepare our youth for a better future.

Congo's history is not known. That's the impression I have, because you'd be amazed at how many outsiders believe Africa is a country. It is up to us Congolese to know how we should be selling our country. Congo is a big country with enormous potential but with an impoverished population. I've just met a young female journalist who told me that when she heard about Goma in the media, she thought it was a village. So it's my job to educate her that while there's war in Congo, it's not all dark. There are brave people fighting for change every day.

CONTACT INFORMATION FOR SYNERGIE DES FEMMES (WOMEN'S SYNERGY FOR VICTIMS OF SEXUAL VIOLENCE):
https://www.facebook.com/synergiedesfemmes

CHAPTER SEVEN

Crimes Against Humanity

Ground Zero

The phrase "crimes against humanity" was first used in response to human rights abuses in Congo. The African American writer and minister George Washington Williams first coined the phrase during a visit in 1890, when he witnessed the cruelty of King Leopold's abusive governing system. The phrase was so apt it was codified into international law in the Hague Conventions in 1899.

There are few parallels in modern world history for what has unfolded in Congo in terms of human suffering over the past five centuries. Crimes against humanity of all kinds have been perpetrated with frequency and total impunity, but this section will focus on two particular human rights crimes: mass rape as a war weapon, and the recruitment of children as soldiers.

PART ONE: MASS RAPE

As Holly Dranginis of The Sentry has written, sexual and gender-based violence has been a defining feature of war in Congo for decades. SGBV is an instrument of war, committed often in tandem with other gross violations of human rights. Social norms regard rape as an unpunishable crime.[234] Holly points out, "The rates of prosecution and conviction for sexual violence are severely low in Congo, and even the cases that do go forward are warped with corruption. Those patterns send a message that it is unimportant or impossible to deliver justice for these crimes."[235]

In 2010 former UN special representative on sexual violence in conflict—and later Sweden's minister for foreign affairs—Margot Wallström memorably and hauntingly called Congo "the rape capital of the world."[236] But Congolese activist Justine Masika wants her country to be known for something else: "I agree with Liberia's Nobel Prize laureate Leymah Gbowee, who called my nation 'the world capital of sisterhood and solidarity.' Congolese women have decided to take our future into our own hands. We have few resources but we have an enormous amount of know-how."[237]

Justine Masika sees inequality and war as driving forces fueling sexual violence: "We women have a huge influence in our communities, yet we are almost entirely excluded from Congolese political life. A lot of this is down to the traditional role of women and a government that ignores article 14 of our constitution, which demands gender equality. Only 8 percent of parliament is female, and we have been almost completely left out of peace-building efforts—apart from the occasional inclusion of one or two women to take notes while men speak. According to the International Peace Institute, the chance of lasting peace increases by 35 percent when women are included in talks, but during times of war, women's political participation tends to decrease while sexual violence increases."[238]

Holly Dranginis explains the legal issues: "SGBV refers to a broad universe of violent acts used in wartime or peace that are connected to sex, gender, or both. SGBV includes rape and certain forms of torture but also extends to sexual threats, exploitation, humiliation, domestic violence, and certain types of enslavement, incest, and involuntary prostitution. Statistics on SGBV often lack precision and accuracy. Low reporting rates and the difficulty of collecting physical evidence degrade the accuracy of statistics, particularly in Congo where census data is scarce and the lack of security and infrastructure hinders investigations. Investigators tend to use two types of data in addition to firsthand testimony: medical and legal case files and population studies. The latter is best for revealing trends, but it is difficult to measure in Congo where there are high rates of displacement and migration and where the last population census was conducted in 1984.[239] Case file data is scarce and anecdotal because of underreporting and confidentiality constraints. Sexual violence survivors often choose not to report crimes for fear of reprisal or stigmatization."[240]

Holly continues with an explanation of legal repercussions: "Evidence suggests rebel and army leaders in Congo may be criminally liable for war crimes and crimes against humanity involving sexual and gender-based violence under the doctrine of command responsibility. High-level officials responsible for these crimes are often the orchestrators, not the direct perpetrators, of the acts, but they are nonetheless liable for their role as intellectual authors of a plan to use sexual violence as a weapon or their failure to prevent perpetration of crimes. For example, judges at the International Tribunal for Rwanda found that in April 1994, Jean-Paul Akayesu, mayor of the Taba commune in Rwanda, directly oversaw the systematic rape of Tutsi women during the Rwandan genocide, failing to prevent, repress, or report the abuses.[241] In Congo, there is evidence that leaders of both rebel and government forces have ordered their troops to commit sexual violence as a deliberate means to gain territory and propagate fear among civilians. The 2013 UN Group of Experts findings suggest that rebel and [Congolese] state army commanders oversaw or orchestrated rape and sexual enslavement while in effective control over their subordinate troops with knowledge that they were committing rape in the context of civilian attacks, triggering their liability for war crimes and crimes against humanity."[242]

Holly focuses on the motivations:[243] "Rape and other forms of sexual violence can be strategic military tools because they manipulate group psychologies and weaken community networks by instilling fear, distrust, and shame at multiple levels of a community, sometimes with a single act. These crimes often traumatize and debilitate the victims as well as the relatives and community members made to commit or observe the acts. Crimes involving SGBV also undermine authority figures traditionally meant to protect women and children in the community.[244] Furthermore, sexual violence both drives and stems from forced displacement: when soldiers and rebels rape civilians, civilians often flee out of fear of repeat attacks or stigmatization. Internally displaced persons and refugees are in turn disproportionately vulnerable to sexual violence in part because they live in IDP and refugee camps that lack security and rule of law."[245]

One of many examples took place in November 2012, when Congolese army soldiers went on a ten-day looting and raping spree in Minova, eastern Congo. Though the number may be only the tip of the iceberg, the rapes of at least seventy-six women and girls were confirmed.[246] The incident generated such an outcry that the Congolese government was forced to pursue legal action against some of the alleged perpetrators. In December 2013, the military court system opened a trial in Goma, with thirty-nine army soldiers and officers charged with various crimes, including pillage and rape. Only two were convicted, and the high-level commanders were never charged, exacerbating the widespread impunity for SGBV in Congo. The case's legitimacy suffered because of three main problems, as summarized by Holly Dranginis: lack of investigation strategy, lack of due process and other defendants' rights for the accused, and apparent political interference in charging decisions.[247] According to reporting by the *Guardian*, in a spate of 2017 prison breaks in eastern Congo, one of the only two men convicted in the Minova case escaped.[248]

As the infamous Rwanda-backed Congolese warlord Bosco "The Terminator" Ntaganda once said, "When you're a soldier, women are free. Everything is free."[249] There may be no other place in the world where the link between consumer demand for products in Europe and America is so directly linked to armed groups perpetrating sexual violence in the countries where the raw materials for those products originate.

Chouchou Namegabe on Mass Rape

"I wish this would not happen to anyone else, I wish this would not happen to another generation, to our children."

These were the words of Nsimire (name altered), a sixteen-year-old Congolese girl, testifying with tears and fear in her eyes, when I first met her around 2005. She couldn't have imagined then that Amani (name altered), her very own daughter, born from rape, would have to face the same treatment a decade later. Oh, my dear Nsimire, if ever you knew what happened to Amani, you would probably find the force to return from the dead where you rest in peace!

It is 2001, in the village of Kaniola, located in the hilly countryside of the South Kivu province in eastern Congo. Nsimire, twelve years old at that time, is raped after an attack by Congo-based Rwandan rebels. During that attack, the rebels killed her father and brothers and took Nsimire and her mother into the forest. After four years of slavery, rape, and other atrocities, she escaped. After reaching Panzi Hospital, a famous center for victims of sexual violence, located in Bukavu, the provincial capital of South Kivu, she realized she was pregnant.

I met her after she gave birth to her baby girl, named Amani. I started to take care of her and her baby. I rented a house for her, but every time the neighbors discovered her story, her child was in danger and she had to move. Nevertheless, Nsimire was recovering fast. She became a close friend of mine, I considered her like my daughter. We were very happy when she found a beloved one and got married. Her husband promised heaven and earth, but the most important thing for her was to take care of her child. Unfortunately, after she gave birth to a son, the husband no longer wanted to take care of Amani and sent her away from the house.

This troubled the mother to a point that a year later, she couldn't hold on any longer, and she died. That was 2013.

Fast forward to May 15, 2017, in New York, at a public debate on the theme "Women and Peace and Security" before the UN Security Council. Jeanine Mabunda Lioko, the personal representative of the president of the Democratic Republic of the Congo in charge of the fight against sexual violence and the recruitment of children, welcomed the significant decline in sexual violence in Congo in just three years. Indeed, sexual violence in Congo has decreased by 85 percent, or so says the UN.

In July 2017, just a few weeks later, in Bukavu, Amani is now twelve years old. I receive a phone call saying that she is at the hospital…because she had just been raped by the security guard of a refugee camp. While the authorities were rubbing their hands that Congo is on the road to being removed from the blacklist of countries affected by sexual violence, poor innocent Amani got raped at the same age as her mother.

I was totally devastated, and full of rage…

We don't want any more statistics, self-congratulations, and punch lines in high-level reports! Every single case is one too many. Every single case is a personal tragedy, devastating the heart and mind of a very awake and promising young girl for the rest of her life.

When I reflect on the story of Nsimire and Amani, it reminds me that this is one story among thousands of forgotten survivors of rape and sexual violence in Congo. I cannot help but also remember all these women who experienced horrible moments and have to live with them until the end of their life. Like the ones who, after being raped, were forced to eat the flesh of their children just killed in front of them, or those women whose vaginas were burned with fuel inside, or those women who were shot in the vagina after being raped by up to ten perpetrators.

This scourge, this disaster that the population has been facing for more than twenty years, has evolved at different scales and in different forms over time. During the repeated wars and conflict that Congo has known, and especially from 1996 to 2008, rape and sexual violence have been used as a weapon and a tactic of war to destroy an entire community. The atrocities that accompany such violence reflect the intention of the attackers: Intimidate and create fear through the bodies of women; use women's bodies as battlefields. The attackers used sexual violence to achieve a triple objective: create fear, take revenge, and force residents to move from their land so that they cede control of lands and mines. Since then, the concept has evolved and, sadly, is not only the modus operandi of rebel fighters anymore. It has spread widely and has become what I refer to as a social sickness.

The control of remote mining areas is an issue of survival for rebel groups, because dealing in minerals provides them with the necessary resources for their struggle. In these areas, the practice of rape as an instrument of terror against the local population is a weapon of choice used by rebel groups to ensure such control.

Between 2013 and 2016 the town of Kavumu in South Kivu province witnessed a series of rapes of baby girls aged from nine months to three years old. The Panzi Hospital stated that forty babies were raped.

Is this a tactic to destroy life at its beginning? How might a pregnant woman expecting a girl feel in such an environment? How could a father sleep when he is worried about his baby being raped? What kind of hopes and dreams could children like Amani have, cursed with the triple trauma of being born from rape, being abandoned by her family, and being raped herself?

Why is sexual violence so frequent in Congo? Some international experts argue that it is related to deep-rooted cultural factors. I don't believe this is true. We didn't hear of any cases of sexual violence before the 1996 and 1998 wars. No, I believe it has more to do with impunity, which is one of the main evil diseases from which Congo suffers. The lack of a reliable, functioning judicial system ensures that there is no clear incentive to stop this plague. The perpetrators are from different categories: from rebels to the police and the army, from UN peacekeeping troops (yes, there have been cases!) to civilians. This impunity above all deepens the wounds of the survivors. Impunity encourages a multiplicity of forms of sexual violence: systematic mass rape committed during all the repeated wars, sexual slavery for the benefit of fighters, prostitution, forced marriage and pregnancy, and sexual assault accompanied by beatings and brutality.

Survivors are seeking justice. There is a dire need to deeply reform the Congolese justice system and combat corruption. This would also require the international community to undertake a serious investigation into these crimes against humanity and bring to justice all the perpetrators, regardless of their rank or nationalities. In the more than twenty years that this has been happening, there have been international courts for Rwanda, the former Yugoslavia, Cambodia, and Sierra Leone. Congo's survivors are still waiting for an International Special Court for Congo.

CONTACT INFORMATION FOR ANZAFRIKA:
www.anzafrika.org

HUGUETTE'S STORY, 2010

(See the full interviews over the course of seven years at www.congostories.org.)

My name is Huguette. I am thirteen years old and I was born in Goma, eastern Congo. This is my home and I live here with my mom and my daughter, Immaculée. My father gave up on us four months ago and left.

I was raped. It happened when I was coming from school. As I was coming from school, I told my friend that I had to go to the bathroom, and I went. Unfortunately, at the toilet, there was a soldier hiding there, and he took me by force. I tried to cry out but he used so much force.

I went home afterward but did not find my mom at home. At the time I was very shy, and I was not courageous enough to speak out, so I just kept it inside me. My mom had gone on a trip. I decided it was useless to speak to my elder brothers. When my mama returned after two months, I told her my secret, that I was raped by a soldier. And my mom asked me why I didn't tell my aunts or elder brothers about it. I went to the hospital for medical tests, and also to the prosecutor's office. At the hospital, unfortunately, I tested positive. I was pregnant.

I was restless and very troubled, and I couldn't speak to anybody. I dropped out of school for a month and my teachers would come to my house and ask why I was not attending school anymore. So when my mom came back from this trip after two months and tried to console me, that's when I told her what happened. But still, the attack has made a big difference between me and my brothers and sisters. They no longer see me as one of their family because of what happened to me. I don't know why they blame me for what happened.

My father came back home, and he kicked my mom and me out of the house, and that's how we came to our uncle's compound here. We have been staying here for four months now. Our uncle offered this place for us to stay. We lodged a case against the soldier, but he was freed later.

My biggest concern today is that people are pointing at me wherever I go, whether at school or home, pointing at me that I have a baby while I am still a child, that I have been raped, so it's very hard. Sometimes, when I go to school, if I come across this soldier, I feel very terrified and I will come back home and not attend school that day.

It's very hard for me when I see my child. Though she's a child, when I see her I feel like killing her, because this happened to me against my will. I feel I am useless. I feel I am broken. Sometimes I would even try to crack open a battery, mix it with water, and drink it, so I could commit suicide, because I don't know why I am living. We have been abandoned by our father, who was providing for our needs, and with my mom and me and the baby, you can imagine it's not easy. It's very tough. Sometimes this child cries, and without having any men to provide for her, it's very tough.

What's very tough for me, very shocking, is that sometimes I find myself in a classroom and I get to thinking about my child and having no means to provide for her. I feel like just going and leaving her in the streets so anybody could maybe take her, so I can live peacefully without thinking any more about her and focus on my education. Stigmatization is the big issue for me, because anywhere I would go, other girls my age would be pointing at me: "Look at Huguette, such a young little girl, she has become a mama." I feel very broken because of that.

I remember that every day since I delivered this child, I have felt like giving her alcohol so that she would die and I could forget totally about this. Man proposes, and God disposes, because if it depended only on me, this child would not have lived. I remember

I have taken all kinds of drugs that I could find so that I could kill myself and this child. But it never worked out. I think it was not God's plan for this child to die.

I was expelled from Lycée Chemchem, where I was attending school, because they said they are only taking care of young girls, not young girl-women, so I had to find another school elsewhere, and that was really shocking.

It's very hard for me, because I would go to this place where other girls are playing, but I can't really enjoy life when I see them and I see my kid, so I ask myself: what is my place? Because of that, I feel I am really useless, I feel I was made for nothing. You can imagine how hard it is when this child is crying and I can't do anything for her. That really shocks me; it makes me remember the entire sequence of the rape—how it happened, and how because of it today I am suffering, today I am being stigmatized.

I have different kinds of dreams. But all of them are tragic. Sometimes I dream of going to school, but when I am in school I am being stigmatized by my friends, my teachers, and things like that, or I would dream I ran into this soldier. If I dream about that day, the following day is very bad.

Mama has been great. She is the only one who has kept siding with me. She has always encouraged me that even though I was discriminated against by my brothers and sisters, I must always stick by them, that's the only way, because if I give in fully to this and get away from them, maybe that would grow deeper. But she always encouraged me to stay with my brothers.

After I attempted several times to commit suicide I came to realize, thanks to the assistance I was getting from friends and lawyers, that there was no other way but to keep on studying and keep on living. My mom, especially, played a big role in that.

Life has become so different for me. Every day I wake up, all of these images come back to me, and I start remembering everything that has happened to me. I must say that I am thankful to this local organization that has been providing assistance to us—psychological assistance—because if it was not for them, I don't know how I could make it.

But what is even more shocking is to see this soldier who raped me free in the street and nobody can do anything against him. Our government didn't do anything, of course. They would not even provide money for me, but at least seeing this guy in jail could be a relief to me, but it is not the case. That's why I feel like committing suicide. It's very hard to accept this.

We started to try to lodge a case in court. I think that if it was not for the help of my lawyers Sadra and Jean-Marie, I would not have made it. I am also grateful to these lawyers because I have gone to different schools where I was rejected because I was a mother, but these guys did all they could to get me into the Goma Institute.

I feel like if I continue my studies I could become a lawyer, so at least I could try to do something. Education is my only way out. I am doing it thanks to these guys who have been providing psychological assistance to me, along with the churches.

I have always been a dedicated student because I knew, and I still know, that only education can be my way out. After what happened to me, I have never been a free girl. I have never enjoyed anything that other girls do, so I had always focused on my education. I didn't have much leisure time as I am coming from a family of moderate means, so most of the time I would focus on studying, exercising, and helping my mom do housework.

I am going to stick with education and that's going to be my way out. I resolved to be resilient and to say I have to live with this child even though this was not my plan, my wish. My lawyers have become a part of this family, providing all the psychological assistance I need.

I'm not the only victim of rape. You often hear personal stories of people who have been raped. There are attempts to lodge prosecutions against the perpetrators, but given the collapse of the justice system in this country, these people are free and nothing is done against them. So I made this decision when I started high school that I'm going to study law in order to try to do something, and I don't know whether it's fate that has come back to affect me. I always thought about being a lawyer.

I must say thank you to these lawyers who did all they could to get me back in school. All I pray for today is that God keeps providing me with the necessary wisdom to make it through this. I have made up my mind that if I finish high school I will do the best I can so that I can attend law school and graduate and become a lawyer, so I could try, at least, to do something positive.

Postscript: Huguette in 2017

I'm now at university, and I'm soon going to major in law. I have also joined a number of local associations, and that's what's keeping me busy. I'm at Goma University in the School of Law. I've gone through a very difficult situation and that pushed me to study law so that I will be able to defend people in need, particularly young girls. I was raped by a young soldier. That's why I decided to study law, so that tomorrow I can be a lawyer and defend my fellow Congolese. People would tell me to stop going to school and stay at home because I have a baby. But I came to believe that I still was meaningful to society and that I should continue with my studies.

I chose to study law to help my fellow citizens. But who knows what my destiny will be. I want to be a humanitarian but also someone well versed in computer science and international languages.

I dream of many things about Congo, because if my dreams of becoming what I intend to be materialize, it will benefit my country. No matter where I'll be, I'll always hold dear helping my country. And I'll call on my fellow citizens to do the same.

As of mid-2018, Huguette was still studying law and was the communications manager of a Congolese human rights group called Peace and Development Humanitarian Action. Her child was in third grade of elementary school.

Fidel's Upstander Story

◇◇

*Through a series of interviews conducted by Fidel,
Congolese Upstanders tell their life stories. All of them are risking
their lives to defend human rights, press for peace,
resist dictatorship, provide education, and prepare a better
future for their fellow Congolese.*

Dr. Denis Mukwege

My name is Denis Mukwege, son of Mukwege Chuma. I was born in Bukavu, South Kivu, in Congo. I was born to a Pentecostal pastor, and my mom's name is Mango. I think there were two parts to my childhood. The first part is the one that I didn't see but was told to me by my mom. And it's true that when I talk about it, I weigh how fortunate I am to be alive today, because a few days after I was born, I caught a severe neonatal infection. And according to symptoms my mom told me about, I had a fever, I had jaundice, I was hardly breathing. When my mom described those symptoms to me, as a medical doctor I understand today that I had septicemia.

Access to health care at that time was not easy. But I must admit that I was fortunate. When I imagine having septicemia back in 1955—I was born on March 1 of that year—and then surviving it, while today in Congo kids still unfortunately die of neonatal infections despite all the medical progress, I always see myself as a survivor.

It was in the 1960s that I witnessed violence for the first time. During that time there was a nationalist leader called Anicet Kashamura who didn't like Europeans. At that time my dad was a pastor with Swedish missionaries, and I witnessed missionaries being taken away from the church by armed men. For me, that was terror I had never seen before. I was crying and yelling, because I couldn't understand why my spiritual father Perloff, a missionary and father of my friend who I grew up with, could be brutally taken away from the church. I think I was five years of age at that time. Even though we were kids, we had previously considered white missionaries as untouchable.

But in fact, something was breaking up in my heart. And my "enough moment"[250] for what I have become today came at the age of eight, when my dad had been called upon as pastor to go pray for a sick kid. And as always in everything my dad was doing, I followed him. And once there, he prayed for the sick kid and then said goodbye to the kid's family. And I was confused. Though I was eight, I stopped my dad and told him, "Dad, I don't understand. This kid is sick!" He had a fever, he was not doing well. I could see that the kid was really sick because he was crying as a result of the pain. So I told my dad, "When I am sick, you pray but also give me medicine. But here you just prayed and then you walk away?" Then my dad looked at me with a really curious eye and simply told me, "Denis, I'm not a medical doctor!" So it was as if my dad had just admitted his impotence, though as a kid I saw him as a jack-of-all-trades, the superman. But that day he showed me his weaknesses. Consequently, I told my dad, "Well, I will do the medicine. That way, you'll be praying and I'll be giving medicine!" And I think that was the trigger of all I'm doing today.

And I look back a bit on the child in distress in front of his parents, who couldn't do anything but call upon my dad. And my dad had opened up my mind because he showed me that what he did for me when I was sick was under the prescription of a medical doctor. So I felt that aspect of vulnerability, unfairness, and revolt. I believe my life path has entirely followed that thread.

My focus would be on injustice and what I can do to repair it. And it's that very day that I made up my mind to become a medical doctor to respond to that injustice! And throughout all my life all I have ever done is to respond to situations of injustice.

I attended high school at a time when Congo was still well organized. Schoolchildren of our time were lucky enough to go to school on a public school bus, we had a meal at school, and inspectors would come to check first where we lived before we could enroll in what was considered at that time an elite school. The schools were good, and today when I see the current state of the Ibanda High School [in Bukavu], I break into tears, because that high school was an idyllic place!

In high school I was close to ending my education and becoming a male nurse, but thank goodness someone advised me to keep on studying biochemistry and maybe medicine at university. I committed to trying to study medicine here in Congo but found myself doing liberal arts. Two years later, I realized that I was completely lost. A generalist is not what I wanted to be.

So I therefore left liberal arts in Kinshasa and moved to Burundi, where I enrolled in medical school. I did my medical courses, and the very first shock I had as a medical doctor was when I came to the Swedish missionary hospital of Lemera and I saw the number of bleeding women who had died giving birth. They had tried to give birth at home, but the placenta didn't come out. Therefore, they were bleeding, and when they reached the hospital, they were already dead. I think that there I had the shock of my life. And it's a shock that I still get as an adult.

I did my thesis in pediatrics with a focus on viral hepatitis, because I really wanted to be taking care of children. And then I came to the hospital and realized that there can only be babies if there are live mothers. If mothers can't be saved, then babies are more likely to die as well, and therefore I won't reach my ideal. Therefore, I took a decision to do obstetrics and gynecology. I said to myself that it was possible anyways to do something! It is possible to fight against maternal mortality!

I packed my suitcases and flew to Angers, France, where I spent five years specializing in obstetrics and gynecology. I then came back home and worked in this hospital, Panzi, for a dozen years, building up the health centers around the hospital and training midwives. I created a nursing school for nurses and midwives, so that they'd know how to do early diagnosis and timely transfers, etc.

Unfortunately, during the 1996 war, my patients were killed in their hospital beds and with them all of the medical staff members. It took me two long years to decide to touch a sick person again.

I felt I had been betrayed, and helpless. You know? I always remember two women I had taken from Bukavu for surgery in Lemera. I left them there after the surgery and came back to Bukavu to evacuate another sick woman, but I couldn't make it back to Lemera because the road was cut off by gunshots fired from Rwanda to prevent any movement.

While I was trapped in Bukavu, the hospital in Lemera got attacked by rebels a few days later, and the sick women I had left there were killed. It was pretty shocking.

I was traumatized because one is a medical doctor to help people live, not lose their lives. I had suffered so much that it required some time before I could practice medicine again. You know, there is a connection between the medical doctor and their patient; it's a kind of fusion between the two. But imagine that you have struggled operating on a patient for three or four hours to help them survive but then they get shot dead at point-blank range. It's like a gunshot right in your own heart!

Nightmares didn't let me sleep for over a year. Every night I would dream of those patients. Also, there were young boys such as Simbi and Kuduguza who had just graduated from the nursing school that I had created who also were killed. They were young men that I had planned to help for their professional future, given their commitment. They had chosen to stay, taking care of the patients, but were killed along with their patients.

I then decided to leave Bukavu after the city was attacked, and I fled to Bunia in northeastern Congo, which also got attacked, and subsequently I flew to Nairobi, Kenya. At that point I was not able to do surgery because those victims were haunting me.

But later on, I made up my mind to come back home. One day, I went walking to a hospital nearby in Bukavu. Then I saw women on a hill overlooking Panzi Hospital. Those women had been transferred for a cesarean section, and one of them was lying dead right in front of me.

At that moment my medical vocation kicked in again and I thought that perhaps I couldn't go back to Lemera, because the hospital was still taken over by the rebels, but at least I could set up at Panzi Hospital and do cesareans to help women from the southern part of Bukavu not have to cross the entire city during war. And that's how Panzi Hospital started with the goal of fighting maternal mortality.

Unfortunately, the first person I took care of here at Panzi was not a maternal case but a rape survivor. She had been sexually assaulted and shot in the vagina. It was a shock, a nightmare, a barbarism and an atrocity that went beyond human understanding. And there I was, thinking that maybe that case was an isolated one. But in the following days, similar cases and more serious ones with baffling tortures started flocking to the hospital. I always remember one of my first cases, which was evacuated from the south. The Red Cross called me and said, "We're bringing you a rape case that has been shot in the vagina after rape, and we just put in a compress to stop the bleeding because it's a big hole, and we're not sure she will make it to your hospital." And when I saw her vagina, it was pieces of flesh. So that's when I started understanding that such rape did not happen by chance. And at that time, I could not imagine that by today I would count dozens of thousands of women I have operated on.

I think that my third shock came when I operated for the first time on a little girl of eighteen months. She had been raped, with the rectum, bladder, and intestines all coming down out of her vagina. It's beyond evil, because even wild animals don't do that to their babies. This time I was not shocked; I was instead outraged.

My life has ever been marked by issues that I feel I cannot run away from. I cannot give up but must always face them and try to find solutions.

Discouragement came, however, when armed men broke into my home, took my kids hostage, and killed my guard, who was trying to protect me. When something like that happens in your home, you feel that is enough. That was the first time in my life when I said, "I give up!" I had decided to leave the country.

Three days later, when I realized that there was no investigation into the crime, I understood that there was something fishy going on. I felt I had to leave to protect my family, my kids. I went through Brussels and settled in Boston.

I came back after I realized that life is not black and white. There are intermediaries, there are good people on earth, and I think that a group of women from Idjwi Island [in eastern Congo] are among the good ones. Their initiative shook me up, and I feel that I owe them a great deal.

These women had acted so powerfully, while I had settled down in Boston with my kids, taking English classes at Harvard. While I was feeling like I had started a new life in Boston, those women from Idjwi Island wrote the Congo president, demanding I come back home. They got no answer. They wrote the then-UN secretary general, Ban Ki-moon. They got no answer. Then the women said, "Whether it rains or snows, he [Mukwege] is our doctor, and we must get him back here." Those women made a decision to come from Idjwi Island every Friday to sell their crops and save the money at Panzi until they had enough to pay a flight ticket to bring me back.

When they deposited fifty dollars for the first time, I asked my wife, "What's our life worth in relation to the lives of these thousands of women demanding we go back home?" I felt I had no choice! I told all the friends who didn't understand me that when I weighed my own life against the lives of thousands of Congolese women who feel given up on and lost, I had to go back. I have so much respect for those women to this day. So I took my flight and came back and decided to fight alongside those women. I want to stay with them, and I feel my destiny is henceforth tied to their destiny.

◇◇

CONTACT INFORMATION FOR PANZI HOSPITAL:

www.panzifoundation.org

◇◇

PART TWO: CHILD SOLDIER RECRUITMENT

Dr. Namegabe Murhabazi on Child Soldiers

My name is Namegabe Murhabazi. I was born in Bukavu on November 18, 1964, and have attended elementary school, high school, and university in Bukavu. I was born amidst a rebellion in 1964 that forced my parents to move frequently. My parents depended a lot on humanitarian assistance at that time, and that's why they named me Murhabazi, which means "he who assists those in need." That name is inspirational to me. During this rebellion in 1964, my parents lost their jobs. However, my mother still did occasional trading to feed us.

There were a lot of children from poorer families in the neighborhood of Bukavu where we lived. And I grew up knowing how to stand in solidarity with others. After school I would share my food with my fellow students and share my clothes and shoes with those who had nothing. I was very sensitive to the conditions of others, even at school.

We grew up during Mobutu's dictatorship, when the public did not know about children's rights and human rights, and nobody could talk about such subjects publicly. I used to rebel when I saw teachers beat my fellow students. I did the same when some men beat their wives with their children watching and crying. Sometimes I stepped in to separate couples fighting in the presence of their children. I grew up with principles that made me a committed human rights upstander, first for my fellow students—before I even knew what I was doing—and then later, in 1989, when I started monitoring the situation of children.

In November 1989, the UN General Assembly adopted the Convention on the Rights of the Child, and Congo was party to the convention as a UN member. I became very interested, and I started convening meetings with students and teachers to discuss the issue. We carried out social surveys and found that there were increasing numbers of street children, while others were dropping out of school, and more and more families couldn't afford to feed their children as a consequence of the socioeconomic effects of the dictatorship. We sought the advice of lawyers, medical staff members, sociologists, psychologists, etc. On March 6, 1992, our organization BVES

(*Bureau pour le Voluntariat au Service de l'Enfance et de la Santé*, or "Voluntary Force at the Service of Childhood and Health") was officially registered by the government, and we set forth as our mission to contribute to the promotion, protection, and defense of the fundamental rights of children who have been socially and economically marginalized.

We started by reaching out to the most vulnerable category of children—street children. Then, in 1994, in the aftermath of the Rwandan genocide, there were many refugee children separated from their families, and they became known as unaccompanied minors. We created a program to reunite Rwandan refugee children with their families in Rwanda.

I began working on the child soldier issue when I saw how the Rwandan forces who had committed the genocide and were now in Congo were forcibly recruiting children, calling them worthless. They were children with dirty clothes and they were drugged to incite them to kill Tutsi and moderate Hutu. We worked to separate them from the genocidal soldiers and coax them back into civilian life to prepare them for a peaceful return to Rwanda and reintegration into society.

Since 1996, we've focused mainly on Congolese child soldiers and war survivors who have suffered sexual violence. We also worked on health, because children were subject to epidemics such as meningitis, measles, and cholera, and we worked hard trying to protect children, who are the most vulnerable.

With ex–child soldiers, we worked out techniques to counter their forced recruitment as well as to liberate them. We worked with armed rebels to sensitize their senior officers against the recruitment and use of children, and then we expanded the program to the governmental forces. With armed militia groups, we'd talk to them and tell them to go about their business but without using children. We'd tell them that according to African tradition, it is the adult's responsibility to protect children, not allowing them to be abused under the pretext that they're contributing to the security of adults.

We also put in place a mechanism for monitoring and reporting on cases of children's rights violations. We do surveillance and observation of these violations that happen in the context of war and poverty. We have advocated to the Congolese authorities to harmonize national laws with the international convention. In January 2009 we won our first legislative battle when the Congolese National Assembly passed a law protecting children, a positive law in that it includes all the rights known to children internationally. We show that law to Congolese government officials and say, "If you don't do this, you're violating children's rights." We're educating political and military officials as well as rebel groups about the law.

All the children we host are children who have carried and used a gun. When we receive children, they are demobilized and have come back to civilian life. Every gun destroyed when a child demobilizes creates room for peace. When they stay in our transit structures, the children are educated to be peacemakers. BVES counts thousands and thousands of children now who have gone through that education process to be peacemakers and become useful to their communities. They contribute to community development to help repair the socioeconomic fabric that has been destroyed by war. Our social reinsertion program consists of empowering children with skills to help their communities build houses or other reconstruction projects.

We have reunified 150,000 children with their families and communities over the years. We have developed informal educational programs for vulnerable children in insecure villages who can't go to school. The programs aim at keeping the children engaged, so that they're not preyed upon by armed groups. We have created literacy centers, and 160,000 children are attending them.

One of the strategies we pursue is to sensitize Congolese army and rebel officers about the protection of children's rights. During the first session that we had with senior officers, the officers broke down in tears when they understood the impact of using children as soldiers. Many swore they'd never again recruit children. Now, the government army has officially stopped recruiting and using children.

There are also cases of government army soldiers forcing young girls to have sex with them and using children as laborers, but these are isolated cases, because soldiers are now aware that if human rights activists find out, they can be in trouble. It's dangerous work and some of our team have even lost their lives trying to make clear to rebel and government army officers that recruiting a child and abusing a child sexually is both a war crime and a crime against humanity.

What is important is when our work leads to young boys and girls from totally different factions and backgrounds singing and dancing together as brothers and sisters instead of fighting. They behave that way after we've told them that no one asked God to create them Tutsi, Hutu, Banyamulenge, Nande, Fuliro, Bembe, or any other ethnic group. Those children eat together, live together, and we've never known any serious security incident in any of our centers. That is a testament that peaceful cohabitation among people in this region is possible, because children are able to show it.

The challenges are enormous for me as a human rights activist and, specifically, a defender of children's rights. With saber rattling and armed conflicts since 1994, war in Congo seems endless, and therefore we cannot rest. After leaving the military, children come to us at BVES feeling hopeless, with no clothes, no shoes, malnourished and sick. We must provide adequate housing for them and then find their families in Congo—a country the size of a continent—or in neighboring countries, and then find a way to reunite them. And the children's reinsertion into the community needs to be supported, because the family's economic situation is usually dire. Then, after the family is reunited, the children must go back to school or learn a craft in order to survive.

Another challenge is our safety. We're in a world where human rights violators do not respect human rights defenders. We live with the possibility of being killed anytime because we stand up for children's rights in a war situation. It is also dangerous for the children, as their former military officers sometimes go after them in their communities because the children have been eyewitnesses to some of the abuses they committed. Security for all of us is a challenge.

We dream of a Congo where respect for children's rights reigns. Congo can be a better place to live. Modestly but steadily, we have been at the heart of the construction of a children's rights awareness movement, and that's why you find so many youths being a part of the pro-democracy movements today. We're helping to build a generation that will be aware of its rights but also its duties. We're helping build a Congo of positive values.

Our big dream is the democratization of our country. We believe that the night will go on as long as it can, but the light will end up shining one day. And we're working through that night so that there is an intermediary light. Our job consists of helping children become aware of the democratic process, claim their rights, and reject that which is being done against them. No matter what the roadblocks are, we believe that the Congolese democratic process will go on and it will be successful.

The support we need from around the world is to join our struggle by helping us pressure the Congolese government and armed groups who are massively violating children's rights. We need people to join us in letting the Congolese government authorities and other armed groups' officers know that the violation of children's rights is both a war crime and a crime against humanity. In addition, we'd like them to support the economic, physical, and psychological rehabilitation of children.

CONTACT INFORMATION FOR BVES:
http://bves-rdc.org/DefaultEn.htm

CLAUDE'S STORY, 2010

My name is Claude. I was born in Masisi in 1986 and I am twenty-four years old. I am an ex–child soldier. I was a Mai-Mai militia commander both in Kisangani and Walikale in eastern Congo. I was forced to join the Mai-Mai group when I was fourteen. It was never my choice to join the army or any armed group. We were kidnapped, and once we arrived at the training camp I realized we were becoming child soldiers. I couldn't find any way to get out of it.

When it happened, I was in grade three and I was going home from school. I was abducted by a militia gang. I would be beaten, beaten a lot. I still have pain in my chest because of the beatings I got. We were forced to commit atrocities, and if you didn't do so, you could get killed. If you were given an order and did not carry it out, there was no way you would not be killed. That's why we committed a lot of atrocities. All this started because of the Rwandan and Congo wars, so we boys were told we were patriots, we were told that we were protecting Congolese land.

How else can you get control of men if you want to acquire their land or whatever they have if you cannot rape their women? I don't want to go into details because my mom is here. It's really shameful. I never wanted to commit these crimes, but we were forced to do it, we had no choice. We were told what to do but without being given any reason. I have changed now, and I am so glad I can live like other human beings, and I would be so grateful if anyone would help to put an end to this war, because it continues.

We would come to a place and find out from the local authorities whether there is any mine that they knew of, and they would show us. We would get tools and start mining. Sometimes, we would not even have to dig deep into the ground, because we would find the minerals just on the surface. So we would get a lot of them, and people would come and give us money for them. You can see the

difference between Rwanda and Congo today, see how developed Rwanda has become. I have no doubt it is because of the minerals we have been selling to them.

The explanation we received for why we were fighting is that tin is used for making bullets and weapons. In addition to tin, we were also mining tantalum and especially gold. Now that I know they're used in cell phones or in laptops, I think anybody who's buying those has a real share in whatever is happening in Congo. I feel these companies and businesspeople, they are human beings just as we are, and I would beg them to invest and make good business, fair business. They should help stop this.

I was in the militia until I was eighteen. When I turned eighteen, I came to visit my family. Unfortunately, I found out that my father was dead and my mom was widowed. I was in a kind of hell, and I am ready to forget that today. I am what I am. If I told you what we have gone through, what we were doing, how brutal we were, I would break down and cry here. I always feel that I can't get out of this because I feel responsible for my father's death, because of the brutalities we were committing in the bush. My father was gunned down because of that. He would be accused: "Look, do you see what your son is doing out there?" For that, he was killed, and I'll never forgive myself for that. I understand it is not my fault, but in the end my dad was killed for that. I wish that I had never been born into this family, because if I had not, then maybe this would not have happened to my father.

I was in a very bad condition when I came back to my family. I had lost weight, but I have been recovering and now I think I'm fine. It has been very hard to make it here, because we were being called ex–child soldiers and viewed as robbers and bandits. I was so lucky because when I got demobilized out of the militia I went to study car repair, and that's how I became a driver. I am so grateful for this international organization called Save the Children. They are the ones who brought me here, helped my demobilization, and helped me get this training. They wanted me to go back to school, but I was too old, so the only option for me was to do technical training.

I am driving this log truck because I have no choice, but it is not the right job for me, given what I have suffered, given my health. I had no choice, because I have to look after my mom. To get a job in this country is something very special. And as I had no choice, I had to handle this driving job. But to be honest, I am very happy about it. I feel proud I can do that job.

I told you how much I was involved in mining, but what difference did it make to my life? None, because all the minerals would go to our commanders. They were doing so well, but I am struggling to make even fifteen dollars now, even though I am a driver. I wish you could go to these commanders to see the beautiful houses they have today. What the international companies have been doing in Congo is useless, because what is the result of [their investments] on the Congolese people?

Sometimes I dream in English, and I feel very proud of that. I've never forgotten what I have been doing in the militia. Sometimes all of these images—people being killed, myself shooting at them—come back to me, and when they do, I spend a very bad day.

Postscript: Claude in 2017

My life is a bit better now. I'm still breathing. I'm alive, and that's enough for me. I am still a truck driver and mechanic. That's still my job. My family is alive, and that's what matters for me. It's enough. We all live together as usual. I'm the one who provides for the entire family. As little as I get from my job, I bring it home for the family. My biggest challenge is the lack of an adequate job. If I could get a good job, life wouldn't be such a burden.

My biggest hope is to find a better job. If I'm lucky enough to find it, I'm sure my life can change for the better. Peace is most needed beyond anything else.

As of mid-2018, Claude was still a freelance driver.

FIDEL'S OWN STORY

My name is Fidel Bafilemba, and I was born in Birere, the mother neighborhood of the city of Goma, on February 22, 1972. That's what my uncle told me, but neither my dad nor my mom ever told me the exact day of my birth, likely because of so much disappointment following the successive loss of my elder brothers and sisters. Celebrating my birthday has always been the least of my priorities. I've never celebrated it and have never celebrated my kids' birthdays either.

I had a turbulent childhood. For a short time I was a happy young kid. Taking a walk down memory lane, I remember being the only young boy wearing Congolese suits, which my dad artfully made for me. My dad, bless his memory, was a famous dressmaker in the region.

When I turned seven, my life was turned upside down. My dad and mom separated, and soon enough I became my own parent and the parent of my brother, who was then five and whose name is Mokilipasi, the Lingala word for "the world is evil." However, apart from my brother, who is my only full sibling, I am the eldest of twenty-seven half sisters and half brothers from my dad's four wives.

After I had unsuccessfully tried to take care of my young brother and myself, I started wandering between my different stepmothers, but none of them could make up for our own mom's love. We soon were turned into donkeys to do most of the housework and fetch water and firewood, or we'd be denied food. All the while, our dad was burying his life in alcohol and barely minding our fate. After more than two years of near-enslavement, my uncle came to our rescue and took me with him. However, he himself had three wives who treated me exactly the same way my dad's wives did.

When I turned thirteen, the bad treatment forced me into the street, where I joined gangs of children living off odd jobs such

as cleaning people's cars and shoes, helping wash clothes, looking after people's goats, and sometimes stealing. Any job was fine, provided that I would be given either food or a bit of money. I soon became a gang leader, not because I was physically strong but rather because I was smart and well-spoken. I smoked weed and taught others how to, and I spent years either sleeping under the stars or in the gutters.

Luckily, I never dropped out of school while living on the streets. Instead, I even encouraged my street fellows to stick with school, telling them there would be no way out for us without education. It was not easy at all, and it would take pages to describe the hardships I went through. Sometimes I had no shoes and no clothes, and I would go to garbage bins and collect whatever I could use. I once was kicked out of the classroom because the teacher noticed that my slippers were loosely tied with scarf pins.

Like people say, necessity is the mother of invention. I was repeatedly kicked out of school for not paying school fees on time. So I started selling bread early in the morning. To make this possible, I'd cross the border into Rwanda every evening and buy bread, package it in plastic bags, and then hang it up on a stick to sell early in the morning. It turned out that I was the first one to introduce this idea of selling bread on sticks along the streets in Goma. The business went so well that it allowed me to rent a house and buy furniture, a bed, and cooking utensils. I later learned how to bake bread and developed my own brand. Problems such as paying school fees, sleeping under the stars and in the gutters, smoking weed, and collecting garbage had become a thing of the past.

However, the bread business seemed to be the only business I had any luck with. Anything else I tried quickly withered away. The bread business led me to study commerce, but when I graduated from high school, I changed my mind and majored in English and African Culture. I had saved enough money, so I set off for the city of Bukavu in eastern Congo and enrolled in the Bukavu Higher Pedagogical Institute.

Two years later, after the Rwandan genocide, in 1996 I joined Professor Rwigamba Balinda and helped restart a high school in Gisenyi, Rwanda. At the same time, I initiated one of the first English-language training centers in Goma and combined that with providing translation and interpretation services to foreign reporters. My childhood life adventure was finished!

———

My entire childhood life was a challenge, but the biggest difficulty was growing up without the love and support of parents. Life rendered me an early adult, and I know I'm so lucky that I was able to pull through. Many of my friends were not that lucky.

At the age of twenty-six, following Rwanda's second invasion of Congo in 1998, I was coaxed into joining the Rwandan-backed rebel movement called the RCD [Rally for Congolese Democracy]. They recruited me and sent me for training with the Rwanda Revenue Authority, or RRA. When I came back home in 2000, I helped replicate the RRA in rebel-held territory in Congo. The Congolese version of the RRA we put in place was known as the Public Revenue Protection Office.

Rebel officials disguised themselves as human rights and democracy supporters and successfully lured many people into their movement. I witnessed the embezzlement of Congo's revenues and assets, which set me off as I decided to become a rebel against the rebels. Eventually, the rebels came after me, and I had to flee to Kinshasa, then Johannesburg in South Africa, and then to London.

When I came back home in 2004, I joined a Mai-Mai armed resistance group. I was appointed a Mai-Mai provincial chairman for North Kivu province in eastern Congo. The Mai-Mai had "magic" water that was supposed to make fighters bulletproof, and that was a very appealing idea, but young boys with little or no military training only served as cannon fodder. The commanders knew the magic water wouldn't stop the bullets, so they often drugged the child soldiers for combat. There was a growing contention between the military leaders and me, and the commanders would not listen. That forced me to quit. It was very depressing!

In 2005 I co-founded SOS Africa, a human rights and development group that aimed to raise international awareness about the Congo's ongoing crisis. I worked diligently to educate the Congolese people about democracy and what it means to be part of the democratic process. Through SOS Africa, I helped design, produce, and disseminate educational materials about the Congolese constitution and how to vote. Additionally, we were in the forefront of calling attention to discrimination against indigenous people like the so-called pygmies, and we fought for their rights. Today, SOS Africa is committed to increasing Congolese awareness about the need for an improved education system and the teaching of critical thinking in schools.

I'm a trained teacher, an activist, and a consultant, and I love doing all these things. However, from the time I joined the Enough Project, research, reporting, and advocacy are what have given real meaning to my life. I believe that working on the issues of natural resources and conflict has had a catalyzing impact on the part of Congo where I live and work. We've been able to remove Congolese army commanders from direct involvement in mining activities and helped build a traceability system for the minerals that used to be a main cause of violence. After my team and I diligently researched and reported on conflict minerals, the US Congress and European Union passed legislation which has begun to remove the violence from the supply chain of these minerals. These international transparency initiatives are a testament that human rights advocates' voices can be heeded.

Our most important success so far has been seeing the Congolese army commanders forced out of the mines because of the US Dodd-Frank legislation. This is an unprecedented shift in the Congolese army commanders' predatory behavior. While army commanders used to control mining sites and force people to work for them at gunpoint, they no longer are able to do that since the passage of the Dodd-Frank Act.

I left the Enough Project in February 2016 to work full-time as the coordinator of a Goma-based civil society coalition of over a dozen organizations, called GATT-RN, a French acronym that means Support Platform for Traceability and Transparency in the Management of Natural Resources. At GATT-RN we are continuing the fight for the rule of law, good governance, and transparency as it relates to natural resources.

The kleptocratic system that builds on systemic corruption and impunity has been the biggest challenge the Congo is facing, whether it is connected to transparency in government or the democratic process in Congo. While the country's economy could benefit a great deal from international transparency initiatives in order to lay the foundation for sustainable development, there has been little political will to do this.

Oversimplifying Congo is what its kleptocratic regimes have been doing best. We can't blame the rest of the world for that. Congo won its independence over half a century ago now, and that should have been enough time for Congo to take off. Instead, Congo has remained dependent on international compassion, mainly because of its own misleaders, the hyenas in charge of the state.

My dream has been to see global activist campaigns on issues of democracy, justice, governance, and conflict minerals in Congo. I dream of a stable and prosperous Congo with democratic transitions of presidential power, a Congo with the rule of law, and a Congo that finally plays the role of the trigger for African development.

For more information about Fidel's efforts to create the first public library in eastern Congo, please go to: www.congolibrary.org

CHAPTER EIGHT

Life Today in One Part of Congo

Goma's Story
by Fidel, a Resident for Life

Goma, an enclave in the foothills of the Nyiragongo volcano, sits on the shores of Lake Kivu, whose waters shimmer with methane gas. The city was a center of trade for centuries—a polyglot crossroads for buyers and sellers of fish, food, and, most recently, weapons and minerals. Crawling with about 1.5 million people, Goma lives in the shadows of the world's largest UN peacekeeping mission. With artillery, armored tanks, drones, and gunships buzzing all over the city every day, the imposing presence of the UN force is a spectacle that amazes Goma residents and leads us to dream of a fantasy peace.

Surrounding Goma in eastern Congo are over seventy armed groups and hundreds of racketeering roadblocks everywhere. The Congolese army—along with other security bodies such as the regular police, the road safety and traffic police, the intelligence agency, and the migration department—man the majority of those illegal roadblocks. In such an environment, succeeding in moving around without being stopped is often a cause for celebration.

Conflict simmers on, erupting everywhere inside and all around the nearby Virunga National Park, forcing hundreds of thousands of people to run for their lives, which ends up expanding Goma's population with these internal refugees. Home-grown rebel groups and others from nearby countries make the lawless forests around Goma their home, while neighbors like Rwanda and Uganda have repeatedly backed Congolese rebellions to promote their own business and security interests. Dozens of local Congolese self-defense groups known as Mai-Mai spring up to fight these rebels but often end up preying on their own communities. Crippled by insecurity and instability, eastern Congo remains one of the least developed regions in the world, with a per capita gross domestic product of only a few hundred dollars per year.

Goma is also home to about 250 international aid agencies, some of which have been around for over twenty years. Goma and war-ravaged areas around it have been a top priority for humanitarian interventions. Hundreds of millions of dollars flow in every year to address the needs of internally displaced persons, fight cholera outbreaks, counter severe malnutrition, support rape survivors, etc. But in a country where successive presidents steal most of the state assets for personal enrichment, these aid agencies can only have a limited impact.

The two active volcanoes around Goma—Nyamulagira and Nyiragongo—tower ten miles north of the city. While the former throws up its lava inside the Virunga park, Nyiragongo sends smoke and steam over the city almost every day, and its looming eruption—occurring every decade or two—warns the city of its impermanence.

Goma, it seems, is used to extremes. Bustling with construction work, our city is living on the edge. Goma faces multiple threats: the two active volcanoes, a potential gas explosion under Lake

Kivu, ethnic conflicts, and political tensions. And with a president clinging to power at all costs, future uncertainty is even higher. We are calm but tense. Goma residents seem desperate to cling to peace after so many years of insurgencies, forced exoduses, cholera epidemics, and refugee influxes.

Life in Goma is sustained by a shimmering hope that a period of peace has come to us as I write at the end of 2017. Today sees a fragile peace, while yesterday bore witness to war and insurgencies. More than fifteen years after the deadly eruption of the Nyiragongo volcano and four years after the Rwandan-spearheaded rebellion known as M23, Goma is still tending its wounds. Most of the city's houses, offices, schools, soccer fields, and roads were swallowed by the lava. Yet, a few weeks after the eruption, Goma residents came back to rebuild. Nyiragongo lava was an ill wind, but the new roads, buildings, restaurants, and hotels in Goma that have been sprouting up like mushrooms owe their building materials to that very lava.

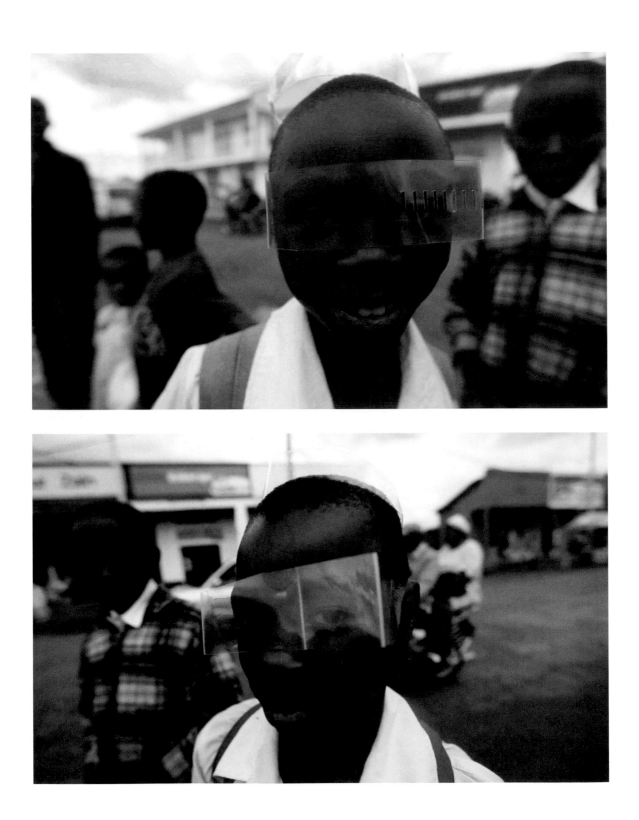

JONATHAN'S STORY, 2010

(Jonathan's full interview and follow-up interviews over the course of seven years are on the book website at www.congostories.org.)

My name is Jonathan. I am seventeen years old. I am studying at the Institut Muzizi in Goma. My normal days are like anybody's days. I wake up at five thirty and I do some exercises. An hour later I take my bath and I get dressed in my school uniform and head to school. We spend something like six hours at school, and it takes me thirty minutes' walking to get there. So I come back home at one or one thirty. If I have a book to read, and if I have no homework, then I listen to music to relax, and then I just sleep. And when I wake up I have to study the lessons for the following day. I have special sports that I like to practice every day.

So by 5:30 p.m. I'm done with schoolwork, and then I go find my friends, so we would relax and maybe talk a little bit. And if I am enjoying visiting my friends, I would stay there late, until 7:00 p.m., and I would invite them to come home with me to share what we have, and then I would take them back to their home. And when I come back to my family, if we have something to share, I will share it, and we'll discuss different kinds of subjects. And then we eat food together and I go to sleep. That's just the cycle of my life.

Regarding my education, people always say that I am intelligent, and I believe I am because I have never gotten poor marks. And I love my education. I have taken up social studies, but people always advise me that I should have taken up writing, because they believe in writing. Maybe that's where I could accomplish what I want. I dream of becoming a journalist, because I can handle the writing. But people say my tribe is made of beggars, so I feel like helping those people. That's why I would like to hold an important position in the political sphere, so I could not only care for my country but also for my people, who have always been stereotyped as beggars. And I always pray to God that my dream will come true one day. And when this dream comes true I will thank God. I will always stick to that, because I don't want to give up on that dream. There are some friends that I have to break away from because I feel maybe they would interfere with my dream.

Since I was a kid, I have loved American songs and some French songs so much, but I'm not very open to Congolese songs. I don't mean I don't like Congolese songs, but most Congolese songs are in Lingala, and I don't speak it. However, with French songs, I can understand what they mean, and I think about American songs in English.

I can't name the titles of songs, but I can name some celebrities whose songs I like. The artists I like are Akon, Chris Brown, Lil Wayne, and Fat Joe. All of these celebrities have their own names, but here in the Congo we call them all "cash men."

I especially love series; I really like action films. And I like reading novels—I think it is the fact that it enriches my French. They also help me to find out about realities in foreign countries. And they help me learn about new words that I don't know. I have a dictionary that helps me look up words I don't know. I think of the world being made up of one humanity. We should take care of Congolese people as brothers and sisters. We should do more instead of just thinking of doing business.

I love my mama, and whenever she is sick I am concerned and do whatever I can to make her feel better. And I think my mama loves me so much. She has been struggling to support me in my studies, my education. And she has always told me that I would go up to heaven. I stick to education with the expectation that maybe I will be an honor to her, as she has been encouraging me through it all.

To come to my mama's struggle, she has gone through very tough conditions. Even though I was still very young, she would sometimes tell me about what she went through. Her struggles started in Bukavu when I was still a kid. It was not even in Bukavu city, but outside in the village. I was there, but I was too young to understand and remember, and nobody has really told me the real sequence of what happened. But people in the family tell me that Mama was raped. I can't really believe it, because I can't distinguish whether it was Interahamwe [the Rwandan militia responsible for the genocide in Rwanda] that did it, as there were a lot of different armed groups there. It has always been very hard for me to believe it. The little bit I heard about, my parents have always encouraged me to forget, but I can't. I still don't believe my ears and my eyes.

I am so proud. Mama is still so strong despite everything that she has gone through. She sticks to us and she still fights for us. I am so glad for that. That has been a real incentive for the work that she is doing today, because she stands up for other women. As I was growing up, I was always amazed by my mama because she wants to value other females. And this keeps me living, it cheers me, and it gives me an incentive to live and to want to help one day. I would also say, "Thank God for my dad," because since he came back to my mama, he has never given up on her again.

Many sexual violence survivors come to see my mama and tell her their own stories of how their families have been split up. They have been scattered, their husbands have given up on them. I really thank God that today my family is still together. I believe Mama is a tremendous woman, because there is so much poverty, and women would come here saying that their children are not attending school and Mama would do what she can for them, even when she is also in need—she would provide help for those children to go back to school. And despite all the wounds we might have in the family, I can't really complain, because I am lacking almost nothing. We don't have as big a house as I would like, but I feel quite good with this. I don't complain a lot, because anytime I need something I just tell it to my mom, and she will struggle to get me what I need. I try also to be moderate, because I can't go beyond what she can afford.

Sometimes I have good dreams and sometimes I have bad dreams. Last night, for instance, I was dreaming gas was coming out of the soil and people were getting suffocated, so it was a real nightmare last night. The dreams are mostly about things I might have spent the day doing, but of course they are mixed… Sometimes the dreams are nightmares. My dreams are often based on what I have gone through during the day. But if I have spent all day here at home, I will sleep like a baby. Sometimes I have nightmares about sorcerers, witchcraft, and death in my family. But if I have nightmares during the night, when I wake up I pray to God and then I wash up and go to school.

I wonder whether American citizens are educated about what is going on here. I wonder how they can just go on with their lives knowing that what they're buying is made from these conflict minerals. How can they feel peaceful with that without questioning why these people are doing this? I can't imagine that people are getting richer and richer from these blood minerals, but I can only hope that maybe one day they will get this message and it can stop and they will find a way to do it right. Congo's wealth should be distributed fairly to all the Congolese people and not just benefit a few individuals. I can only hope that one day our government will be held accountable, so that it stops individual enrichment and ensures that this business is organized so that it is formal and benefits all the Congolese people. I learned that North Kivu province alone, which is just a part of the Congo, is so wealthy that it could even help other countries to develop.

Postscript: Jonathan in 2017

I'm twenty-four now. Earlier, I enrolled in the university, studying law at the University of Goma. Since I was very young, I've always wanted to do either law or journalism. But given that there's nowhere I can do journalism here in Goma, I went for law. It's a dream I held since I was a little kid.

At university I've started seeing things differently, and that is a major change in my life.

We still live in the same house. I learned to like it. I've never been pretentious. It's true it's not a fancy neighborhood, but I like the people we live with and the neighbors, despite the insecurity. I learned to appreciate and enjoy what life gives me.

The family is doing well. Nobody is sick. My dad is currently in Bukavu, and my mom is at home with my elder sister with her three kids. Everybody is doing well. My mom is still running here and there looking for funding for her projects. The biggest challenge our family faces is unemployment. Dad and Mom are both jobless. That doesn't make life easy at all. My siblings can hardly go to school, and I'm the only one going to university because I was fortunate enough to meet you guys. My other siblings are experiencing a number of problems. And I think all of it stems from my parents' unemployment. Jobless as they are, they can't even educate their children. I think that's the most difficult challenge the family is facing.

I wouldn't say we eat to our satisfaction, but our mom manages the best she can to get us food. Of course, it happens sometimes that we don't eat, but at the end of the day, we eat something.

Things have changed in Goma. Visibly there have been some positive things because the youth have woken up to Congo's political situation. The youth are creating their own political parties and pro-democracy groups opposing the way the ruling authorities are leading the country. Such awareness from the youth was not possible earlier. There are a lot of youth groups sprouting up and they're pressuring the government for change. I support them, and soon my colleagues and I will be creating our own political party. We're still brewing the ideas, but I think soon after we're done with the university, we'll see how to go about it. First we'll be looking for people whose way of seeing things politically intersects with ours. And our party will focus mainly on educating the people so that they can be aware of their rights and duties vis-à-vis the ruling authorities. We believe that raising the awareness of the people to know their rights and duties is the most important instrument for change. The goal is to be of help to the country. If our destiny will lead us to be part of the ruling class, I'll happily do it. But the goal first is to assist with raising awareness.

I dream of the rule of law in Congo because there are so many rights violations. The country is in really bad shape justice-wise! So much corruption. So, my dream for this country is to see all such things stop.

In September 2017 Jonathan graduated from law school, and as of mid-2018 he was training with a Congolese law firm.

MARIE'S STORY, 2010

My name is Marie. I was born in Bukavu in eastern Congo on June 6, 1972. I am married to Jonas. I have eight children—among whom are five sons and three daughters, including twins whom I've just had seven days ago.

I am a survivor of rape. The FDLR forced the door open and took me by force. They held a knife to my husband, as you can see by the cut on his face. I still have a scar on my breast and on my leg, where they branded me. They raped me in front of my children. I felt really traumatized, and my husband was traumatized.

We struggled against them; we fought the best we could. But a soldier would take one leg and another soldier the other leg, and one would come in between and then the second one would come and so on. It was the same for my daughter and the other women. It is so very discouraging because we came as guests to this village where it happened; we were there to help them. My daughter Aline was fifteen years old at the time. I would say maybe these soldiers had become insane.

They just left, they didn't even steal anything. It is as if they just came to rape.

I think the intent of the FDLR is to destroy the community through rape so they can keep hold of the mines.

The difference between civilians and soldiers when they rape is at least civilians do not torture you while raping. A civilian would rape but they would not take a machete and cut into women's vaginas. But the FDLR soldiers torture women and use machetes and sticks. I can remember at the same time as I was being raped, my neighbor was also being raped, but unfortunately for her they took a weapon and dug into her vagina and it would come out with intestines, and she was killed. I realized that these men no longer wanted women to live.

With my wounds, I was welcomed by Mama Mathilde, the head of the Olame Center in Bukavu, who did a great job helping me psychologically and physically. Otherwise, there was no free medical assistance at that time.

My husband, Jonas, decided to leave us, to leave me alone with our children. He left me while I was two weeks pregnant and he was thinking that maybe this was a pregnancy resulting from the rape by the FDLR soldiers. Because Jonas wrongly believed that the pregnancy was from the rape, he was demanding that I have an abortion. Being a woman and knowing myself, I told him he was wrong and that I was already pregnant.

Jonas went across the border to Rwanda and was welcomed there by a priest named Father Jean-Pierre from Congo, who helped to de-traumatize him. The priest helped him understand that it was not my fault that I was raped. So he encouraged my husband to come back to me. And that is how he came back to me after three years. By the time he came back, the child was already two years old.

I'm now the president of my own women's organization, *Mamans Organisées pour le Développement* (Mothers Organized for Development—MAODE), which I founded in 2000 as a survivor of sexual violence. When I was raped, I was traumatized. I was helped by nurses who helped me medically. I felt I needed to set up something myself so I could encourage other women who have suffered the same thing I went through. I decided to create this association so that these women could also access medical assistance.

Three months after I had been raped, I decided to create this association. I would visit agricultural fields and meet with women, sensitizing them about the consequences of staying unhealed or untreated. They were quite excited about the idea of seeking assistance, but transportation was always a big problem. So with other mothers in the organization, we were collecting money to buy antibiotics.

My husband, Jonas, began working with me in my organization. He was still feeling ashamed because people were pointing out that his wife had been raped. Throughout the region, men were giving up on their wives who had been raped, so Jonas was encouraged to help me sensitize these men to come home to their wives. This is how Jonas joined me in the work to sensitize men. Other men joined Jonas, as they have learned from his courage. I get really encouraged by that. This is how we kept our family together.

Educationally, I have chosen to do law. I did it out of a need to advocate and fight for women and children. I came to notice that whenever there was any trouble in any family, it was the women and children who were suffering the most. This year I have just gotten my BA in law.

My personal dream is to provide education for my children. I want them to become doctors, to become lawyers, to become representatives, and why not president?

For Congo, I think peace is the pillar for real development. Give people peace and you're going to see how they will prosper. Now you don't know whether you are going to make it to tomorrow morning. You're always traumatized, always afraid. If you hear something strange outside, you're afraid it's the militia coming to your door. So peace is the only key for the Congolese people, and that's what I'm dreaming of for all of us.

Postscript: Marie in 2017

People should not be jailed in central prisons for petty crimes. When family members of such people come to me in our office, I go see the judicial authorities—magistrates, judges, prosecutors—to discuss the different cases, and sometimes they order the detainees to be freed. I feel very proud when that happens.

Negotiating the freeing of detainees requires you to be brave, and I am. But sometimes I feel that I'm like John the Baptist preaching in the desert, because sometimes judicial authorities just ignore my pleas. It's frustrating!

People need to be trained for the future of Congo. The next Congolese president should be someone who bears and feels the suffering of the population, someone whose team helps him work first for the best interest of the people. We Congolese boast about our country's wealth. But where does that wealth go to? Congolese people would not be begging for assistance if that wealth was managed transparently.

Marie's main objective now is to be elected to Congo's parliament. The story of Marie's husband and Jonathan's father, Jonas, is on the book website at www.congostories.org.

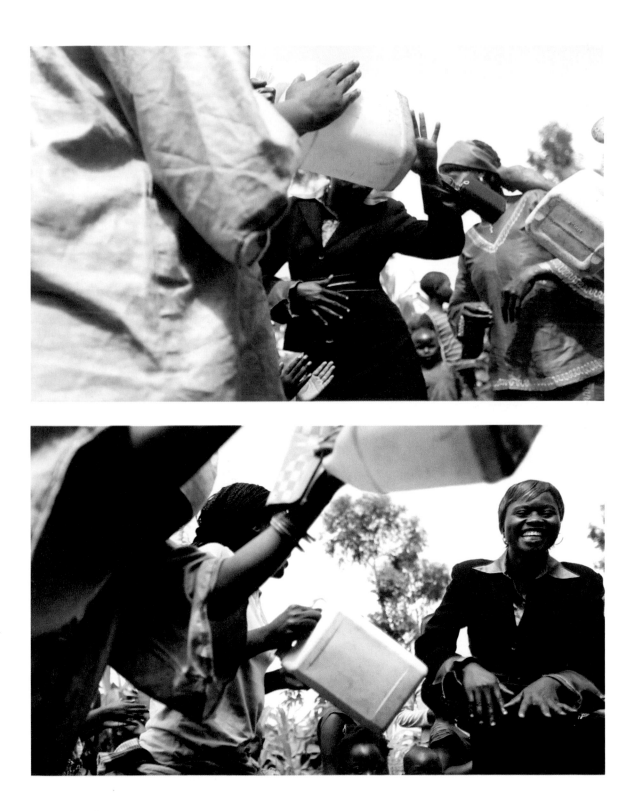

CHAPTER NINE

Congo Responds to the Onslaught

The Whistle for Change

The situation in Congo may seem hopeless to some, but here's the good news: many heroic Congolese are now rejecting the poisonous status quo and are working to build a more peaceful future. These include human rights and environmental activists, women's and youth groups, church leaders, reform minded politicians, local journalists, and many others.

The most powerful driver of change in Congo is the reform efforts of Congolese themselves on the front lines of the battles for human rights, democracy, peace, equal opportunity, and an end to corruption. With Congolese intentions and battles as the foundation, the real multiplier effect comes when those reform efforts on the ground link into global movements for change.

In fact, there is a long history of resistance by Congolese people and civil society groups to the unfair and oppressive governing and economic arrangements put in place by everyone from King Leopold II of Belgium in the 1880s right up to President Joseph Kabila, the latest kleptocrat to inhabit the Congolese presidency. Congolese people have not taken the abuse sitting down, even while their efforts at organizing for change have been met by successive governments with extreme violence and repression. Congolese groups and coalitions have formed to provide resistance, make demands, and promote recommendations and alternative visions for their country's future. Civil society groups have a long history of vitality and influence in Congo. They soldier on, against great odds.

Congolese historian Georges Nzongola-Ntalaja elaborates: "The democracy movement in the Congo is a struggle for political freedom and economic prosperity. Thus, the independence struggle of the 1950s, the popular insurrections for a 'second independence' in the 1960s, the fight against Mobutu's one-party dictatorship, and the current struggle against new forms of dictatorship and external oppression have, as a common denominator, the demand for expanded rights politically and for a better life economically."[251]

Congolese Youth and Women's Movements

Youth movements have been at the forefront of efforts to alter the course of Congo's history, driven by high levels of unemployment and anger at corruption. In recent years, two movements are worth noting. In response to a crisis of inadequate drinking water, Lucha (*Lutte pour le Changement*, or "Struggle for Change") was formed in May 2012 in Goma. Lucha soon became focused on broader social action and innovative protest. Social media has been Lucha's primary means of communication, and its roots are mostly middle-class in the eastern Congolese city of Goma. Symbolizing the reactionary nature of the Congolese state regarding any challenge to the status quo, the Congolese governor of North Kivu, Julien Paluku, once called them "tomorrow's terrorists."[252] Lucha branches have popped up across Congo, in Kinshasa, Lubumbashi, South Kivu, and elsewhere. Their members and leaders have been imprisoned numerous times for peaceful democratic protests. One of Lucha's founders, Ghislain Muhiwa, who himself spent six months in jail and spent the time teaching other inmates how to read and write, explains the focus of the group: "People here think it is normal to have no water, no electricity, to be killed by militias. Our job is to convince them it is not normal."[253]

In 2015 Lucha was instrumental in supporting the creation of Filimbi ("whistle"), inspired by other youth movements across Africa whose activities could be studied by Congolese activists as a result of the proliferation of social media channels and access. Filimbi members were also called "terrorists," this time by the Congolese government's information minister. Filimbi operates in Kinshasa and throughout the country.

In addition to social media, text messages are a favored organizing tool. One of the protest phrases is *telema* ("stand up" or "arise"), which was used by Citizen Front 2016 at a number of public events, such as soccer matches. Another theme in the pro-democracy youth movements has been *Les Congolais debout!*, or "Congolese, stand up!" which builds on a line from Congo's national anthem. Paper tracts are often used to organize in advance of protests. Music remains a medium of choice for challenging the status quo.[254]

Similarly, women's movements and organizations are driving change from the neighborhood to the national level. There is an incredible diversity of women-led activism for change throughout Congo. Illustratively, Justine Masika wrote:

> "[In September 2017] my organization coordinated 65 women leaders from every province to come to our capital city, Kinshasa, to start a Congolese Women's Forum for peace and equal political representation. . . . It felt incredible to have so many people listen to us.
>
> "Less than one week after the event we started to see progress. Six women from our group and 80 local women were included alongside militant groups in peace talks in the Kasai Region, a hotbed of violence, where an estimated 3,300 people have been

killed by warring forces in [2017]. Collectively, women made up around 20 percent of those in the room—a huge contrast with similar previous events.

"We are now focused on increasing this further, against all the challenges.

"Every day I put my life at risk by speaking out, but I have no choice but to keep going. Congolese women need to be taken seriously so the DRC can finally witness the peaceful future that we have all dreamed about for many years. A part of that is in our hands."[255]

Congo's Catholic Church

Congo's Catholic Church has often been at the center of mobilization, through its priests, nuns, lay leaders, and schools. Congolese cardinal Laurent Monsengwo and the Congolese Conference of Catholic Bishops have been at the forefront of opposing authoritarian rule in Congo for many years. Leaders of the organization, known by its acronym, CENCO, took a key role in advocating for democratic processes and reforms, as well as adherence to the rule of law. The church has conducted large-scale peace, voter, and civic education programs. And when the country faced an electoral crisis at the end of 2016, CENCO mediated an agreement that averted catastrophe. CENCO has been a unifying force for civil society in Congo. In 2017, CENCO leaders asked the Congolese people to stand up and take democracy into their own hands.

Catholic groups, particularly the Catholic Lay Committee (CLC), upped the ante in late 2017/early 2018 by organizing large-scale demonstrations in support of free and fair elections, despite the government's ban on demonstrations. Predictably, they were met by massive crackdowns by the state security services, which fired into church grounds and killed at least eight worshippers as they knelt and sang hymns.

Resisting Dictatorship[256]

Congolese popular movements have been particularly active in demanding a democratic presidential transition. According to the Congolese constitution, the end of President Joseph Kabila's second term was supposed to be December 19, 2016. That should have ushered in Congo's first peaceful democratic transition of power—from one elected president to a new one—in the country's history. Using a variety of tactics, however, President Kabila did not leave office.

Beginning in January 2015, Congolese grassroots movements in support of free and fair elections gained strength, staging peaceful protests, workshops, and panel events in cities around the country, keyed in part by Lucha and Filimbi. That surge of activism also brought on an escalation of violent crackdowns against pro-democracy groups and other civilians joining marches and protests calling for elections to happen on time. According to Human Rights Watch, during the week of January 19, 2015, the government used "unlawful and excessive force to crack down on protests," and "36 people, including one police officer, were killed during the demonstrations in Kinshasa, Congo's capital. Of these, Congo's security forces fatally shot at least 21 people. Additionally, on January 22, at least four people were killed during demonstrations in the eastern city of Goma."[257]

In another notable moment in the evolution of civil society's growing pro-democracy movement, protestors and pro-democracy groups again took to the streets during the week of September 19, 2016, two months before elections should have taken place. This was a flashpoint date that grassroots groups used to encourage civilians out into the streets, since it marked the time when the elections commission should have officially announced the beginning of election preparations. As anticipated, the announcement was not made, symbolically sealing the fate of Congo's faltering democracy. Elections would not be held on time, and Kabila would stay in power beyond the constitutional limit. Again, violence occurred, disproportionately perpetrated by government forces against civilians.[258]

Government crackdowns continued into 2017 and 2018. On July 31, 2017, according to Human Rights Watch, "Congolese authorities arrested at least 128 people in nine cities across the country today as youth movements and opposition parties called for nationwide demonstrations to protest the announcement that elections will not be held this year."[259] Arrests of hundreds of pro-democracy protestors and police killings of many others, including prominent activist leader Rossy Mukendi, have continued into early 2018. Furthermore, as Freedom House notes, "Journalists and human rights advocates continued to face threats, unlawful detention, and beatings by state security forces and rebel groups around the country."[260]

At the time of this writing, Congolese elections were scheduled for the end of 2018, and Kabila's regime was utilizing all the usual delaying tactics to either postpone the poll again or rig it to the ruling party's advantage. Congolese resistance efforts by civil society were intensifying in response.

Hope for the Future

A positive example of local organizing efforts combining with international advocacy pressure is the December 2016 deal struck between the Congolese government and the opposition, averting major violence around postponed elections. Congo's Catholic bishops provided highly competent mediation, but the negotiations also needed to be ripened, as the parties did not always see it in their interest to come to agreement. This leverage came in local and international forms: determined activism by the Congolese pro-democracy movements Lucha, Filimbi, and others, who continued demonstrations in the face of protest bans and the arrest of their leaders; carefully escalated international pressure and elevated policy attention from the US and Europe, in particular coordinated targeted sanctions spearheaded by President Obama's special envoy Tom Perriello and Belgian envoy Renier Nijskens; regional diplomacy and pressure, especially by Angola; compromises by the opposition and the government; and, in the US, a significantly larger bipartisan congressional, activist, and NGO constituency for democratic change than had ever before been seen for Congo which pressed the Obama administration to act in support of peace and democracy.

Upping the Pressure

In June 2017, 195 Congolese civil society organizations welcomed international sanctions against Congo's leading officials in response to their subversion of democracy and peace.[261] This is reminiscent of the anti-apartheid struggle in South Africa, when South African organizations led the movement at great personal risk and supported international sanctions against South Africa's leaders. Despite years of repression and violence, eventually the South African activists prevailed—with the support of the global anti-apartheid movement—and that vile governing system of racial domination was dismantled.

Illustrative of the challenge to the regime presented by civil society, on August 18, 2017, in Paris, forty leaders of Congolese civil society and citizens' movement organizations launched a manifesto, *Manifeste du Citoyen Congolais*, calling for Kabila's exit (accessible in English at www.manifesterdc.com/manifeste/). The manifesto is the result of strategic organizing and analysis, as well as staggering bravery on the part of its authors and supporters. "Under the existing regime, terror has once again become the preferred method of government, making it impossible for the Congolese people to claim their rights," it reads.[262]

Civil society groups and activists in Congo will continue to organize in support of human rights and democracy at enormous personal risk. Their courage and commitment have no limits.

Fidel's Upstander Story

◇◇

*Through a series of interviews conducted by Fidel,
Congolese Upstanders tell their life stories. All of them are risking
their lives to defend human rights, press for peace,
resist dictatorship, provide education, and prepare a better
future for their fellow Congolese.*

Douce Namwezi

My name is Douce Namwezi N'Ibamba. I was born in Bukavu in 1989 into a family of eight children, and I'm the second. I had the common childhood of any Congolese kid. I was born when Mobutu was kicked out as president, so after that the rest of my childhood was in the war. I went to primary school, secondary school, and university in the same city. When I was eight we had to flee with my family because of the 1996 war. I was a child, so I didn't really realize how risky it was, because I was on the back of my father and I didn't know where we were going. But when we arrived at the place we went, after two days there was no food and water, so my uncle told me to go to the market and steal some food so we could eat.

I lost two years of school while we were refugees. The situation didn't get better after we went home, because so much was destroyed. I went back to school at a place with a lot of refugees. By the time I started secondary school I wanted to become a journalist, but that was a no-no because women journalists are not common in our society. Women who are journalists are called a lot of nicknames: prostitute, complicated, whatever. So it wasn't easy for me when I said to someone, "I want to study journalism when I finish secondary school," and they would say, "No, you don't have to become that strange woman. You can just study for other kinds of work that women do." At the time there were very few women journalists, but I said, "No, this is the kind of work I want to do."

Often I would listen to the radio with my father and I would ask him, "Why do we always listen to men's voices? Why do we not listen to women's voices?" He told me that not many women were interested in journalism, that it's not easy work. You have to wake up early. You have to work hard. Come home late.

I didn't have a lot of friends when I was a child. I had some colleagues, the ones we were studying with, but I was just focused on my studies, so it wasn't like I had time to go and joke and play and do a lot of things. I was just studying.

I was inspired by the only two women journalists whose voices were heard on the radio here in Bukavu. When I got my diploma I said, "I want to study journalism." Unfortunately, there was no school of journalism here; we had to go to either Bujumbura or Kinshasa to study journalism—but my father didn't have the money for that. So I decided to study international relations at the local university. When I was in the first year, I learned about the women's media association AFEM, an organization of women that is working to promote women's rights and fights against sexual and gender-based violence. I went to AFEM and met one of the co-founders, Chouchou Namegabe, and I told her I wanted to become a journalist. She said I could join them and learn how to produce radio shows. I didn't even know how to edit, so I learned by doing. I began going in the field, interviewing people, writing their stories, and the adventure began. AFEM now has its own radio station, which I am managing. I went from a simple reporter to the manager, and I really love it. I realized I could be part of changing the way people tell stories about Congo, to give a more positive image of Congo, how to tell positive stories, and how to be an active citizen through media.

The context we are working in is not really easy for journalists, especially for women journalists. There are a lot of stereotypes of women and women journalists, because society wants women to stay home, to cook, to take care of their family. So when a woman is interviewing a politician or participating in a panel with men, giving opinions, people say this is not a normal woman. The problem is not the strength or the power that women have, it's the way people perceive that power. People ask, "How can she combine work, home, blah blah blah, traveling? When she travels, her husband stays home alone. Who's cooking for him?"

Our biggest success is having the first thematic radio station in Congo. Before we created the radio station, we made an assessment, monitoring gender in the media. How many media outlets are there in South Kivu? How many of them are led by men and how many by women? We went through their programs and looked at their gender sensitivity. And we found very few women, and the programming in general was not so gender sensitive. We asked if they had debates, and they said they did. We asked how many women participated. And they said, "Oh no, women don't come, they are lazy, they don't know how to talk, or they don't want to talk about politics." They had to justify why women didn't take part in the shows or the debate. So we concluded that there was a need to have a thematic radio station led by women where we could try to introduce other perspectives.

Creating the station—Mama Radio—was very challenging. No one thought we would succeed without a man leading the project. And when we started broadcasting, and when a journalist would make just one mistake, people would say, "Ah, women again." And there were constant questions about why we were so focused on women. So we just went about our work, coaching and training women journalists. In February 2017 we were one year old, and we celebrated that success. Many women journalists were coming to AFEM to learn or participate. A lot of young people have come to the radio station to be trained, to learn journalism, and we encouraged a lot of women also, especially girls, to build a media strategy. So we are like a reference.

Once, when AFEM was going into the field and talking to women about their situation and the way they are affected by the conflict, we went to Kamituga and met an older woman with eight children who was working in the mines. We talked to her about the sexual violence and abuse there. She explained that the mine owner controlled when the miners could leave the mines to go home. He could even put his hand inside their vaginas to make sure that they didn't hide gold or any other mineral. We talked with her about whether she would want to do other work and asked her if she wanted to work at the local radio station. She didn't think it was possible but gave us permission to ask the station manager. We went back a year later and we could hardly recognize her. She was really transformed. She was happy, she was smiling. She wanted to do more training. AFEM sent her to Bujumbura for an internship, and when she came back she worked to transform the way they were doing journalism. She denounced what was going on in the mines in her community, so other NGOs working in the mines became more interested in addressing the violence against women in the mines.

My dream is to see a Congo where men and women are equal and where men and women are more sensitive to the situation of women. And I see the world equal at different levels. Do I see her or him as an enemy or as a potential force that can also help me? And how do I look at my children, boys and girls together? Do I consider the boy the one who has to be the leader, the one who has to drive the car? And do I educate my girl just to stay home? I want to see parents consider their children as equals; to see teachers who consider all their pupils as equal; to see professors encourage women to do architecture or any other work that is stereotypically men's work; to see churches that preach equality; to see media talking about gender equality in all spheres of life; to see men and women together, hand in hand, working to change the country. So I dream of that kind of Congo.

To improve our situation depends on Congolese people first of all, but not only Congolese, because we know that some Western people also benefit from our situation, and they're maybe not ready to let go of that. They want to continue stealing, they want to continue destroying, so they can continue doing their business. We need examples of the positive side of Congo. There are a lot, even if we don't see them at first sight: we have parks, we have lakes, we have rivers, we have mountains, we have a lot of gifts that nature gave us. We can show the Congo that welcomes people, the Congo that wants to trade and exchange with the world, the Congo that is learning, the Congo that is developing itself. We can provide examples of Congolese businessmen and women who are trying to bring new ideas, new technology, new things to Congo, and who are helping the people here. We can show the image of the Congo where even with only ten dollars, women are able to send their children to school, to feed them. There are a lot of examples that we can give to other people, not only war and violence. But this is not easy. That context is not helped by the other one, the sociopolitical one. We want elections, we want peace, but there are no elections. Even if you talk, you cry, and you yell, there still are no elections. I think there are a lot of things that must go together. Just because you are a mzungu [someone of European descent], you cannot be expected to talk positively about Congo. When foreigners come to Congo there are no roads, no running water, no electricity, lots of armed groups. How do you want them to talk positively about Congo? When you arrive in Sweden, you don't need people to tell you to talk positively about the roads in Sweden, or talk positively about gender in Sweden, for example.

It's important to wear Congolese clothes to be more able to talk about Congo, because it's easier to come from the outside for a visit, to judge, to condemn, but without really trying to understand the root causes of the situation. It doesn't mean you have to stay a year or five years in Congo, but it means to interact with Congolese. For example, in journalism, if there is no war or killing, we are not interested. If you want to talk about Lake Kivu, "What is Lake Kivu? We don't care about Lake Kivu." But if it is about a new armed group, we are more interested. Professional journalism doesn't mean you kill your own heart, you are no longer sensitive to the situation you're reporting on and you're reporting just to report, not to change. That is not the work of journalism. The journalist should be attempting to understand the situation and deciding to talk about it so it can change. If you're just reporting to be famous but not to change the situation, for me this is not professionalism. So it's kind of a debate or discussion: "You're an activist, you're not a journalist." But I say, "Good journalists are activists."

◇◇◇

CONTACT INFORMATION FOR AFEM:
www2.afemsk.org/en/

◇◇◇

CHAPTER TEN

Davids and Goliaths

Global Rights Activists vs. the War Profiteers

This chapter examines two major international solidarity movements sparked by atrocities in Congo. The first popular movement formed at the end of the nineteenth century in response to the "rubber terror" unfolding under King Leopold's rule. The second movement, driven by American students, focused on conflict minerals at the beginning of the twenty-first century. Although separated by a century, the two movements have many things in common.

PART ONE: THE FIRST GLOBAL HUMAN RIGHTS MOVEMENT OF THE TWENTIETH CENTURY

What is striking about the first movement is how a relatively small number of people with the courage to speak out managed to expose Leopold's many injustices, building an international people's movement and eventually bringing an end to the Belgian king's personal ownership of the Congo territory. Over time, this helped end some of the worst atrocities being perpetrated by the armies of the Belgian colonial authorities and their commercial allies.

Because the many Congolese who fought and died in this struggle are anonymous to history, the narrative in this section is necessarily limited to the contributions of non-Africans.

An Unrelenting Activist

Edmund Morel worked for a British shipping company that had cornered the market on all goods moving by sea to and from the Congo Free State. Over time, Morel noticed that the Belgian ships were leaving Congo overflowing with ivory and rubber, but they were returning with ammunition, guns, and soldiers. Morel deduced from this that there must be massive forced or slave labor extracting that rubber and ivory, and that the trade was riddled with extreme corruption, with enormous profits being spirited away off the books.[263]

Morel was unrelenting in his efforts to publicize the Congolese crisis. He helped mobilize hundreds of mass meetings in Britain and the United States focused on protesting slave labor in Congo. He met with President Theodore Roosevelt and demanded that the US government do something. He brilliantly used the media of the time to keep the story alive for audiences all over Europe and America.[264]

There were also African American activists who seeded the ground for this protest movement to flourish. Historian and journalist George Washington Williams and missionary William Sheppard were critically important in getting the story out about the horrors unfolding in Congo. Williams wrote the first exposé of what was unfolding in Leopold's Congo at the time. Williams exposed Leopold's anti-slavery rhetoric as hypocrisy, as he accused the king's government of being "engaged in the slave-trade, wholesale and retail. It buys and sells and steals slaves."[265] Williams concluded that Leopold's Congo state had perpetrated "crimes against humanity," a term he coined for the ages.[266] When Williams went to Congo in 1890, there had already been roughly a thousand European and American visitors to that territory, but Williams was the first to denounce what was happening there.[267]

There were some African American missionaries in Congo as well. Protestant missionaries came to Congo from the US, UK, and Sweden. They had front-row seats to the violence that was unfolding in Leopold's colony. William Sheppard was perhaps the first missionary to publicize the atrocities in Congo, writing a series of articles that were very damning of the authorities' human rights violations, including the cutting-off of hands and mass killings.[268] Sheppard took a series of photos with a newly acquired Kodak camera, with which "he recorded the atrocities in a series of gory images that would shock the Western world."[269]

Many missionaries fed information to Morel's campaign efforts, and the photographs were particularly damning, documenting children whose hands and feet had been cut off, among many other depredations. The Baptist missionaries were particularly effective in publicizing the atrocities, holding "magic lantern" slide shows in Scotland even before any real organized movement was created.[270]

At the same time, other missionaries were part of Leopold's colonial enterprise and were complicit in it.[271] Leopold wrote a famous letter to missionaries in 1883:

"Evangelize the savages so that they stay forever in submission to the white colonialists, so they never revolt against the restraints they are undergoing. . . . Convert always the blacks by using the whip."[272]

In addition to anti-slavery missionaries, there were also human rights organizations that protested what Leopold was spawning in Congo. The Aborigines Protection Society and the Anti-Slavery Society used the media to educate the public about the territory's misdeeds. Morel's agenda differed from the global scope of these two groups in that he believed that Congo was "a case apart, an entire state deliberately and systematically founded on slave labor."[273]

The campaign gained the most traction in the United Kingdom, so much so that in May 1903, the British House of Commons passed a resolution in a unanimous vote urging that Congo's "natives should be governed with humanity."[274] It was as firm a denunciation as a fellow imperialist state could make.

The resolution led the British government to authorize its diplomatic representative in Congo, Roger Casement, to go on a fact-finding mission into the interior of the territory. Instead of the usual public relations tour most visitors were taken on, Casement went on his own, traveling for over a hundred days throughout the interior of Congo, observing firsthand some of the worst depredations of the rubber terror, and he pressed his case upon his return with fury and passion, inspiring others in his circles.[275]

It was only a matter of time before Casement and Morel became allies, and eventually close friends. (In their letters, Casement was "Dear Tiger" and Morel was "Dear Bulldog.") They drew up plans during a meeting in Ireland for a global campaign to expose the brutalities that so horrified them both. Shortly thereafter, Morel created the Congo Reform Association, and using funds supplied by Casement, he bought a typewriter and other supplies. The association was endorsed by an array of public figures, including politicians, faith leaders, nobility, and businessmen. A thousand people attended the organization's first meeting in Liverpool.[276]

————

The campaign that Morel led was unrelenting. Without money or position, he challenged governments around the world. He smartly tailored his message to particular audiences and their unique concerns, from the business community to the clergy to parliamentarians.[277]

In one six-month stretch in 1906, Morel wrote 3,700 letters about Congo. By that time, over sixty resolutions had been adopted at mass meetings condemning Leopold's resumption of slavery and demanding action from the British government. Congo Reform Association employees Reverend John Harris and Alice Seeley Harris, returned Baptist missionaries who had taken many of the photos used by the campaign, spoke publicly about Congo some six hundred times over a two-year period.[278]

Because the United States was the first country to recognize Leopold's authority over Congo, Morel asserted that the US was obligated to respond to the catastrophe unfolding there. He traveled to the US, saw President Roosevelt, and helped establish the American Congo Reform Association, which soon attracted notables such as Booker T. Washington and Mark Twain, the latter traveling to Washington, DC, to lobby on three occasions after meeting Morel. Twain wrote a particularly effective and popular takedown of the Congo Free State, penning a satire called *King Leopold's Soliloquy*, which was a harsh condemnation of the tactics and motivations of the king.[279] During and after Morel's visit, his Baptist missionary employees Reverend and Mrs. Harris spoke at over two hundred gatherings in nearly fifty cities in the US.[280]

Leopold Strikes Back

King Leopold counterattacked in the US with money and religion. Leopold gave concession rights in Congo to a number of wealthy, prominent, and influential men. He also worked with the Catholic Church to counter the Protestant human rights advocacy. And he employed a number of lobbyists throughout the United States. However, Leopold's zealous defense proved to be his undoing, as one of the lobbyists he used and then tossed aside released publicly a trove of damning documents about Leopold's efforts to manipulate American public opinion and bribe US legislators, which turned official sentiment strongly against the king—an early data dump that has a familiar ring to it.[281]

King Leopold II died in 1909, not long after giving up in the face of the campaign and unrelenting international public pressure and condemnation, finally selling "his" Congo to the Belgian government after Belgium's parliament annexed the territory in August 1908. Forced labor in Congo continued, albeit on a somewhat diminished scale, but unfortunately the human rights campaign was having trouble sustaining itself without its chief architect and villain, Leopold, still in the picture.

Morel was able to recruit the immensely popular Sir Arthur Conan Doyle of Sherlock Holmes fame to the campaign. Conan Doyle spoke to large crowds and authored a book about Congo with the help of Morel, asserting that the tragedy unfolding in Congo was "the greatest crime which has ever been committed in the history of the world."[282]

With Leopold removed from the equation, Morel and the campaign focused on ending the forced labor system that had so devastated Congo. The Belgian colonial administration began to institute reforms regarding forced labor and other abuses. By 1913, Morel was able to announce to the world that the atrocities, the rubber tax, and forced or slave labor were officially at an end.[283]

The person who has best documented this international human rights campaign, Adam Hochschild, should have the last word here when assessing the importance of this people's movement:

> "Today we are less likely to speak of humanitarianism, with its overtones of paternalistic generosity, and more likely to speak of human rights. . . . The Congo reform movement at its best not only helped to shape and strengthen this set of beliefs; it went beyond them. . . . E. D. Morel talked…about causes: above all, the theft of African land and labor that made possible Leopold's whole system of exploitation. . . . The larger tradition of which they are a part goes back to the French Revolution and beyond; it draws on the example of men and women who fought against enormous odds for their freedom, from the slave revolts of the Americas to the half-century of resistance that brought Nelson Mandela to power in South Africa. During its decade on the

world stage, the Congo reform movement was a vital link in that chain, and there is no tradition more honorable. At the time of the Congo controversy a hundred years ago, the idea of full human rights, political, social, and economic, was a profound threat to the established order of most countries on earth. It still is today."[284]

PART TWO: A TWENTY-FIRST-CENTURY STUDENT-LED MOVEMENT FOR CONGO

In the United States, a people's movement has evolved over the past decade that pressures companies and governments to change their policies toward Congo. Such movements have altered the course of human history over the last century. Without the civil rights, labor, women's, environmental, peace, and LGBTQ movements in the US, it's hard to imagine what the social fabric of the country would look like today. And beyond influencing what happens in their own countries, Americans and Europeans—in solidarity with Africans—together contributed to global and local people's movements that helped dismantle apartheid in South Africa and end the blood diamonds wars in West Africa.

The connections between the minerals found in our laptops, cell phones, and other electronics products and the terrible violence in eastern Congo inspired a people's movement focused on removing conflict and violence from the supply chains of those products. The movement is led by students but supplemented by faith-based organizations, human rights groups, academics, investigative journalists, principled politicians, and celebrities. These global efforts coordinate closely with Congolese reformers on the ground who are standing up in the face of great risk and danger to press for change. Just like with the anti-apartheid and blood diamonds movements, the global people's movement addressing conflict minerals has helped give Congo's upstanders further hope that change will come and their struggle for freedom will succeed, because the international sources of their repression and exploitation are finally being called to account.

The impacts of this movement against conflict minerals have been significant. Government policies have changed, corporate supply chains have been cleaned up and become much more transparent, and the number of Congolese armed groups and the money that sustains them have been dramatically reduced. The market has cratered for three of the four conflict minerals (tin, tantalum, and tungsten) just as it did for blood diamonds as companies have insisted that their raw materials not underwrite violence. The most destructive militia over the last decade, a Rwandan-backed insurgency called the M23, is no longer operating in Congo as a result.

Enough Project colleagues Annie Callaway and Sasha Lezhnev, who have both been at the forefront of corporate engagement and campaigning on Congo from campuses to board rooms to the halls of Congress, spell out the origins and the tactics of the conflict minerals movement, in the following account.

Conflict Minerals Campaign Story

by Annie Callaway and Sasha Lezhnev

In the early to mid-2000s, it was clear that the world was not paying attention to Congo, despite the staggering levels of violence and violations of basic human rights. Conflict in Congo was often portrayed internationally as too complicated to understand, which made it difficult for would-be solidarity activists to connect with each other and with Congolese in the diaspora in order to advocate for an end to the violence. During that time, we read report after report from the UN and Congolese civil society groups about how armed groups wreaking havoc in eastern Congo were making millions of dollars from controlling the minerals trade. The UN Panel of Experts called minerals "the engine of the conflict,"[285] a Congolese civil society group cited minerals as "a major source of income and of conflict in North Kivu as in the whole of the DRC,"[286] and a third said they were "the principal method used by FDLR to raise funds."[287] A major part of the profits was also going to the patrons of these armed groups in Rwanda and Uganda and to elites in Kinshasa and eastern Congo. Despite peace agreements being signed by diplomats, the fighting continued unabated. It was clear that there was an economic incentive to continue the war that needed to be changed.

At the Enough Project, we increasingly recognized this problem and convened a meeting between UN experts and NGOs working on Congo in mid-2008 to delve more deeply into this problem of minerals, economics, and war, trying to gather who knew what about the problem and what was being done about it. As it turned out, there were very important gaps in knowledge of both the problem and the solution. So we decided to embark on a thorough research project to learn which minerals were helping the deadly armed groups profit and in which products these minerals were used, utilizing information from the UN Group of Experts, Congolese civil society reports, interviews with industry experts, and our own field research at mines in Congo.

UNDERSTANDING THE ISSUES

Our team spent the next eight months talking to Congolese civil society groups, minerals traders, government officials, UN experts, tech firms, industry gurus, and minerals refiners, as well as writing to minerals associations, traveling to Congo to do research at the mine sites, and meeting regularly as a team about what we learned. We realized that although Congo contains many different types of minerals, four "conflict minerals" in particular were responsible for sustaining armed groups' profits in eastern Congo. These four minerals were tin, tungsten, tantalum, and gold, which at one of our team meetings at Enough we decided to call "the 3Ts and gold" for short. In 2008 alone, the Enough Project estimated that armed groups' profits from the conflict minerals trade was $185 million, based on extensive reporting from the UN and Enough field research.[288]

After many industry interviews, we came to understand that the supply chains for the 3Ts and gold looked like an hourglass. At the beginning of the supply chain there were thousands of mines, and at the other end there were thousands of companies selling and manufacturing the final products. But globally there were only a few hundred smelters and refiners pinched in the middle of the hourglass. The smelters turn rock ores into metals usable for electronic devices, autos, jewelry, and many other products. And we learned that US-based end-user companies had powerful supply chain influence over those smelters and refiners, because they were their main customers and they paid a better price than Chinese end-user companies. Importantly, smelters and refiners knew where in the world they purchased minerals from, because it was their business to find minerals for a low price and then smelt or refine them. This meant that smelters and refiners could be the key to uncovering which minerals were funding armed violence in Congo.

If the end-user companies could pressure the smelters to change their purchasing decisions, to require that the rock ore minerals they purchased to process must come from conflict-free mines in Congo, we posited, that could dry up a major source of income for armed groups and army commanders in Congo. There was a relatively small group of smelting and refining companies that tech corporations would need to influence to start making this change, but first we would have to get the tech companies to care enough to take action. We knew that other industries, such as aerospace and defense, industrial manufacturing, and automotive, also consumed conflict minerals, but we also knew that tech would be an important way in to help leverage reforms in those other industries, and future conflict minerals legislation would capture several of those industries as well.

CAMPAIGN STRATEGY

We decided to attempt to influence tech companies through major consumers and social influencers such as students and celebrities. We also collaborated closely with faith-based groups such as Catholic Relief Services and World Vision, and we began engaging colleges, cities, and states, all of which make major technology purchases on a regular basis. We knew that tech companies marketed aggressively to students and young people, who also happened to make up the majority of the Enough Project's activist base. So we thought that a new student driven campaign could potentially influence the economics driving violence in Congo by pressuring tech companies to make their minerals supply chains more transparent, conflict-free, and responsible through consumer demand and legislative action.

While an advocacy campaign could have been built around any of the many serious dynamics impacting Congo's conflict, such as the use of rape as a weapon of war or child soldier recruitment, the conflict minerals entry point offered two key dynamics that would ultimately contribute to its successful growth as a movement:

1. While not the original cause of the conflict, profits from the deadly trade in conflict minerals added very important fuel to the fire and allowed armed groups and their sponsors in Rwanda, Uganda, Kinshasa, and eastern Congo to sustain themselves and their brutal campaigns of violence. By focusing on this funding source, the conflict

minerals campaign was able to open up space for broader issues to be addressed once the violence abated.

2. The connection between minerals in Congo and minerals powering cell phones, laptops, etc. is a bona fide connection, not something cobbled together for the sake of a coherent campaign narrative. It was (and remains) true that most people in the US owned at least one product that could contain minerals from Congo fueling conflict, and the fact that we as consumers should have the right to know whether that was true became a compelling argument for activists.

RESEARCH-BASED CAMPAIGNING

We knew we wanted consumers and students to take action, but we needed them to have the most accurate information about what was happening in Congo, how the minerals were used, and what the supply chains looked like. After nearly a year of in-depth research and interviews with key players in both Congo and the relevant industries, Enough published a report in April 2009 that spelled out how action addressing conflict minerals would support peace in eastern Congo through a comprehensive strategy.[289] We analyzed what would be the most important actions that tech companies, the Congolese government, the United Nations, and the US government could take that would combat the conflict minerals trade, and how those actions would concretely help resolve the conflict in eastern Congo.

The key three-part solution we outlined was trace-audit-certify. We advocated that companies should trace where the 3Ts and gold were in their products, independently audit the smelters of these minerals so that conflict-free smelters could be differentiated from dirty smelters, and help build the certification process in Congo and the broader Great Lakes region to help demilitarize mines and assess which mines were conflict-free and which were not. We published a series of articles and reports that laid out the connections between conflict minerals and electronics step-by-step, as well as op-eds in Silicon Valley and national newspapers.[290] Among other media outlets, we also worked with Scott Pelley and his *60 Minutes* crew from CBS on a segment called "Congo's Gold" in 2009,[291] which was nominated for an Emmy Award. This education was critical for activists and companies alike, and it generated momentum. By the end of 2009, the term "conflict minerals" was one of the *New York Times* "buzzwords of the year."[292]

COMPANY ENGAGEMENT

Speaking directly to executives and officers at companies that worked with minerals suppliers had to be part of the strategy, because these were the people who could actually reform the supply chain. After consulting with Congolese civil society leaders and organizations that were raising awareness about the conflict minerals issue and working toward solutions for it, we began reaching out to companies with our research. We then sent a letter on behalf of a wide NGO coalition to the CEOs of the twenty-five largest tech companies in early 2009, asking them to engage in solutions. We offered to meet with them or their teams to discuss the problem and solutions in detail. That letter made it to several executives' desks and hit the press. Although many didn't respond, we had very constructive exchanges with Intel, HP, Motorola, AMD, and RIM (the makers of BlackBerry).

During this process of dialogue, it became clear that some companies were much more interested in taking action than others. HP offered a number of supply chain reform proposals, Intel flew its corporate officers to far-flung corners of the globe where the 3Ts were being smelted in order to urge smelters to action, and Motorola and RIM supported congressional legislation on conflict minerals supply chain reporting requirements.

We then established criteria for ranking the largest tech companies on what they were concretely doing (or not doing) regarding conflict minerals. We published our first conflict minerals company rankings in 2010, and HP came out on top, with Intel in second place.[293] The rankings also showed that there was a long way to go on the solution, as the top score was only 32 percent.

The story of Steve Jobs of Apple that follows this section demonstrates the impact of activists, led by students, engaging with corporations.

CONGRESS

Legislation was also critically important in order to get companies across the board to reform their supply chains. We knew, based on lessons from the blood diamonds campaign, that leading companies with major brands would probably take action, but that without regulatory requirements, thousands of manufacturers might not. Members of Congress were interested from the beginning, following trips to Congo by Senators Sam Brownback (R-KS) and Dick Durbin (D-IL) in the late 2000s. Senators Brownback, Durbin, and later Russ Feingold (D-WI) wanted to take action to stem the flow of conflict minerals, and they introduced a bill on tantalum and tin in mid-2008.

The House of Representatives soon joined the fight, led by Jim McDermott (D-WA) along with Frank Wolf (R-VA), Barney Frank (D-MA), and others. Their Conflict Minerals Trade Act was introduced in late 2009 and included strong provisions in support of Congolese miners' livelihoods. This legislation was ultimately altered and inserted into the 2010 Dodd-Frank Wall Street Reform and Consumer Protection Act as Section 1502. Essentially this legislation required companies to report on their supply chain due-diligence efforts with regard to conflict minerals. It did not require companies to source from conflict-free mines or change anything at all about their business operations except mandating that they publicly release information about their conflict minerals supply chains each year. The logic was that this public reporting would encourage companies to begin sourcing conflict-free minerals so that they wouldn't be criticized for continuing to contribute to Congo's violence through their purchasing policies.

Getting the legislation passed was a classic David vs. Goliath effort and took a monumental effort by congressional staffers, activists, and senators. While some tech companies supported the bill, major industry lobbying behemoths such as the US Chamber of Commerce and the National Association of Manufacturers financed efforts to kill the legislation. Their reasoning was mainly that this bill would open a Pandora's box of regulation. They didn't want Congress to begin exposing the secrecy of corporate supply chains, fearing that environmental and other social issues would then be regulated as well. Those lobbyists tried hard to use their relationships on Capitol Hill to stop the bill from being passed, but they failed. There were several activist write-in campaigns at key points in the congressional process to push back against the industry lobbyists.[294] Toby Whitney from Representative McDermott's office played a critical role in shepherding offices together in the House of Representatives and helping fold the provision into the Dodd-Frank bill due to investor interest in the issue, as did Peter Quaranto in Senator Feingold's office and Maggie Fleming and Kody Kness in Senator Brownback's office.

There was a critical juncture in early 2010 when Sen. Blanche Lincoln of Arkansas was vocally opposed to the bill, and yet it still moved through the congressional conference committee for the Dodd-Frank bill, of which she was a member. Activists from the Enough Project, Lisa Shannon's organization Run for Congo Women, and other groups mobilized in Arkansas and across the country and posted repeatedly on Senator Lincoln's Facebook page to encourage her to change her stance on the bill. Within days, Lincoln reversed her position, and the bill moved through the Senate committee. This kind of grassroots activism was repeated across the country and resulted in a number of legislators changing their position and supporting the bill. It was finally folded into the Dodd-Frank bill by Senator Brownback in May 2010, passed as part the bill, and signed into law by President Obama in July 2010.

Importantly, the law was supported by many people in Congo who believed that a conflict-free minerals trade could help end the violence in their country. Congolese environmental activist Dominique Bikaba reflected on this and how he has seen the changes begin to take place: "For me, this law—even though it was an American law—had shown a great impact on mining in Congo. And I think the improvements we are seeing today in terms of the reduction of illegal mining in the region, or traceability, I think it's thanks to this law. If this law hadn't passed in the US, I don't know where we would be today. Not just for people, but also for wildlife and forests."

THE SEC

Dodd-Frank Section 1502 succeeded in creating a law that required publicly traded companies in the US to report annually on their supply chains with respect to conflict minerals. Though the law was passed in 2010, it took two years for the Securities and Exchange Commission (SEC) to write the corresponding rule, and companies did not file their first reports until 2014.

Despite losing the battle in Congress, the National Association of Manufacturers and the US Chamber of Commerce went on to sue the SEC over the rule. However, after a long, drawn-out court battle, they ultimately lost this fight as well. Only one small piece of the rule—the descriptor requirement—was ruled unconstitutional, leaving the majority of the rule, including the due-diligence reporting requirements, intact.

In response to attempts to weaken the rule in early 2017, 111 different Congolese civil society organizations wrote to the SEC in support of the rule, warning that if it were to be weakened or disappear altogether, it could lead to increased instability and violence in Congo's mining areas.[295] One coalition of thirty-one civil society groups based in South Kivu noted how the law helped reduce violence: "Cut off from the illegal extraction of minerals, which was a major source of funding, armed groups are significantly less active. In the east of [Congo], around 8,500 children left armed groups between 2009 and 2015."[296]

Congolese leaders like Dr. Denis Mukwege, founder of Panzi Hospital, also spoke out in support of conflict minerals legislation: "A conflict-free minerals industry would contribute to ending the unspeakable violence the people of Congo have endured for years. Government must not only enact strong legislation, they must be willing to enforce the law. Companies bear the responsibility of compliance and public disclosure and act transparently, as consumers are increasingly aware of conflict-free components on the market. Tens of thousands of legitimate miners would benefit from a clean, transparent minerals industry....The mineral trade is one of the components that drive suffering in Congo."[297]

STUDENT LEADERSHIP

In order to engage electronics companies on the issue of conflict-free sourcing, we focused on leveraging student activism in particular, for the following reasons:

1. Electronics companies aim to instill brand loyalty at an early age.

2. Students and young people generally pay more attention to emerging technology trends and are among the first to comment on them.

3. Students have a connection to and therefore an influence (directly or indirectly) over their school's technology purchases. So while individual student conflict mineral awareness is important, even more so is their collective power as a group that can shape their school's procurement policies.

Enough's Conflict-Free Campus Initiative (CFCI) was established in partnership with the student anti-genocide organization STAND in order to capitalize on these unique interdependent relationships between student activism, schools, electronics companies, and minerals from Congo. Activities were held and chapters were established at hundreds of campuses. These resolutions modify institutions' procurement policies to commit the schools, cities, or states to preference companies that are working to source conflict-free minerals from Congo for their products.

Jacqui Johns is one of many examples of students who—once they learned about their connection to the Congo through their cell phones and laptops—became engaged in the conflict minerals movement. Jacqui became a campus organizer (CO) with Enough's CFCI in the 2014–15 school year after learning about the movement from Georges Nzabanita, a Congolese student who was studying with her at Georgetown College in Kentucky. Georges had traveled to the US to study but was still looking for ways to support peace in his hometown of Rutshuru in eastern Congo. He came across CFCI and quickly began working to pass a resolution at Georgetown College.

Because of his intrepid activism, he later had the opportunity to travel to Washington, DC, and meet with then US special envoy to the Great Lakes region Russ Feingold to discuss the ways he felt a conflict-free minerals trade in Congo would help end the violence he and his family had lived through for many years.

Although Georges graduated before Georgetown College passed a resolution, Jacqui took up the mantle and remained involved with CFCI as a CO for three more years. During that time, she succeeded in passing the campus resolution Georges had initiated, and she ultimately spearheaded the process of successfully passing a city resolution as well. Jacqui became a leader among her peers, as others in her group on campus and COs across the country looked to her for her guidance and leadership skills. Her experience with CFCI helped guide her to work with refugees (from Congo and elsewhere) in her community, which is something she has pursued since graduating in 2017.

— JACQUI'S STORY —

"When I started college, I knew nothing about the conflict in Congo, let alone anything about the country. However, because of an introduction to a passionate Congolese student trying to bring the Enough Project's Conflict-Free Campus Initiative (CFCI) to Georgetown College during my first semester there, I can easily say that the movement to end conflict in Congo has fueled my passion and efforts for the last four years as a student activist. CFCI is a student-led movement that works with campus administrations to pass procurement resolutions that commit the school to prioritizing purchasing from companies that are working to source conflict-free minerals from Congo for their products. Conflict minerals have fueled and continue to help sustain armed violence in eastern Congo, linking them to the deadliest conflict globally since World War II. Since that first introduction, even if I had wanted to, I could not escape the reality of this conflict, as it touched other aspects of my life beyond my work with CFCI. Having two internships at Kentucky Refugee Ministries during my college career brought me face-to-face with Congolese refugees who had been forced to flee from their homes because of the violence and being resettled in Kentucky.

"Over my three years as a CFCI campus organizer, I took on a new goal each year. My first year, I worked with university and high school students across the Midwest region in the United States to guide them in their endeavors to bring CFCI to their schools and pass campus-wide conflict-free resolutions. My second year, I focused on my own campus, helping build our college's CFCI chapter and ultimately passing Georgetown College's conflict-free campus resolution. Through this process, I discovered just how vital it was to create our group's presence on campus and to build relationships with those who could serve as our support system and with those who would have a say in passing a resolution. On May 11, 2016, Georgetown College approved a resolution[298] to support a procurement policy that addresses the use of conflict minerals in the school's most commonly purchased electronic items.

"During my third year as a campus organizer, I sought to pass a conflict-free resolution in my college town, Georgetown, Kentucky. I had no clue how to even begin this process, but my fellow CFCI students and I worked with the Enough Project on the steps involved and felt that we were up for the challenge. Over the course of two semesters, our CFCI chapter organized community support, researched our city, wrote a letter to the city council, and communicated with all of the council members and the mayor's office regularly—sometimes emailing multiple times a day! In our initial communications, we received pushback, hesitancy, and a sense that our requests were falling on deaf ears, but we kept pushing, and when the time was right, we finally presented our proposed resolution at a city council meeting.

"On June 12, 2017, just over a year after my campus went conflict-free, the Georgetown city council passed a conflict-free resolution. The resolution commits the city to consider whether the electronics products it purchases contain conflict minerals from Congo and, where possible, to favor purchasing from companies that are working to source verifiably conflict-free minerals for their products. I didn't realize it at the time, but the past three years of dedication, hard work, and even the ups and downs with CFCI were building up to this point. There were definitely moments of discouragement and feelings of defeat that at times had me wondering if it would be possible to pass such a resolution. In the end, however, as the city council acknowledged, it was our CFCI students' persistence that won them over.

"Having my beloved college town pass a conflict-free resolution means more to me than I can explain. CFCI and the success of passing a campus-wide as well as a city-wide conflict-free resolution have left me encouraged to continue to stand up for causes

I believe in, even when it may be half a world away, for this process has illustrated that each one of us has a voice, and I never want to let mine fall silent."

CELEBRITY INVOLVEMENT

A number of other actors, musicians, and athletes have been supportive of the campaign. These well-known personalities have had a positive impact on the issue, contributing to the progress so far in creating a conflict-free minerals trade in Congo. Celebrities are very effective recruiters to the cause, raising awareness among a broader audience than human rights groups can reach on their own. They can take the spotlight shining on them as celebrities and redirect it to the causes they care about. When done in a responsible way, celebrity activism can drive education efforts and accelerate impact.

Actors, athletes, and musicians who have been involved with the Congo campaign besides Ryan include pro basketball players Serge Ibaka and Bismack Biyombo; pro football players Aaron Rodgers and Andy Mulumba; actors Emmanuelle Chriqui, Robin Wright, Don Cheadle, Ashley Judd, Javier Bardem, Mariska Hargitay, Ben Affleck, Iman, Andie MacDowell, Kristen Bell, Emile Hirsch, George Clooney, Mia Farrow, and Rosario Dawson; and musicians Sheryl Crow and Joel Madden.

IMPACTS SO FAR

Much has changed since we first began examining the conflict minerals issue in the mid-2000s. We've seen progress both in the transparency of corporate supply chains and, more importantly, in breaking the links between minerals and violence in Congo. As of December 2017, 495 mines have been certified conflict-free in eastern Congo.[299] When we first started working on this issue, that number was zero—there was no system to inspect or certify mines. To be sure, the certification system is not perfect and must still be improved, and there must be more work done on conflict gold and on mine safety. But having independent teams go to mines and inspect them for armed groups and child laborers is a revolutionary change from a decade ago.

There has also been important progress in making tech and other companies' supply chains more transparent to positively impact the minerals trade. Over 75 percent of the world's smelters and refiners for the 3Ts and gold have now passed third-party independent audits, and more and more are participating in these audits almost every day. Again, when we first began this work, that number was zero. And whereas in 2010 the UN Group of Experts for Congo found that "in the Kivu provinces, it appears, almost every mining deposit is controlled by an armed group,"[300] in 2016 an independent study from the International Peace Information Service concluded that over three-quarters (79 percent) of 3T miners surveyed in eastern Congo were working in mines where no armed group involvement had been reported.[301]

Thanks to consumer activism, corporate engagement, legislation, and support from Congolese activists in mining communities, we're beginning to see the tide turn away from a minerals trade controlled by violence toward one that benefits the Congolese people.

Much more work remains, especially with regard to combating the conflict gold trade and to providing support to Congolese miners and their families to ensure they are able to benefit fully from the conflict-free trade, but the momentum is gathering. And the small but dedicated people's movement, which continues to be led by students, will maintain its solidarity with Congolese who are pressing for change.

Fidel's Upstander Story

*Through a series of interviews conducted by Fidel,
Congolese Upstanders tell their life stories. All of them are risking
their lives to defend human rights, press for peace,
resist dictatorship, provide education, and prepare a better
future for their fellow Congolese.*

Neema Namadamu

I grew up in the village of Itombwe, and life was really wonderful. I contracted polio when I was three years old. It was really difficult for me because there were no roads, no crutches, and no running water. I had a loving mom who would take me to the toilet near our house.

I never liked the word "survivor," and I don't really like to be the victim. I have always looked at things positively. My focus was not on my polio. My focus was on solutions.

I began to work with other women a long time ago. I focus on empowering women through technology to give them education, so they can see a future for themselves. In order to change, you first have to change your mind. And this is my work every day: to empower women through technology and also to give women hope for a future. We have perhaps five thousand women now who are members of Maman Shujaa ("Hero Women").

In the work that I do, I am challenging the current culture, the patriarchal system. In African countries, especially Congo, this system is really very strong. That is where I focus, because this patriarchal system sends the message that women don't have the capacity to manage organizations, especially women with a disability and against a backdrop of tremendous gender-based violence. Before I was able to build my organization, when I went to the offices of different authorities, they thought I was coming to beg, and they would shift me from one person to the next without meeting anyone that would give consideration to my proposals.

When I see the women we work with smiling, I feel I'm doing something good. I want to see every human being live a better life, have water to drink, have medicine, and have safe conditions for birth. I have a few role models. For example, [former president of Ireland] Mary Robinson is a great example to me of someone who listens and tries to help.

Some people say I am successful at my work, but for me, I'm not yet there. I don't see myself as successful as long as my sister doesn't have crutches or doesn't have a toilet, and I can't stop.

When I went back to my home village of Itombwe after twenty-five years away, I saw how girls continued to be subject to early marriage and rape. I had a meeting with the women and we had to sit outside of the office because women are not supposed to be in the office. They told me why girls can't be in school. They said that the school is far away, and when the girls get their periods, there is no solution for them: they just don't go to school for a week and so they fall behind and fail. And once they have their period, then people say, "Well, she's a woman now, so it's time for her to get married." But we came up with some solutions for those girls and helped keep them in school. People saw that there were solutions and the girls were so happy. I'm keeping girls in school. Now I'm going to build a school for girls in Itombwe.

I have a really big hope: I hope that tomorrow we will have a new Congo. That is my hope.

People don't really know Congo. They only talk about our challenges and problems. People have a bad image of Congo. When I went to conferences in the White House and talked to people there, they said, "Forget Congo. It's a lost cause. Don't talk about it."

And I said, "What?!"

I like to compare Congo with my life. When I got polio when I was a baby, people would say, "She's a lost cause. She's nothing." This is how I see Congo. People say, "Congo is a lost cause. Don't talk about Congo. Forget it." I say, "No!!" We are here. We are Congolese. And we believe Congo will soon be associated with dignity and not with shame; there will no longer be any shame in having a Congolese passport, which always brings questions now. But we are innocent—Congo is innocent. Congo is full—full of potential, full of opportunities. My job is to change the challenges to opportunities.

In Congo—in our country, in my culture—we don't have a word for rape. And now people get that bad image and everyone thinks that Congo is only rape, it's only war, and that affects us. This is hurting us. But Congo is not a lost cause. We are not a lost cause.

I would like the world to know that Congo has the second-greatest forest in the world after the Amazon. Congo can help save the world. This is our opportunity to help the world with climate change. Please don't cut down trees. They are our only source of oxygen. We need to preserve that. We need to protect that. I invite you all to protect Congo. Protect the Congo forest, because with it everyone can breathe. Because we have one world, we have one problem, we will have one solution, and the solution is Congo and Africa. Thank you.

◇◇◇

CONTACT INFORMATION FOR MAMAN SHUJAA:
www.herowomenrising.org

◇◇◇

CHAPTER ELEVEN

Steve Jobs and Conflict Minerals

*Apple and
Corporate-Driven Change*

In 2009, as the Enough Project began ramping up its conflict minerals campaign efforts, Enough wrote letters to the top twenty-five consumer electronics companies in the world, confronting them about the conflict minerals that they were sourcing in Congo. Many of the companies didn't take the letters seriously, probably thinking that a small NGO in Washington, DC, and a handful of student activists wouldn't create enough of a stir to require any action.

Apple was one of the companies that initially responded primarily with lip service. Apple was letting industry associations and other companies lead on the conflict minerals issue. Enough Project staff had a couple of meetings with some of Apple's team members, and the takeaway impression was that Apple was comfortable sitting on the sidelines.

Enough began to work with grassroots activists like Lisa Shannon to put Apple on the spot, calling for the company to use its enormous power and influence to push its supply chain in the right direction. In response, a PR representative at Apple's head-quarters told Lisa that their products were "already conflict-free" because "they ask their suppliers to provide a certificate," clearly not a credible response.

Enough then moved into high gear with its campaigning, including among many other things a student-led protest at the opening of the first Apple store in DC; student video contests with Hollywood judges; and a video spoofing the ubiquitous "Mac versus PC" ads, which Nicholas Kristof featured in his *New York Times* column and which quickly racked up hundreds of thousands of views on YouTube.[302] It was also right at the time when con-flict minerals legislation, which previously stood little chance of advancing through Congress, was added as an amendment in the Dodd-Frank Wall Street reform bill.

Still, little response was forthcoming from Apple. Staff at Enough soon learned that the policy guidance on this issue came straight from the top of the company. As fate would have it, Apple CEO and founder Steve Jobs would occasionally answer emails from customers. One week after the student-led protest in Wash-ington, DC, Wired.com published one such query to Jobs about conflict minerals in Congo, and Apple's answer to it. In his answer, Jobs basically disavowed responsibility.[303]

Letter from Wired.com Reader Derick Rhodes:

Hi Steve,

I'd planned to buy a new iPhone tomorrow—my first upgrade since buying the very first version on the first day of its release—but I'm hesitant without knowing Apple's position on sourcing the minerals in its products.

Are you currently making any effort to source conflict-free minerals? In particular, I'm concerned that Apple is getting tantalum, tungsten, tin, and gold from Eastern Congo through its suppliers.

Looking forward to your response,
Derick

Reply from Steve Jobs:

Yes. We require all of our suppliers to certify in writing that they use conflict free materials. But honestly there is no way for them to be sure. Until someone invents a way to chemically trace minerals from the source mine, it's a very difficult problem.

Sent from my iPhone

This meant that it wasn't just some PR person making Apple's policy about conflict minerals; it was the founder himself. We at Enough decided to use this as an opportunity to engage directly with the man himself.

The first email Enough sent to sjobs@apple.com was respectful and educational, though harboring little hope that it would ever be seen by Jobs personally. In his response to *Wired* and in his PR people's comments, there was a misunderstanding of the supply chain dynamic. It would be much easier than Apple was claiming to trace their supply chain back to Congolese mines of origin for their raw materials. Enough staff had been to the mines, to the middlemen, to the smelters, and to the manufacturers, and knew what was possible. In the note to Jobs, Enough told him it would only be through the efforts of leaders like him that real industry progress could be made, and offered a briefing should he be interested.

The response was swift and clear, stunningly coming from Jobs himself: "I'm happy to chat with your CEO."

A few of us Enoughers huddled around a speakerphone and called his direct number, and—of course—he picked up. Jobs berated us for attacking Apple, claiming that we did so because the conflict minerals legislation was not going to go anywhere in Congress and, amid the verbal barrage, called our ideas "stupid."

We laid out our arguments, noting that the conflict minerals bill was now part of the Obama administration's centerpiece Wall Street reform bill, and explained how Apple could make a difference. Although far from persuaded, Jobs told us to send him a memo answering a series of his questions and then we would take it from there. The memo went to Jobs early the next week, and soon thereafter he invited us to see him and his team at Apple headquarters in Cupertino.

When we arrived at the Apple campus, we were escorted through the atrium and up a series of suspended walkways to the top floor.

Once inside the conference room, we were shortly joined by Apple's team, consisting of the current CEO, Tim Cook, who at the time was the chief operating officer; Bill Frederick, vice president of AppleCare and Logistics; Jeff Williams, vice president of Operations; and Cathy Novelli, vice president for Worldwide Government Affairs. Jobs would enter by himself ten minutes later.

Jobs jumped right in and made it very clear that he was skeptical of this issue and had no desire for Apple to have to take up other social causes. The gist of his message was that he understood the supply chain problems, but we were going to have to sell him on what he could do about it.

We then proceeded to give a slideshow presentation, which Enough's Sasha Lezhnev, David Sullivan, and Aaron Hall had created. After the presentation, filled with slides of destitute miners and communities existing in slave-like conditions in eastern Congo, Jobs was still resistant. We pressed forward with our points about supply chains, global impact, corporate responsibility, and the natural resources that allow Apple to be Apple, where they come from, how they are sourced, and what happens between coming out of the ground and being soldered to a computer or phone motherboard somewhere in Asia.

Jobs hammered on the point that Apple does more than anyone to map and understand their supply chains, and that he had created an industry leader in that regard and we should be thankful for that.

We answered that even if Apple was an industry leader in general supply chain management globally, what mattered to us and to the people of Congo for the purposes of this meeting was how Apple dealt with its specific supply chain of minerals from Congo. We were concerned with grave human rights abuses and decades of conflict in Central Africa that have been, in part, perpetuated by the extraction, illegal taxation, and smuggling of minerals that end up in Apple products.

We proceeded to discuss in more detail the conflict mineral supply chain: how material was currently being extracted in eastern Congo; how it moved through the region en route to Malaysia and other smelters in Asia; who moved the minerals; who benefited; and how that perpetuated the conflict and corruption destroying communities in Congo.

We then told Jobs that we'd love to see Apple make a public commitment to trace, audit, and certify its supply chains for gold and the 3Ts (tin, tantalum, and tungsten), and that we'd love to see Apple be an industry leader in setting standards for corporate social responsibility as it relates to the ongoing humanitarian crisis in Central Africa that is directly linked to these supply chains.

Jobs explained that Apple doesn't publicly tell anyone what they are going to do. Rather, Apple first *does* something, and then afterward tells you they've done it. He told us the culture at Apple is about being able to produce and progress. Forward movement and innovation reign. Do you provide added value? Can you not only do the job you were hired to do but make it better? Yes? Great, you're hired; I don't care what you dress like or how "profession-ally" you carry yourself. Are you not producing? Are you unable to perform? Are you slowing the cogs on the front line of American technological creativity? Yes? Then you're gone.

Then, right there on the spot, without consulting anyone, Jobs proceeded to make a commitment to be the first company in the world to map its supply chains for the 3Ts and gold materials to their source of origin where possible, and to be the first company to map and identify all the processing facilities Apple and its component manufacturers under contract use to process 3Ts and gold material for Apple use.

The commitment was game-changing. This was a quantum leap forward in responsible sourcing of raw materials. And it was Apple, the biggest end user of conflict minerals in the world.

Jobs and his team stayed true to their word of "doing something, then telling you we've done it." Jobs, Tim Cook, and Jeff Williams did everything promised that day—and more. Apple made a radical 180-degree shift in the right direction, becoming the first company to require its suppliers to source only from audited conflict-free smelters and kicking out smelters who refused to be audited; working tirelessly to bring transparency to the minerals bag-and-tag system in Congo and the region; supporting a number of conflict-free minerals and human rights projects in Congo; and having the highest percentage of conflict-free smelters in any industry in its supply chain. In Enough's most recent company rankings on conflict minerals in November 2017, Apple is at the top, scoring higher than any other tech company in the elaborate survey. In the wake of Mr. Jobs's death, the Enough Project continues to keep in touch with senior people at Apple and their teams to support further progress, not just on these conflict minerals but cobalt as well.

CHAPTER TWELVE

War Crimes Shouldn't Pay

Lessons from Al Capone to al-Qaeda

"Give us peace, peace, peace, please!
And you're going to see how tremendously this country can develop.
We only need peace. Because of conflict,
we can't send our children to school, and you know
education is the future of any country.
We can't dream of any development
without these children going to school. So give us peace!"

—ESTHER, WHOM THE THREE OF US MET IN
AN INTERNALLY DISPLACED PERSONS CAMP

"I think there is an ethical way to come to the help
of Congo instead of providing weapons and buying smuggled
minerals. You should come to Congo and do ethical business.
In addition to ethical investment, there should be prosecution of all
these greedy people who have been getting profits out
of these minerals, because those who have killed so many people are
the ones who have been rewarded to become kings.
And here you can't dream of becoming a VIP until you shed the
blood of others. Many of our soldiers are no different

from those who committed the genocide in Rwanda. Nobody has ever
tried to prosecute them. In this camp, most of the
women are widows. It doesn't mean that their husbands have died of
natural causes. They were slaughtered. Our leaders in
Kinshasa can speak of peace, but we don't know what peace
means to them. These leaders are flying airplanes, driving beautiful
cars, living in beautiful houses, and that's peace for them.
They should come see our 'peace' here. If I would be given a chance
to speak to the leaders in America and Europe, I would ask them to
prosecute all of the people who have been bringing trouble to Congo."

—EMMANUEL, THE LEADER OF THAT SAME
DISPLACED PERSONS CAMP

This chapter explores solutions to the conflict, exploitation, and the extreme corruption of the Congolese state. We outline the Al Capone approach to taking down a kleptocratic network and how that provides a ray of hope for Congo, offering a new way to counter human rights crimes and support lasting peace. The situation is complex, but there are solutions. It is not hopeless.

In Congo and its surrounding region, massive attacks targeting civilians, child soldier recruitment, mass rape, and the blockading of humanitarian aid have all been routine tactics of war. A common denominator for all of them is the lack of an effective international response that targets the root causes, whether it is Congo, Sudan, South Sudan, the Central African Republic, Somalia, Burundi, or other violence-affected neighbors.

Popular narratives notwithstanding, the primary driver of violence and conflict in Congo and its neighbors in east and central Africa isn't religious, racial, ethnic, or environmental in origin. Those factors can certainly be accelerators and mobilizers of extreme violence, and they need to be addressed as part of a solution. But the big prize—the real impetus for deadly competition—is the way that governing institutions have been hijacked and repurposed for the private gain of the leaders and their international commercial collaborators, who feed off the immense natural resource wealth of these countries.

Those committing and profiting from mass atrocities and mass corruption in Congo can be stopped by targeting their illicit finances. These thieves of state are benefiting financially and politically from the violence and the absence of the rule of law, making a killing off war through the illicit exploitation of Congo's natural resources. None of our current policies effectively influences the cost-benefit calculations of these leaders and their international collaborators. Therefore, the leaders ignore peace agreements they've signed, commit war crimes, steal elections, obstruct humanitarians and peacekeepers, and block justice without any consequence.

However, the top Congolese officials responsible for these human rights atrocities and their international commercial partners are vulnerable and exposed in one main way: they try to hide their ill gotten wealth in other countries and use US dollars and euros to launder their dirty money through the international banking system, which is a crime that can instigate prosecution or the seizure of assets. There are relevant policy tools that are used to battle terrorism, nuclear proliferation, drug trafficking, and other organized crime by following the money and shutting offenders out of the international financial system. But we never use these effective tools to counter mass rape, child soldier recruitment, and other atrocities in places like Congo that are perceived to have little strategic significance.

Al Capone's downfall is a helpful metaphor for part of an alternative strategy. Capone was the head of a huge criminal organization that was responsible for deadly violence, major corruption, and massive profits, mostly hidden through nontransparent financial arrangements. After all of the crimes Capone was directly or indirectly responsible for, federal prosecutors were finally only able to convict him on tax evasion charges, but that was enough to remove him from circulation and prevent him from doing further damage. His conviction was built on rigorous financial investigations, following the money, finding one piece of evidence at a time until enough was compiled for a meaningful conviction.

Congo's leaders and their international collaborators committing human rights crimes can be countered by aggressively enforcing top-level targeted network sanctions (i.e., sanctions that don't just go after individuals but rather target the entire network responsible) and ensuring banks implement anti–money laundering measures. That is the successful policy cocktail: network sanctions plus anti–money laundering actions. While we work to ensure that these war criminals and their commercial collaborators face their destiny in a court of law for the atrocities they have committed or benefited from, law enforcement and regulatory officials can go after the money they have stolen and hidden in banks, real estate, and shell companies. The ultimate goal of these tools of financial pressure is to shift the cost-benefit calculation of these leaders and their international collaborators away from mass violence and mass corruption and toward peace and good governance.

Imposing real consequences so that war crimes no longer pay would be a game-changer in supporting Congolese struggles for peace, human rights, and good governance. This isn't an argument for regime change. It's an argument for *system* change, for dismantling the kleptocratic and authoritarian governing system that is the main engine for conflict, deepening poverty, and state looting.

What to do about the Violent Kleptocracy

As billions of taxpayer dollars of humanitarian and peacekeeping aid pour into Congo and other crisis-stricken African countries every year, billions of stolen dollars are siphoned off by the leaders causing the crises along with their international facilitators and enablers. There needs to be a more serious effort to create stinging financial consequences for the looting and destruction and to bring any stolen money back to these countries.

Anti–money laundering tools, network sanctions, and asset recovery measures have not yet been used widely in the service of peace and human rights in Africa, but they could and should be. Regular individual sanctions have been mostly ineffective in Africa because of weak approaches to targeting and a lack of enforcement, often because there is very little reliable, actionable information generated on the assets of sanctioned officials. This is being addressed in part by The Sentry (www.thesentry.org), co-founded by George Clooney and John, which is compiling just this kind of information for regulatory and law enforcement authorities in governments around the world as well as for global and regional banks.

The ultimate objective is not just to freeze a few assets but rather to shut war criminals and their accomplices out of the international financial system altogether. These networks move their ill-gotten gains into the international banking system, and banks do not want to be associated with money laundering—the reputational and brand risks are too high, just as they are for Apple or other companies. Nobody wants to be perceived as supporting warlords through sourcing conflict minerals. It suddenly becomes in the core financial self-interest of banks to enforce measures that support human rights and peace. This is revolutionary, because it gives international policymakers and diplomats a major new point of leverage to impact the calculations of those willing to commit mass atrocities to maintain or gain wealth and power.

If international policymakers are to have a real impact in helping Congolese reformers actually reform the system, they need to shift lenses. They must understand that the current situation in Congo is simply the latest iteration of a longer pattern of violence and corruption, and respond accordingly. Policies should focus on creating significant consequences for those most responsible for the system of violence, corruption, and the undermining of democracy.[304] This isn't just an effort to change behavior in the short term. It's really about dismantling the kleptocratic system and ultimately disincentivizing personal enrichment as the primary goal of holding power.

For more, see www.congostories.org

What to do about the 3T Conflict Minerals

As a result of the people's movement described in chapter 11, important progress has been made in addressing the violence and corruption around the mining of the 3T conflict minerals—tin, tantalum, and tungsten. In recent years, evidence unearthed by the International Peace Information Service, the UN Group of Experts, the Enough Project, Global Witness, and others shows an expanding traceability and certification regime for the 3Ts.[305] This has led to a significant reduction in opportunity for the army, militias, and other criminal networks to benefit from the exploitation and illegal taxation of the 3T minerals.[306]

As more and more 3T mine sites have been validated as conflict-free, with the associated implementation of traceability and certification, 3T producers in Congo have benefited from increased access to international markets.[307] While reports by the UN Group of Experts on Congo have expressed concern about indications of the smuggling of minerals from non-certified mines (which are not conflict-free) into the legitimate supply chain,[308] there remains a broad consensus among industry, civil society, government, and other observers that there has been major progress in removing armed groups from the 3T supply chain.[309]

Throughout eastern Congo, smugglers have been discouraged, mines have been demilitarized, and armed groups have been partially defanged.

For more, see www.congostories.org

What to do about Conflict Gold

Conflict gold has become the number one financier of armed rebels and abusive Congolese army units in eastern Congo,[310] and so it is critically important to focus on solutions to this challenge. The Enough Project has engaged in nearly a decade of field and industry research on how to tackle the conflict gold problem,[311] realizing that many have key roles to play in the solution to this thorny problem: jewelry and tech companies, the US and European governments, activists in Congo and around the world, neighboring African governments, investigative journalists, and banks.

One key part of the solution lies with jewelry retailers. Corporate and consumer behavior can lead to increased demand for responsibly sourced, conflict-free gold and can promote investment in positive mining initiatives in the region. That is an important part of the equation, because demand can spur further investment in pilot conflict-free gold projects in Congo that are starting up now. As the largest end user of gold, accounting for over 50 percent of worldwide gold demand,[312] jewelry companies have the ability to increase demand for conflict-free gold from Congo and the region. Jewelers in the United States and Europe should spur such demand by using conflict-free artisanal gold from Congo in their jewelry lines.[313]

————

In late 2017 the Enough Project ranked companies for their responsiveness to concerns about conflict minerals. Two jewelry retail companies in particular—Tiffany & Co. and Signet Jewelers—demonstrated clear leadership in beginning to address the conflict gold issue by taking proactive steps to set up supply chain controls and support the communities affected by mining and violence in Congo. Other jewelry retailers are starting to follow suit, but in general, Enough found the jewelry industry is lagging far behind leaders in the consumer electronics industry when it comes to developing responsible, conflict-free sourcing practices. Signet was the only jewelry retailer Enough surveyed in 2017 to receive credit for actually sourcing conflict-free gold from Congo, compared with eight out of ten surveyed electronics companies.[314]

For more, see www.congostories.org

What to do about the Armed Groups

There have been times when eastern Congo was so rife with armed militias that analysts and policymakers saw very little hope of altering the situation. But there are examples of how concerted Congolese and international action together can make a difference and remove an armed group from the scene. One prime example is the M23 militia.

In 2012 the M23 took control of Goma, the largest city in North Kivu, eastern Congo; controlled key parts of the Congo/Rwanda/Uganda border region; and at times had the clear upper hand in its war with the Congolese government. But a year later, the M23 was defeated, retreating across neighboring borders, largely dismantled and neutered. What happened? Three variables were decisive, and lessons can be derived from all three for how to deal with other recalcitrant armed groups.[315]

First, the international community came together in an unprecedented way to demand an end to external support for the M23. After numerous human rights and UN investigative reports had fingered Rwanda as the main source of support to the M23, the US, UK, and other donor governments suspended parts of their Rwandan aid programs, in particular blocking renewal of World Bank direct budget support, and made strong appeals to Rwanda to cease all support for the M23, support that Rwanda had consistently denied providing.[316]

Second, then UN special envoy Mary Robinson, then US special envoy Russ Feingold, and key African states supported Congolese civil society calls for army reform and accountability for war crimes. As a result, the Congolese government sent new commanders to the front line, rotating out a number of highly corrupt senior officers. In particular, Congolese army colonel Mamadou Ndala played a heroic role as a positive force, highly rare in the Congolese army. His efforts, which were extremely popular in eastern Congo, are portrayed at length in the documentary film *This Is Congo* by Daniel McCabe.[317] (This film was one of three documentaries made around the same time that focused on different aspects of Congo's unique situation. The others are *When Elephants Fight* by Michael Ramsdell and *Merci Congo* by Paul Freedman.) The diplomats also demanded that no amnesty be given for the commission of war crimes, something that was routinely doled out in the context of past peace deals. The new spirit of reform and accountability had an empowering effect on the Congolese army's performance, strongly backed by an African-led "UN Force Intervention Brigade" that helped turn the tide militarily against the M23 in a way that wasn't possible before.

Third, the previous source of illicit rebel financing—violent and illegal extraction of conflict minerals—was vastly diminished by a combination of reforms catalyzed by the Dodd-Frank transparency law. This made the money available to the M23 from the minerals trade much lower, since they would not be able to sell the 3T minerals that in previous years they would have easily looted and sold off as Rwandan minerals with no questions asked. Since the legislation was enacted, a series of actions taken by regional governments, multinational companies, and local civil society organizations removed much of the profitability of rebellion.[318] Violence was no longer as lucrative as it once had been, as the warped war economy was finally being addressed for the first time since the Europeans began looting Congo's wealth five centuries ago.

What to do about Legal Accountability

There are a number of ongoing efforts and initiatives surrounding legal accountability that are trying to break the cycle of impunity that has marred Congo's history. These include a proposal in the Congolese legislature for a "mixed chamber" that would combine Congolese and international jurists; assistance to improve Congo's military justice system; cooperation with the International Criminal Court; efforts to prosecute crimes of pillage; and a United States Institute of Peace initiative focused on prosecuting economic and environmental crimes.

For more, see www.congostories.org

CHAPTER THIRTEEN

Vanquishing the Vampires

What You Can Do

Many of the crises in Africa have ended or been diminished in part as a result of people's movements in the US and around the world providing support to local activists and frontline upstanders pressing courageously for peace and human rights.

- The blood diamonds campaign helped stop the smuggling of those precious stones into the international market from West Africa's war zones and as a result contributed to ending wars in Sierra Leone, Liberia, and Angola.
- The global anti-apartheid movement helped free Nelson Mandela, end the system of institutionalized racial discrimination in South Africa, and promote the first free and fair election for all of South Africa's citizens.
- The Save Darfur campaign was not able to help bring an end to the war in Sudan's western region of Darfur, but it did ensure that life-sustaining humanitarian aid was delivered for years in a country where the government has frequently used starvation as a weapon of war. As a

result, hundreds of thousands of Darfuris are alive today that might have perished had the government not been so publicly spotlighted and challenged in its efforts to blockade humanitarian aid.

- ONE, an international campaigning and advocacy organization founded by U2 singer Bono and whose president/ CEO is now Enough's co-founder Gayle Smith, has ensured major investments in the treatment and prevention of HIV/ AIDS, as well as helped wipe out hundreds of millions of dollars in crippling debts in Africa. ONE members played huge roles in securing passage in Congress of the Electrify Africa Act and Global Food Security Act.

- The student-led Invisible Children movement, together with Enough and Resolve, pressed for changes in the policies of a number of governments—including the US and key European governments—that in turn led to broad international support for a dramatically successful African initiative to sharply reduce the military capacity of Joseph Kony's Lord's Resistance Army militia. The United States deployed forces to train and support Ugandan and other African forces in their efforts. The success of this mission has allowed millions of refugees and internally displaced persons to go home in peace and thousands of former child soldiers to be freed or to escape and return to their communities in northern Uganda.

- The student-led conflict minerals campaign for Congo has been documented earlier in the book, and its impacts have been important as well.

This is an incredibly positive legacy of activism making a major difference throughout Africa. When you question your ability to effect change, reread that list above. Millions and millions of people's lives were impacted by these movements and campaigns, when people around the world simply decided that enough is enough and we need to get involved and try to do something in support of the changemakers on the ground in Africa.

Indeed, the changes will be made in Congo by Congolese, but global people's movements and activism can provide critical support to turn the tide.

Most of the major positive changes in the United States during the last century have come about as a result of people's movements—the labor movement, the women's movement, the civil rights movement, the environmental movement, the peace movement, the LGBTQ movement; the list goes on. If we can help tell or amplify the story that Congo and other war-torn African countries are much more than the worst things that are happening, if we can tell the story that Congo is not hopeless, that Africans have critically important ideas and are leading the calls for change, that Africa is not that different from the rest of the world in terms of its post-independence historical trajectory, and that Africa is full of transformative examples of hope, then the global effort required to support Congo's and—more broadly—Africa's struggles for peace and human rights becomes a whole lot more viable.

This is our challenge: To help tell the whole truth about Congo and its people. And to believe there is hope based on that truth. And to demand from our political leaders and the companies we buy products from that they support positive change and partner with Africans as equals in an interconnected world.

The Positive Impact of Activism

Here's the bottom line: it isn't up to the US and Europe to solve Congo's problems, but US and European governments, corporations, and citizens can play a major role in supporting the Congolese to find solutions.

John had the honor of working with the late Nelson Mandela after he retired as president of South Africa and was chief mediator of the Burundian Civil War. When John worked at the White House, President Clinton sent the late Howard Wolpe and him at one point to support the mediation efforts of President Mandela, who told many riveting stories about the long and lonely anti-apartheid struggle. And President Mandela said that he never gave up hope, in part because people around the world were behind him and the struggle. He recalled getting messages while he was an inmate in Robben Island prison about students and other activists in America and Europe who were demonstrating, writing letters, and getting arrested undertaking civil disobedience in support of the anti-apartheid campaign. He was personally moved by that support from thousands of people he did not know, thousands of miles away, simply on the basis of principle. And that support helped fuel and buttress internal efforts for change, which led to the release of President Mandela from prison, the dismantling of the apartheid system, and the holding of free and fair elections in which all South Africans had an equal vote.

Change is possible. In the late 1990s/early 2000s, Sierra Leone and Liberia were countries in turmoil, ripped apart by battles in part over control of the lucrative blood diamond business. Today, Sierra Leone and Liberia are peaceful democracies. They still have corruption and governance problems, but they are no longer engulfed in deadly conflict. The horrors there led the world to get serious about stopping the blood diamond trade and the wars that it financed. The same thing can happen in Congo with the right government policies, responsible business reforms, and consumer awareness and pressure.

Chip and Dan Heath write about the phenomenon of these positive examples, these "bright spots," and how they can help drive change. "But if you're trying to change things, there are going to be bright spots in your field of view, and if you learn to recognize them and understand them, you will solve one of the fundamental mysteries of change: What, exactly, needs to be done differently." The Heaths continue, "Big problems are rarely solved with commensurately big solutions. Instead, they are most often solved by a sequence of small solutions, sometimes over weeks, sometimes over decades." And they conclude, "These flashes of success—these bright spots—can illuminate the road map for action and spark the hope that change is possible."[319]

Our book website has fresh and updated recommendations for actions readers can take: **www.congostories.org**. In a dedicated section on the website, the Enough Project's Annie Callaway and Sasha Lezhnev provide some pointers on specific ways you can make a difference for Congo and more generally on issues that you care about.

While there are so many memorable quotes from Dr. Martin Luther King Jr. about why we need to stand up in the face of darkness, consider this one, which comes from a speech in which he outlines the basics of a complete life:

> "Be a bush if you can't be a tree. If you can't be a highway just be a trail. If you can't be the sun be a star. It isn't by size that you win or fail. Be the best of whatever you are."[320]

Countering Myths and Stereotypes

Josephine's Story[321]

Early one morning in a village in eastern Congo, Josephine lay sleeping in her hut, dreaming about selling her crops. In the distance, she heard people singing victory songs. She thought it was part of her dream, but gunshots jolted her awake. She could see in the light of dawn that the village next to hers was on fire. She saw people fleeing toward her village, some being shot as they ran.

She quickly herded her four children into the tall grass, where others from her village were already hiding. They watched their village torched by that singing militia, known as Raia Mutomboki, one of the myriad militias that have ravaged eastern Congo for over a generation.

During her family's first day of hiding after the attack, Josephine sent her eldest son, Emmanuel, back to the village to get food from their storehouse. He was discovered and shot. The militia began to hunt the villagers in the tall grass, again singing victory songs, using hoes and machetes to kill whomever they caught. Josephine, her remaining children, and other survivors from the village fled the only place they ever knew as home and walked for days to an internally displaced persons camp, where Josephine's second son, Avarino, soon died of malaria.

"I can't understand how human beings can treat other human beings this way," Josephine told us.

This story echoes what so many Congolese have suffered for so long. When we asked Josephine why all this was happening, she replied, "The war is about the minerals, nothing else."

In the middle of this internally displaced persons camp, someone who wasn't a renowned historian summarized a perspective that doesn't often get heard: that of a Congolese person who is part of a long, shocking story of greed, slavery, exploitation, war, heroism, and perseverance. This is the story of Congo and its relationship with America and Europe.

Josephine continued, "People around the world should do all they can to stop those instigating war in my country. That is the only way we can be at peace. If I hear my village is at peace, I will drop everything and go home with my children."

All of us who now know what we know about Congo and how connected we are to Congo should heed Josephine's clarion call to support peace and human rights in her country.

The Hopelessness and Helplessness Narratives

The usual narrative about war-torn African countries centers on hopelessness and helplessness, portraying these countries as a huge net negative globally in terms of how dependent they are on massive aid flows going into the country with little recognized or acknowledged value coming out. This stereotype is deeply flawed, especially as it pertains to Congo.

The Congo mythology is driven by a mixture of ignorance, historical revisionism, and racism. Congo and its people in fact represent a huge net positive in terms of their contribution to global progress, and the United States and Europe have been the primary beneficiaries of this contribution.

But as you can see, the Congolese people, wildlife, environment, and state institutions have paid a terrible price for these gifts to the world.

A pervasive narrative depicts America and Europe as having developed as "superior" or "exceptional" nations that have magnanimously provided assistance to African countries in need. However, this narrative does not account for the extraordinary levels of exploitation of other regions of the world that made rapid development gains possible in America and Europe, leaving some of those other regions, in particular Africa, incredibly disadvantaged in today's global economy. Injustices are justified or hidden due to that narrative. Instead of accepting the status quo as inevitable, we might instead ask, What history created this status quo? What structures sustain it? What ingredients are necessary for change? In order for injustices to be fully visible and ultimately addressed, that false narrative has to be challenged.

See our book website at www.congostories.org for stories about how white superiority over Africans has been inculcated into American and European culture. For example, Ota Benga, a young Congolese, was put on exhibit in the monkey house at the Bronx Zoo, and Belgium created a human zoo of Congolese people at the 1958 World's Fair. See Pamela Newkirk's fascinating book *Spectacle* for insightful commentary.

Ways to Counter Those Narratives

Against the backdrop of this representation of a helpless Africa and a superior America and Europe is a far more dynamic reality. This book has attempted to rewrite false and damaging narratives about Congo in a few specific ways:

1. **False idea:** Congo is inherently poor and hopeless.
   Our counter-narrative: Congo is inherently rich in natural

resources and human capital, but both have been co-opted by unfair global structures of extraction. As the book's Congolese Upstander stories demonstrate, Congolese are striving in all kinds of unique and courageous ways to address the injustice and inequity that lie at the core of their country's relationship with the world.

2. **False idea:** Congo needs charity and the US and Europe are its saviors.

   Our counter-narrative: The preceding pages have attempted to outline the historical context and the international role in where Congo is today. Historian Adam Hochschild sums it up perfectly: "From the colonial era, the major legacy Europe left to Africa was not democracy as it is practiced today in countries like England, France, and Belgium; it was authoritarian rule and plunder. On the whole continent, perhaps no nation has had a harder time than the Congo in emerging from the shadows of its past."[322] However, Congolese people are writing their own futures in the face of incredibly inequitable global forces, and the US and Europe can support their efforts by working to address the manner in which they as outsiders contribute to mass corruption, unfair exploitation, and undemocratic processes in Congo.

3. **False idea:** Congo is a place of war and powerlessness.

   Our counter-narrative: Congo is a bright and vibrant country, and the arts, music, culture, and movement-building have thrived not only in spite of war but because of it, as a way for people to hold on to hope and build a better future. Congo has not just been impacted by the world over these past few centuries; it has also been the impactor. The precolonial Kongo Kingdom sent diplomats and gifts to European nations with innovations in art, textiles, and other arenas. The rubber terror during the venal King Leopold's reign led to the first international human rights campaign of the twentieth century. Congolese soldiers participated in victories during both World War I and II, and Congo played a unique and until recently unknown role in ending World War II. Congo was the first African country to insert itself into the Cold War. Congolese activists allied with global activists have forced major changes in the way multinational electronics companies source their raw materials, and hopefully will have the same impact on the jewelry and automobile industries. And the ready supply of Congolese minerals has allowed much faster technological and industrial progression on a number of fronts throughout the last century. As historian David Van Reybrouck concludes, "Congolese history has helped to determine and form the history of the world."[323]

Beyond Congo, much of Africa is on the move. Struggles marking Congo today have been replicated in other African countries, and progress is beginning to show. Many African countries are experiencing a rapidly growing middle class. Democratic elections are being held in countries across the continent. Civil society is organizing and growing by leaps and bounds. Communication modalities are exploding. There are over 700 million mobile phone subscriptions in Africa—a number that will soon surpass Europe[324]—and they're pioneering social media innovations. There is a burgeoning entrepreneurial class. During the first decade of the twenty-first century, six out of the world's ten fastest-growing countries were in Africa. A number of countries are developing manufacturing and service economies. Poverty rates are falling in many African countries, and death rates for under-five children are dropping. There is real, measurable progress. It just isn't newsworthy, apparently.

———

Another way to counter the negative stereotypes is to look at what Africans are striving for. The latest Afrobarometer poll on democracy from 2016 seeks to track that through regular, professional polling. Afrobarometer found that 82 percent of Africans reject one-man rule; 68 percent support democracy over any other form of government; 77 percent reject military rule; and 75 percent oppose single-party rule.[325]

———

Finally, the centrality of African leadership in crisis response should be highlighted. The stereotype remains prevalent that Africans need to be saved from themselves. But in most emergencies, anyone taking a closer look would see the absurdity of that stereotype. Africans are on the front lines of humanitarian efforts, distributing life-saving aid in dangerous environments. Africans comprise the vast majority of peacekeepers in civil conflicts in Africa. Africans lead peace negotiations for the wars being fought in Africa. Africans are the park rangers protecting the elephants from poaching. Africans are the health-care workers caring for those stricken with epidemic diseases. And the list goes on.

History Repeats, but It Doesn't Have to

Europe and America for hundreds of years suffered the bloody wars that made states and borders. Europe's violent invasion of Africa, occupation, slave trading, and further exploitation interrupted Africa's own historical path.

Congo has been an independent nation-state for less than sixty years. When the United States was sixty years old, newly enlarged by wars with its neighbors, its army was busy fighting Native Americans, ethnically cleansing them from their homelands. Slavery was legal and fueling a major agricultural boom; enslaved families were the main financial asset in half the country, with farms and industries relying on their unpaid labor. The US Civil War had not yet been fought, one of the deadliest wars in per capita terms in human history. In short, the US too was built through slavery, ethnic cleansing, colonialism, and war. Perhaps this helps add a bit of perspective on some of the horrors being perpetrated in contemporary Congo, and makes it less easy to judge events unfolding in Africa.

Wars in Europe and the lands around the Mediterranean were even more destructive of human life, involving centuries of deadly wars and genocides to determine current borders. Europe's Thirty Years' War killed millions and destroyed wide swaths of the continent. World Wars I and II were among the deadliest in human history.

Finally, wars of state formation in Congo and certain other African countries are occurring at a time in which armaments are far deadlier and more accessible than they were during the great wars in America and Western Europe.

Moreover, after only a few decades of independence from the European colonial rulers, the majority of African nations are striving to create multi-party electoral democracies where disputes are beginning to be addressed through processes other than war. Democratic transitions of power have occurred throughout Africa, as seen in recent years in Senegal, Ghana, Gambia, and Malawi, for example. Since some parts of Africa remain beset by extreme violence and authoritarian rule, most dramatically Congo, those countries draw more attention in a world where anything that bleeds, leads.

But Congo is not the norm in Africa; it is an outlier. In fact, it is Africa's most extreme outlier.

Hollywood, the News Media, and Africa

> *"It was the best of times, it was the worst of times,…*
> *it was the season of Light, it was the season of Darkness,*
> *it was the spring of hope, it was the winter of despair."*

These words written by Charles Dickens about the period leading up to the French Revolution seem quite applicable to Congo, and more broadly Africa, today. In the first decade and a half of the twenty-first century, large swaths of the African continent experienced a spring of hope. But for many trapped in zones of Africa marked by deadly conflict, appalling corruption, poverty, and authoritarianism, it remains truly a winter of despair. This book has attempted to explore how to understand and address that winter of despair without reinforcing crushing, racist, disempowering, and ahistorical stereotypes—the "heart of darkness" theme that so many commentators and storytellers fall into, a theme that leads to hopelessness and inaction.

As a result of these crises and the focus of mass media on the gloom-and-doom agenda, Africa is widely perceived as hopeless, beset by wars that are only explained through "tribal" or other racist and oversimplified identifiers. This image of a hopeless continent reinforces the belief that not much can be done and that the problems are insoluble, which in turn reinforces a global policy response that is stunning in its lack of creativity, energy, or innovation. When there is a belief that something cannot be fixed or changed, few resources are invested in building toward a solution. Given the media messaging we're all exposed to, it's easy to understand why the "Africa is hopeless" narrative is so accepted.

Although Hollywood gets blamed for a lot, and it should for some of the racist and stereotyping movies it has made about Africa, it certainly isn't the only culprit for representing Africa as a basket case. Remember the mass media mantra of many newspaper or website editors and television producers: "If it bleeds, it leads!" The bias is overwhelmingly toward crisis and tragedy—the worse it is, the more coverage it gets. According to a *Columbia Journalism Review* study, in one five-month period in 2010, the ten most-read US papers and magazines carried 245 articles about poverty in Africa, but only five mentioned economic growth.[326] Humanitarian organizations can contribute to this, as they often focus not on what has been accomplished but rather on what they need to raise money for. Understandably, they need to attract funding, but the messaging and imagery can reinforce the helplessness motif.

The incentives are built in to highlight doom and gloom. There is a tremendous competition for scarce funds. Journalists who are operating on tight budgets often are dependent upon agencies with funding agendas to get access to stories. As foreign correspondent

Lauren Gelfand summarized, "It's easier to sell a famine than to effect real, common-sense policy change."[327] For example, John was first compelled to go to Africa in his early twenties when he saw pictures of starving Ethiopians. Only later, by being there, did he learn that the story was so much more complicated than drought-stricken Africans who needed charity.

Making a Difference

In this increasingly interconnected world, it is impossible to avoid our links to grave human rights issues. It is also impossible to conclude that our actions have no consequence. A difference has been, can be, and will be made. Genocide, mass atrocities, and conflict can be effectively countered and stopped. We need the right tools, enveloped in the correct peace strategy, to address the properly diagnosed root causes and critical drivers of conflict. Only when sufficient political will is built can this highly promising policy approach ever be deployed. Political will is built not by bystanders, but by upstanders. That is all of our responsibility.

And when it comes to Congo, that political will has been impacted by the combination of Congolese standing up against oppression along with Americans and Europeans standing in solidarity with them. Through the use of social media, participation in demonstrations, writing letters, engaging companies, signing petitions, meeting elected officials, and many other innovative actions, corruption and human rights crimes have been exposed, solutions have been offered, company behavior has been altered, and policies have been changed.

Congo doesn't fit neatly into the history books written in America or Europe. The slave trade, the colonial history of extraction, the scramble for Congo's resources, the Cold War, and the continuing demand for Congo's raw materials for the innovations of global industries don't have an easy-to-categorize headline for textbooks, newspapers, websites, YouTube videos, or cable television shows. Congo is a wealthy country, not inherently poverty-stricken, but its people are among the poorest. Billions of looted dollars pour out of Congo illicitly, while billions go into the country to clean up the humanitarian mess created by the kleptocrats and their armed henchmen stealing Congo's vast resources, with vast profits accruing to multinational corporations, banks, arms dealers, and other opportunists.

For five centuries, it has been this way.

But we can *change* it.

Postscript by Dave Eggers

This book about what has happened, and is still happening, in the Democratic Republic of the Congo—and about the industrialized world's long complicity in the country's sorrow—can send a reader into a spiral of guilt and inaction. But I want to give you a few lessons of hope I've been taught by two people I've been fortunate to know, both of whom work in similarly fraught places. One is an education visionary working in the nonprofit realm, transforming attitudes in South Sudan one student at a time. The other is an entrepreneur using direct trade as a lever for social change in rural Yemen.

And crucially, both of these stories start and end with the importance of scale. That is, change can start on a very small scale; indeed, it almost always does.

First there is the story of Valentino Achak Deng. He was born and raised in what is now South Sudan, in a small village that was frequently raided by militias on horseback. As part of a concerted effort to destabilize the south, the government of Sudan empowered these militias to burn towns, kill men and boys, and seize women and children to be sold as slaves.

Valentino eventually joined a caravan of children who sought safety in then-peaceful lands, walking hundreds of miles by foot to refugee camps in Ethiopia and Kenya. Hundreds of children died along the way. But thousands survived.

Many of the survivors, now in their thirties, having been given citizenship and educations in countries such as the United States, Canada, and Australia, are now back in South Sudan, helping the new country find its way to stability. South Sudan is still the youngest of countries, and its first years have been exceedingly difficult. There has been civil war and massive displacement as former military commanders jockey for power and scarce resources.

Amid all the sadness and upheaval there are stories of noble courage, of people working for the good of the most vulnerable. Valentino Deng is one of those people. Though he could have stayed in the United States and grown old in easy comfort, he has chosen to return to his home village, to build the first secondary school in the region. In a country where 97 percent of women are illiterate, and where most girls are married before their sixteenth birthday, the Marial Bai Secondary School has dedicated itself to educating girls, and to fighting to keep them in school.

Deng has been so successful as a school builder and administrator that the government of South Sudan has repeatedly handed other schools to him—most of them long-shuttered or not functioning well—so he and his team can restart and operate them efficiently. Valentino combines local knowledge, a deep compassion for every young person, and a bit of American entrepreneurial spirit, and this combination is rare and extremely powerful in a region where bureaucratic impotence and kleptocratic corruption can stall or end any well-meaning project.

Valentino gets things done, period, and his ability to do so has inspired many other former refugees from South Sudan who have also returned to effect change in the nascent nation. Today there are dozens of projects, from new wells to new schools and medical clinics, that have sprung from the zeal and ingenuity of South Sudan's so-called Lost Boys, who were born and raised under the most dire of circumstances and who now are integral to the country's hopes.

Crucial to remember in Valentino's work, and in the work of so many young South Sudanese women and men, is that instead of trying to build a massive organization, and instead of attaching himself to a global nonprofit, Valentino kept his operation small, local, and lean. He solicited community input, came up with a plan and tight schedule, and then put his shoulder to the wheel. His first school campus was built from scratch and was educating teenagers in under a year—an astonishing achievement for any nonprofit operating in South Sudan.

For those readers wondering how to support comparable enterprises in the DRC, there are hundreds of similar small-scale and hyper-local nonprofits run by Congolese idealists who are getting the work done on the ground: the upstanders who have been highlighted in this book. And as much as the international community should, and must, support the many storied large-scale humanitarian nonprofits that have long dominated headlines and fund-raising, we should be looking to support and to fund—early and enthusiastically—local projects conceived and run by local residents. They tend to get things done quickly, cheaply, and with local buy-in.

Yemen too finds itself seized by civil war, with no way out. The hopes of the Arab Spring gave way to the rise of a rebel group, the Houthis, who have overtaken much of the country and have spawned a proxy war between Saudi Arabia and Iran, with millions of Yemeni innocents caught between their dueling agendas. Tens of thousands have died, food insecurity affects millions, and unemployment is catastrophic.

It would seem to be wholly irrelevant to worry about the coffee-growing industry at a time like this. But this is precisely what Mokhtar Alkhanshali, a young American of Yemeni descent, is doing. Before the Houthis took over much of the country in 2015, plunging the long-troubled country into a new stage of chaos and deprivation, Alkhanshali had begun exporting high-end coffee from the hills of Yemen's fertile central provinces. The high price paid for this coffee greatly improved the quality of life for his heretofore impoverished farmers. But when civil war overtook much of the country, it would have been tempting to pack up and cease his coffee business until the war was over.

But that's precisely the wrong impulse. Even a country at war with itself needs enterprise, needs real revenue, and farmers need to make a living. Though exporting coffee from a country like Yemen, where the seaports are routinely bombed and always contested by warring factions, is exceedingly difficult, the farmers depend on revenue from these exports for their livelihood. And so Alkhanshali continues to get the coffee out however he can and to pay the farmers for their crops.

Key to Alkhanshali's work is direct trade. Readers might be familiar with fair trade, a crucial term for consumers to know. But one step further is direct trade, where a buyer in the consuming country—in this case Alkhanshali—is working directly with the farmers on the ground in the country of production. Alkhanshali has cut out the many loan sharks who typically prey on small farmers, keeping them in a state of permanent debt not unlike indentured servitude. By buying coffee beans directly from farmers, and paying a premium for them, Alkhanshali gives the farmers a chance to feel proud and empowered by their work, as opposed to being forever under the thumb of exploitive middlemen.

Socially conscious capitalism is Alkhanshali's way of addressing the sorrow wrought by civil war. International aid plays a role in alleviating the suffering of a nation like Yemen, but preserving some semblance of economic enterprise is perhaps a more durable way forward. It gives Yemenis self-determination, and lays the groundwork for a post-conflict economy.

Which brings us to the Democratic Republic of the Congo. As noted in previous chapters, consumers have real power. In Alkhanshali's words, buyers in consuming countries have the choice, every time they shop, "to exploit or to uplift." They can look the other way when it comes to potential abuses and exploitation resulting from their purchases, or they can make a conscious choice to support enterprise that actually helps the producers.

And here's where we can do something very concrete. We can boycott plenty of products, and that has a real effect on curbing abusive business practices. But we can also actively choose to spend our money on those businesses, however small, that we know are doing the right thing. Avoiding and even protesting the worst abusers in Congo, for example, is one thing. But seeking out and spending money on those enterprises that do the right thing, that source their raw materials ethically and sustainably, that are locally owned and provide fair wages, is another.

So while we're thinking of what we can do, wherever on the globe we stand, to combat all the evil that's been done in Congo, look for even the smallest seeds of change—entrepreneurial and humanitarian—and help them grow. Seek out the changemakers and commit your support directly. Buy something that's ethically sourced and made. Such an action, so easy to accomplish in our interconnected world, is a humane and even intimate way to state your rejection of a history of soulless corporate exploitation. You do have this power. Don't ever think you don't.

Afterword by Chouchou Namegabe

I was born and raised in Bukavu, one of the most beautiful places in the world. It is a small corner of paradise, with its very clement weather all year round, its mountains overlooking the city, and its five bays like five fingers of the hand embracing the welcoming waters of Lake Kivu. From the inside, I admired my city, I enjoyed living there—without having a clue about all the valuable resources we were sitting on—until several waves of repetitive wars and violence came along to steal our tranquility. This natural wealth that does not benefit the population became one of the sources of all its misfortune. But on the other hand, the difficult times that we Congolese have gone through over the years have strengthened our resilience and ability to innovate, to find solutions and adapt our livelihoods to a fast-moving environment.

Women in particular pay the heaviest price of these repeated wars, disasters, and violence. They are the ones who deserve to be praised for their ability to cope. Strong and enduring, they have always fought for the survival of the community and never have given up. They never gave up working, never gave up taking care of their family. They even never gave up smiling! And that is the foundation of my hope. I hope that change in Congo will come through the women. They are the foundation of the families, communities, and the economy, and I'm strongly convinced they have the power to go the extra mile and transform the country at large.

The influence of women has the potential to change the way the country is managed. On the security front, they can demand a responsible, republican, well-trained, and well-equipped army and police force, capable of ensuring protection, peace, and security. On the justice side, they can institute a strong, independent, just, and equitable legal system that can put an end to all forms of impunity and can especially fight corruption! On the economic level, everything has to be restructured. Women can put in place policies to improve economic development, starting with agriculture. With its nine months of rain, this great green country as big as Western Europe could conceivably feed the entire African continent! Then, with women in the lead, Congo could negotiate as equals with those who are interested in our mineral wealth, so that the development of that wealth respects our environment and rebuilds our country.

Congolese women would be proud advocates of our country on the international scene, talking with the developed countries on equal terms. Congo would no longer be considered as underdeveloped, but rather as a great power thanks not only to its great forests, abundant water resources, and mineral wealth underground, but also to its people! To all of you who would like to help Congo, my message is simple: please invest in women!

This country, *my country*, is so wonderful, and its people, *my people*, deserve way better than the crumbs of development that fall off the table. We have suffered too long. Governance needs to be rethought, from top to bottom. Don't get me wrong—there are already plenty of innovative initiatives and things that are working well and have the potential to transform our society. Those promising efforts need to be scaled up. There are already strong Congolese leaders—men and women, young and old—who continue to think positively and have great hopes for this country. They need to be empowered.

This is a project, an objective, a movement that we can pursue together, in Congo and around the world.

For more information, further Congolese upstander stories, multimedia content, a curriculum for teachers, illustrations by Congolese artists, and other ways to get involved, please visit our website at

www.congostories.org

Acknowledgments

We want to express our profound gratitude to the incredible people we met or got to know better as a result of the multiple roads that brought us finally to this book. We are humbled by the complexity of the issues facing Congo and daunted by the forces working against that country's progress. But seeing the ingenuity, bravery, and determination of the Congolese people profiled in this book—and so many others whose stories are not recounted here—gives us enormous hope for the future of this embattled country. We also want to express our appreciation for the staff at the Enough Project and The Sentry, who contributed to the content and production of this book in many ways, particularly Sasha Lezhnev, Holly Dranginis, Annie Callaway, Carl Bellin, Greg Hittelman, Jennifer Lonnquest, and Megha Swamy. We want to recognize our traveling companions in Congo: Sia Sanneh, Steve Petty, and Lauren LeBeouf. We were greatly assisted by comments on early drafts by Samantha Power, Joe DiStefano, and Sia Sanneh, and in the finalizing of the photographs by Hama Sanders. And we are indebted to the wonderful people at Grand Central Publishing, in particular our editor Gretchen Young, who kept the fires burning during dark nights, as well as Katherine Stopa, Emily Rosman, Rick Ball, Mari Okuda, and Flag Tonuzi, and Paul Nielsen and his design team at Faceout Studio.

A "Geological Scandal" Results in a Governing Disaster

Congo is one of the world's richest countries in terms of natural resources. In the words of a Belgian geologist in the 1890s, it is a veritable "geological scandal." But in a classic case of the "resource curse,"[i] Congo's governing system has been repurposed for the benefit of those in charge and their international facilitators, leaving the people impoverished and governing institutions hijacked or cratered. The illustrations and graphics here depict manifestations of that resource curse.

As the political scientist and Congo expert Pierre Englebert observed, "Congo is still understood more as a resource to be plundered than as a state to be built, and grassroots Congolese continue to shoulder the burden of such a system."[ii]

■ **Natural resources overall**

○ Contains 1,100 minerals,[iii] particularly copper, cobalt, diamonds, tantalum, tin, gold, uranium,[iv] timber, oil, water for massive hydroelectricity, and 80 million hectares of arable land.[v]

○ Natural resource wealth estimated at $24 trillion.[vi]

■ **Copper**

○ In 2016, produced 1,021,634 tons of copper.[vii]

○ Value of output in 2015 nearly $6 billion.[viii]

○ Reserves estimated at 20 million tons.[ix]

■ **Gold**

○ Estimated $28 billion worth of gold reserves.[x]

○ Gold produced from industrial mines 31.8 tons in 2015.

○ Estimated value of gold output: $2,192,250,881.[xi]

○ The UN Group of Experts estimated that 98 percent of gold produced by artisanal miners is smuggled out of the country (10–12 tons worth approximately $400 million) and is mainly smuggled to Uganda and Dubai, UAE.[xii]

■ **Cobalt**

○ Largest producer of cobalt globally, accounting for 50–60 percent of global production in 2015. World's leading source of mined cobalt.[xiii]

○ In 2015, estimated value of output nearly $2.5 billion.[xiv]

■ **Diamonds**

○ "Second largest producer of industrial diamonds [in the world] in 2015, contributing about 24 percent of global production behind only Russia."[xv]

○ Congo holds the second largest reserves after Australia.[xvi]

○ Production in 2016 (from the Kimberley Process statistics):[xvii]

● 23.2 million carats (volume) produced at a value of $246.7 million.

● 14.7 million carats (volume) exported at a value of $229.5 million.

○ More than 800,000 artisanal miners estimated to be employed in diamond mining in 2014.[xviii]

■ **Tantalum**

○ Accounted for about 32 percent of global tantalum production in 2015.[xix]

○ Estimated value of production in 2015 over $135 million.[xx]

■ **Tin (Cassiterite)**

○ Total estimated production value of over $172 million in 2015.[xxi]

○ Contains one of the world's largest tin mines, Bisie.

■ **Tungsten (Wolframite)**

○ Total estimated production value of over $1.7 million in 2015.[xxii]

■ **Zinc**

○ Total estimated value of over $23.5 million in 2015.[xxiii]

■ **Land/Forest**

○ Land mass roughly one-fourth the size of the US.[xxiv] Eleventh largest country in the world.[xxv]

○ Has half of Africa's forests and water reserves.[xxvi]

○ Sixty-seven percent forest.[xxvii] The Congo Basin forest is the second-largest area of dense tropical rain forest in the world, containing one quarter of the world's remaining tropical forests, as well as a spectacular array of biodiversity—10,000 species of plants, 1,000 species of birds, and 400 species of mammals, many of which exist nowhere else on earth.[xxviii]

○ Timber sector is worth $95 million annually, with an estimated 40 million people's livelihoods linked to the country's forests.[xxix]

■ **Rivers**

○ Congo River 3,000 miles long.[xxx] Volume second only to Amazon River.

○ Thirteen percent of the world's hydropower potential.[xxxi]

○ Forty thousand MW of 100,000 MW hydroelectric potential concentrated at Inga site on the Congo River.[xxxii]

○ Congo utilizes just two percent of its estimated 100,000 MW of hydroelectric potential.[xxxiii]

○ The Congo River is the second-longest river in Africa and the second-largest river in the world as measured by discharge.[xxxiv]

○ In the Congo River, more than 300 species of fish have been identified, 30 percent of which are found nowhere else on the planet.[xxxv]

■ **Oil**

○ Produced approximately 23,000 barrels of oil per day in 2014 (seventy-eighth in the world), and new reserves are being discovered offshore and onshore in both the west and east.[xxxvi]

○ Estimated value of petroleum output in 2015: over $450 million.[xxxvii]

DEATHS
- Conflict-related: 5.4 million people dead as a result of war-related causes as of 2008. Number has not been credibly updated since then. Highest deaths by war globally since WWII.[xxxviii]

REFUGEES/DISPLACED
- Refugees
  - 537,000 Congolese refugees as of 2016.[xxxix]
  - Congo represented the sixth-largest country of origin of refugees globally at the end of 2016.[xl]
  - 475,000 foreign refugees in Congo, as of August 2017.[xli]
- Internally Displaced Persons
  - As of October 2017, 3.9 million Congolese were internally.[xlii]
  - According to the 2016 *Global Trends* report by UNHCR, Congo had the seventh most forcibly displaced individuals in the world.[xliii]
  - During 2016, more than 1.3 million people were newly displaced in the DRC, more than anywhere else in the world (ahead of South Sudan at 865,000, Libya at 630,000).[xliv]
- Trafficking in Persons
  - Congo is a source, destination, and possibly a transit country for men, women, and children subjected to forced labor and sex trafficking; forced recruitment of children into army and armed groups.[xlv]

UNEMPLOYMENT
- Roughly 80 percent of the active population operates outside the labor market and the unemployment rate is 73 percent.[xlvi]

INFANT MORTALITY
- 69.8 deaths/1,000 live births in 2016, ranked twelfth highest in the world.[xlvii]

MATERNAL MORTALITY
- 693 deaths/100,000 live births in 2015, ranked seventeenth highest in the world.[xlviii]

SCHOOLING
- Primary school dropout rate—44.6 percent as of 2013.[xlix]

DISEASE
  - HIV/AIDS: ranked fifteenth in the world in deaths.[l] TB: ranked fourth in the world.[li] Malaria ranked fourth in the world.[lii]

CORRUPTION
- Out of 174 countries on the Transparency International Corruption Perceptions Index in 2016, ranked 156th, a score that has worsened over time.[liii]
- Ranked forty-sixth out of fifty-four African countries in the Mo Ibrahim Foundation's annual governance index.[liv]
- The United Nations estimates that $64 million to $121 million from the artisanal minerals trade goes to criminal enterprises each year.[lv]
- "Each year, up to $10 billion worth of copper and cobalt is dug up from Congo's soil and sold abroad. However, [Global Witness'] analysis shows that as little as 6 percent of annual mining exports reach the country's budget."[lvi]

INEQUALITY
- Ranked 153rd of 188 countries on Gender Inequality Index in 2015.[lvii]

LIFE EXPECTANCY AT BIRTH
- 57.7 years in 2017, ranked 210th of 224 in the world.[lviii]

CHILDREN/YOUTH
- Under-five mortality rate per 100,000—98 (2015), ranked ninth highest in world.[lix]
- Moderate or severe stunting percentage of those under age five)—42.6%.[lx]
  - Child labor: over 38 percent of kids were working between 2009 and 2015.[lxi]
- Ranked ninth in the world in under-five mortality rate in 2015.[lxii]

EDUCATION
- Government expenditure on education as percentage of GDP: 2.24 percent, which ranked 156th out of 176 countries in 2016.[lxiii]

INCOME
  - GDP per capita was 227th out of 230 in the world in 2017, roughly $800 a year.[lxiv]
  - Population living below income poverty line, over 77 percent.[lxv]
  - Congo ranked 176th out of 188 countries in the world in the UN Human Development Index in 2016.[lxvi]
  - Inequality is rising.[lxvii]

GDP
  - GDP per capita: $800 in 2016, 227nd in the world (only Burundi, CAR, and Somalia were lower).[lxviii]

i   Term coined by Richard Auty in *Sustaining Development in Mineral Economies: The Resource Curse Thesis* (London: Routledge, 1993), describing the paradox that developing countries with the most mineral wealth tend to be the poorest and least democratic.

ii   Pierre Englebert, *Democratic Republic of Congo: Growth for All?* (Johannesburg: The Brenthurst Foundation, 2014), Discussion Paper 6, p. 3, available at https://pierreenglebert.files.wordpress.com/2014/11/brenthurst-paper-2014-06-final.pdf.

iii   World Bank, "Overview: Democratic Republic of Congo," available at http://www.worldbank.org/en/country/drc/overview (last accessed August 2017).

iv   Some of Congo's uranium was used to make the atomic bombs that were dropped on Japan in World War II. Patrick Marnham, "Tracing the Congolese Mine that fuelled Hiroshima," The Telegraph, November 4, 2013, available at http://www.telegraph. co.uk/culture/10416945/Tracing-the-Congolese-mine-that-fuelled-Hiroshima.html.

v   World Bank, "Overview: Democratic Republic of Congo," available at http://www.worldbank.org/en/country/drc/overview (last accessed August 2017).

vi   UN News Centre, "DR Congo: UN advises prudent use of abundant resources to spur development." 10 October 2011. Accessed 8 August 2017.

vii   Export.gov, "Congo, Democratic Republic – Mining and Minerals," available at https://www.export.gov/article?id=Congo-Democratic-Republic-Mining-and-Minerals; accessed 15 August 2017.

viii   Sasha Lezhnev, "A Criminal State: Understanding and Countering Institutionalized Corruption and Violence in the Democratic Republic of Congo," Enough Project report, October 2016, available at https://enoughproject.org/files/A_Criminal_State_Enough_Oct2016_web.pdf; Statistics from: The sources for this table are: Fédération des Entreprises du Congo, (FEC), Chambre des Mines, "Industrie Miniere en RDC: Rapport Annuel 2015," available at http://www.congomines. org/system/attachments/assets/000/001/086/original/CdM_ annual_Report_2015 _FR_-_0902_2016_-_web.pdf?1455110717; Banque Centrale du Congo, Condensé statistique, August 2015, available at http://www.bcc.cd/index.php?option=com_ content&view=section&id=9&Itemid=58; Sara Geenen, African Artisanal Mining from the Inside Out, (Abington, UK: Routledge, 2015), pp. 5, 9; The annual average commodity prices are estimates from different sources and graphs published by FEC.

ix   U.S. Geological Survey, "Copper," accessed August 2017, available at https://minerals.usgs.gov/minerals/pubs/commodity/copper/mcs-2017-coppe.pdf

x   "River of Gold," Global Witness, 5 July 2016, available at https://www.globalwitness.org/en/campaigns/conflict-minerals/river-of-gold-drc/

xi   Sasha Lezhnev, "A Criminal State: Understanding and Countering Institutionalized Corruption and Violence in the Democratic Republic of Congo," Enough Project report, October 2016, available at https://enoughproject.org/files/A_Criminal_State_Enough_Oct2016_web.pdf; Statistics from: The sources for this table are: Fédération des Entreprises du Congo, (FEC), Chambre des Mines, "Industrie Miniere en RDC: Rapport Annuel 2015," available at http://www.congomines. org/system/attachments/assets/000/001/086/original/CdM_ annual_Report_2015 _FR_-_0902_2016_-_web.pdf?1455110717; Banque Centrale du Congo, Condensé statistique, August 2015, available at http://www.bcc.cd/index.php?option=com_ content&view=section&id=9&Itemid=58; Sara Geenen, African Artisanal Mining from the Inside Out, (Abington,

UK: Routledge, 2015), pp. 5, 9; The annual average commodity prices are estimates from different sources and graphs published by FEC.

xii   U.N. Security Council, "Final report of the Group of Experts on the Democratic Republic of the Congo," 23 May 2016, p. 33, available at http://www.securitycouncilreport.org/atf/cf/%7B65BFCF9B-6D27-4E9C-8CD3-CF6E4FF96FF9%7D/s_2016_466.pdf

xiii   U.S. Geological Survey and U.S. Department of the Interior, "Mineral Commodity Summaries 2016," available https://minerals.usgs.gov/minerals/pubs/mcs/2016/mcs2016.pdf and Washington Post, 'The Cobalt Pipeline,' 30 September 2016, available at https://www.washingtonpost.com/graphics/business/batteries/congo-cobalt-mining-for-lithium-ion-battery/

xiv   Sasha Lezhnev, "A Criminal State: Understanding and Countering Institutionalized Corruption and Violence in the Democratic Republic of Congo," Enough Project report, October 2016, available at https://enoughproject.org/files/A_Criminal_State_Enough_Oct2016_web.pdf; Statistics from: The sources for this table are: Fédération des Entreprises du Congo, (FEC), Chambre des Mines, "Industrie Miniere en RDC: Rapport Annuel 2015," available at http://www.congomines. org/system/attachments/assets/000/001/086/original/CdM_ annual_Report_2015 _FR_-_0902_2016_-_web.pdf?1455110717; Banque Centrale du Congo, Condensé statistique, August 2015, available at http://www.bcc.cd/index.php?option=com_ content&view=section&id=9&Itemid=58; Sara Geenen, African Artisanal Mining from the Inside Out, (Abington, UK: Routledge, 2015), pp. 5, 9; The annual average commodity prices are estimates from different sources and graphs published by FEC.

xv   Export.gov, "Congo, Democratic Republic – Mining and Minerals," available at https://www.export.gov/article?id=Congo-Democratic-Republic-Mining-and-Minerals; accessed 15 August 2017.

xvi   U.S. Geological Survey, "Diamonds (industrial)," available at http://minerals.usgs.gov/minerals/pubs/commodity/diamond/ mcs-2015-diamo.pdf (last accessed August 2017).

xvii   Kimberley Process, "Annual Global Summary: 2016 Production, Imports, Exports and KPC Counts," accessed August 2017, available at https://kimberleyprocessstatistics.org/static/pdfs/public _statistics/2016/2016GlobalSummary.pdf

xviii   Thomas Yager, "2014 Minerals Yearbook: The Mineral Industry in Congo (Kinshasa)," accessed 31 August 2017, available at https://minerals.usgs.gov/minerals/pubs/country/2014/myb3-2014-cg.pdf

xix   U.S. Geological Survey, "Tantalum," accessed August 2017, available at https://minerals.usgs.gov/minerals/pubs/commodity/niobium/mcs-2017-tanta.pdf

xx   From Enough Project report: https://enoughproject.org/files/A_Criminal _State_Enough_Oct2016_web.pdf; Statistics from: The sources for this table are: Fédération des Entreprises du Congo, (FEC), Chambre des Mines, "Industrie Miniere en RDC: Rapport Annuel 2015," available at http://www.congomines. org/system/attachments/assets/000/001/086/original/CdM_ annual_Report_2015_FR_-_0902_2016_-_web.pdf?1455110717; Banque Centrale du Congo, Condensé statistique, August 2015, available at http://www.bcc.cd/index.php?option=com_ content&view=section&id=9&Itemid=58; Sara Geenen, African Artisanal Mining from the Inside Out, (Abington, UK: Routledge, 2015), pp. 5, 9; The annual average commodity prices are estimates from different sources and graphs published by FEC.

xxi   From Enough Project report: https://enoughproject.org/files/A_Criminal _State_Enough_Oct2016_web.pdf; Statistics from: The sources for this table are: Fédération des Entreprises du Congo, (FEC), Chambre des Mines, "Industrie Miniere en RDC: Rapport Annuel 2015," available at http://www.congomines.org/system/attachments/assets/000/001/086 /original/CdM_ annual_Report_2015_FR_-_0902_2016_-_web .pdf?1455110717; Banque Centrale du Congo, Condensé statistique, August 2015, available at http://www.bcc.cd/index.php?option=com _ content&view=section&id=9&Itemid=58; Sara Geenen, African Artisanal Mining from the Inside Out, (Abington, UK: Routledge, 2015), pp. 5, 9; The annual average commodity prices are estimates from different sources and graphs published by FEC.

xxii   From Enough Project report: https://enoughproject.org/files/A_Criminal _State_Enough_Oct2016_web.pdf; Statistics from: The sources for this table are: Fédération des Entreprises du Congo, (FEC), Chambre des Mines, "Industrie Miniere en RDC: Rapport Annuel 2015," available at http://www.congomines.org/system/attachments/assets/000/001/086 /original/CdM_ annual_Report_2015_FR_-_0902_2016_-_web .pdf?1455110717; Banque Centrale du Congo, Condensé statistique, August 2015, available at http://www.bcc.cd/index.php?option=com _ content&view=section&id=9&Itemid=58; Sara Geenen, African Artisanal Mining from the Inside Out, (Abington, UK: Routledge, 2015), pp. 5, 9; The annual average commodity prices are estimates from different sources and graphs published by FEC.

xxiii   From Enough Project report: https://enoughproject.org/files/A_Criminal _State_Enough_Oct2016_web.pdf; Statistics from: The sources for this table are: Fédération des Entreprises du Congo, (FEC), Chambre des Mines, "Industrie Miniere en RDC: Rapport Annuel 2015," available at http://www.congomines. org/system/attachments/assets/000/001/086 /original/CdM_ annual_Report_2015_FR_-_0902 2016_-_web .pdf?1455110717; Banque Centrale du Congo, Condensé statistique, August 2015, available at http://www.bcc.cd/index.php?option=com _ content&view=section&id=9&Itemid=58; Sara Geenen, African Artisanal Mining from the Inside Out, (Abington, UK: Routledge, 2015), pp. 5, 9; The annual average commodity prices are estimates from different sources and graphs published by FEC.

xxiv   Central Intelligence Agency, "The World Factbook: Democratic Republic of Congo," available at https://www.cia.gov/library/publications/the-world -factbook/geos/cg.html

xxv   USAID, "Democratic Republic of the Congo: Power Africa Fact Sheet," accessed August 28 2017, available at https://www.usaid.gov /powerafrica/democratic-republic-congo

xxvi   http://www.unep.org/disastersandconflicts/news/unep-study-confirms -dr-congos-potential-environmental-powerhouse-warns-critical-threats

xxvii   World Bank (2016). "Country Profile: Congo, Dem. Rep.", accessed 28 August 2017, available at http://databank.worldbank.org/data/Views /Reports/ReportWidgetCustom.aspx?Report_Name=CountryProfile&Id= b450fd57&tbar=y&dd=y&inf=n&zm=n&country=COD

xxviii   John Katunga, "Minerals, Forests, and Violent Conflict in the Democratic Republic of the Congo," Wilson Center, July 7, 2011, accessed 31 August 2017, available at https://www.wilsoncenter.org/sites/default/files /Katunga12.pdf

xxix   "Exporting Impunity," Global Witness, June 3, 2015, available at https:// www.globalwitness.org/en/campaigns/democraticrepublic-congo /exporting-impunity/

xxx   Robert Draper, " The Main Road Through the Heart of Africa is the Congo River — For those who dare to take it," National Geographic, October 2015, available at http://ngm.nationalgeographic.com/2015/10/congo-river /draper-text

xxxi   USAID, "Democratic Republic of the Congo: Power Africa Fact Sheet," accessed August 28 2017, available at https://www.usaid.gov /powerafrica/democratic-republic-congo

xxxii   USAID, "Democratic Republic of the Congo: Power Africa Fact Sheet," accessed August 28 2017, available at https://www.usaid.gov /powerafrica/democratic-republic-congo

xxxiii   USAID, "Democratic Republic of the Congo: Power Africa Fact Sheet," accessed August 28 2017, available at https://www.usaid.gov /powerafrica/democratic-republic-congo

xxxiv   Kevin Obert, John Shelton, Ned Gardiner, P. Ryan Jackson, "Discharge and Other Hydraulic Measurements for Characterizing the Hydraulics of Lower Congo River," July 2018, p. 1, accessed 31 August 2017, available at https://hydroacoustics.usgs.gov/publications /Measurements4LowerCongo-6.pdf

xxxv   Kevin Obert, John Shelton, Ned Gardiner, P. Ryan Jackson, "Discharge and Other Hydraulic Measurements for Characterizing the Hydraulics of Lower Congo River," July 2018, p. 1, accessed 31 August 2017, available at https://hydroacoustics.usgs.gov/publications /Measurements4LowerCongo-6.pdf

xxxvi   Congo produced 8,374 million barrels in 2014, according to its EITI report, which rounds out to 22,900 barrels per day. Initiative pour la Transparence des Industries Extractives, "Republique Democratique du Congo - Comite Exécutif de L'iniative pour la Transparence dans les Industries Extractives-Rapport ITIE RDC 2014," (December 2015), available at https://eiti.org /files/rapport_ de_conciliation_itie_rdc_2014_-_final.pdf; Africanvault, "Top 20 Oil Producing Countries In Africa," available at http://www .africanvault.com/oil-p

xxxvii   From Enough Project report: https://enoughproject.org/files/A_Criminal _State_Enough_Oct2016_web.pdf; Statistics from: The sources for this table are: Fédération des Entreprises du Congo, (FEC), Chambre des Mines, "Industrie Miniere en RDC: Rapport Annuel 2015," available at http://www.congomines. org/system/attachments/assets/000/001/086 /original/CdM_ annual_Report_2015_FR_-_0902_2016_-_web .pdf?1455110717; Banque Centrale du Congo, Condensé statistique, August 2015, available at http://www.bcc.cd/index.php?option=com _ content&view=section&id=9&Itemid=58; Sara Geenen, African Artisanal Mining from the Inside Out, (Abington, UK: Routledge, 2015), pp. 5, 9; The annual average commodity prices are estimates from different sources and graphs published by FEC.

xxxviii   International Rescue Committee, Mortality in the Democratic Republic of Congo: An ongoing crisis. (New York, US: IRC, 2008).

xxxix   UNHCR (2016). UNHCR Global Trends 2016, p. 19. Accessed 23 August 2017, available at http://www.unhcr.org/5943e8a34.

xl   UNHCR (2016). UNHCR Global Trends 2016, p. 19. Accessed 23 August 2017, available at http://www.unhcr.org/5943e8a34.

xli   USAID Fact Sheet on the Democratic Republic of Congo, August 2017, available at https://reliefweb.int/sites/reliefweb.int/files /resources/08.25.17%20-%20USAID-DCHA%20DRC%20Complex%20 Emergency%20Fact%20Sheet%20%234.pdf

xlii   Central Intelligence Agency, "The World Factbook: Democratic Republic of Congo," available at https://www.cia.gov/library/publications/the-world -factbook/geos/cg.html

xliii   UNHCR (2016). UNHCR Global Trends 2016, p. 6. Accessed 31 August 2017, available at http://www.unhcr.org/5943e8a34

xliv   UNHCR (2016). UNHCR Global Trends 2016, p. 35. Accessed 31 August 2017, available at http://www.unhcr.org/5943e8a34

xlv   Central Intelligence Agency, "The World Factbook: Democratic Republic of Congo," available at https://www.cia.gov/library/publications/the-world -factbook/geos/cg.html

xlvi   African Development Bank, "Congo, Dem Rep. 2012," p. 15, available at https://www.afdb.org/fileadmin/uploads/afdb/Documents/Publications /Congo%20Democratic%20Republic%20Full%20PDF%20Country%20 Note.pdf

xlvii   Central Intelligence Agency, "The World Factbook," available at https:// www.cia.gov/library/publications/the-world-factbook/rankorder/2091rank .html#cg

xlviii   Central Intelligence Agency, "The World Factbook: Democratic Republic of Congo," available at https://www.cia.gov/library/publications/the-world -factbook/geos/cg.html

xlix   United Nations Development Programme, "Human Development Reports Congo (Democratic Republic of the)," available at http://hdr.undp.org/en /countries/ profiles/COD (last accessed August 2017).

l   Central Intelligence Agency, "The World Factbook: Democratic Republic of Congo," available at https://www.cia.gov/library/publications/the-world -factbook/geos/cg.html

li   United Nations Statistics Division, Sustainable Development Goals Indicators Database. http://data.un.org. Accessed 31 August 2017, available at http://data.un.org/Data .aspx?q=tuberculosis+Congo&d=SDGs&f=series%3aSH_TBS _MORT%3bref_area%3aCOD%2cCOG

lii   United Nations Development Programme, "2016 Human Development Report," available at http://hdr.undp.org/en/indicators/102506

liii   Transparency International, "Corruption Perceptions Index 2016," 25 January 2017, accessed 31 August 2017, available at https://www .transparency.org/news/feature/corruption_perceptions_index_2016

liv   Transparency International, "Corruption Perceptions Index 2015," available at http://www.transparency. org/cpi2015; and Mo Ibrahim Foundation, "A Decade of African Governance, 2006-2015," 2016 Ibrahim Index of African Governance (IIAG) (2016), available at http://s.mo.ibrahim . foundation/u/2016/10/01184917/2016-Index-Report.pdf?_ga=1.1 31307078.839743015.1475756933

lv   This is in addition to other criminal natural resource smuggling of wildlife, charcoal, and timber. UNEP-MONUSCO-OSESG, "Experts' Background Report on Illegal Exploitation and Trade in Natural Resources Befitting Organized Criminal Groups and Recommendations on MONUSCO's Role in Fostering Stability and Peace in Eastern DR Congo," (April 2015), pp 3-4.

lvi   "Regime Cash Machine,"Global Witness, July 2017, available at https:// www.globalwitness.org/en/campaigns/democratic-republic-congo /regime-cash-machine/

lvii   United Nations Development Programme, "Human Development Report 2016," p. 216, available at http://hdr.undp.org/sites/default/files/2016 _human_development_report.pdf

lviii   Central Intelligence Agency, "The World Factbook," available at https:// www.cia.gov/library/publications/the-world-factbook/rankorder/2rank .html#cg

lix   UNICEF, "The State of the World's Children 2016 Statistical Tables," 27 June 2016, available at http://data.unicef.org/resources/state-worlds -children-2016-statistical-tables/

lx   United Nations Development Programme, "Human Development Reports Congo (Democratic Republic of the)," available at http://hdr.undp.org/en /countries/ profiles/COD (last accessed August 2017).

lxi   UNICEF, "The State of the World's Children 2016 Statistical Tables," 27 June 2016, available at http://data.unicef.org/resources/state-worlds -children-2016-statistical-tables/

lxii   UNICEF, "The State of the World's Children 2016 Statistical Tables," 27 June 2016, available at http://data.unicef.org/resources/state-worlds -children-2016-statistical-tables/

lxiii   World Bank, "World Development Indicators," Excel spreadsheet accessed 31 August 2017, available at http://data.worldbank.org/data-catalog /world-development-indicators

lxiv   Central Intelligence Agency, "The World Factbook," accessed 31 August 2017, available at https://www.cia.gov/library/publications/the-world -factbook/rankorder/2004rank.html

lxv   UNDP, "Human Development Report 2016: Human Development for Everyone," p. 218, accessed 31 August 2017, available at http://hdr.undp .org/sites/default/files/2016_human_development_report.pdf

lxvi   UNDP, "Human Development Report 2016: Human Development for Everyone," p. 200, accessed 31 August 2017, available at http://hdr.undp .org/sites/default/files/2016_human_development_report.pdf

lxvii   IMF, 2015: 4-7. There are signs, however, that the macroeconomic context is deteriorating in the wake of declining commodity prices. See Congo Research Group, "Just What Kabila Did Not Need: A Bad Economy," April 19, 2016, available at http:// congoresearchgroup.org/just-what-kabila -did-not-need-a-badeconomy/. [In nominal value terms. International Monetary Fund, "Democratic Republic of Congo: Staff Report for the 2015 Article IV Consultation," Washington, DC, August 17, 2015, p. 2, available at https://www.imf.org/external/pubs/ft/dsa/pdf/2015/dsacr15280. pdf; and Africa Confidential, "Congo-Kinshasa," available at http:// www .africa-confidential.com/browse-by-country/id/53/CONGOKINSHASA]

lxviii   Central Intelligence Agency, "The World Factbook: Democratic Republic of Congo," available at https://www.cia.gov/library/publications/the-world -factbook/geos/cg.html

Notes

Epigraph

1   Howard Zinn, *You Can't Be Neutral on a Moving Train: A Personal History of Our Times* (Boston: Beacon Press, 2002), p. 258.

Chapter 1

2   The militia was the Democratic Forces for the Liberation of Rwanda (or the FDLR), remnants of the group that had perpetrated the genocide in Rwanda in 1994 and crossed over the border into Congo after being defeated in Rwanda's civil war.

3   Paul Collier and Anke Hoeffler, "Greed and Grievance in Civil War" (World Bank Policy Research Working Paper 2355, World Bank Development Research Group, Washington, DC, May 2000), available at http://documents.worldbank.org /curated/en/359271468739530199/pdf/multi-page.pdf.

4   Term coined by Samantha Power in her Pulitzer Prize–winning book, *"A Problem from Hell": America and the Age of Genocide.* See Samantha Power, *"A Problem from Hell": American and the Age of Genocide* (New York: Basic Books, 2002).

Chapter 2

5   Alisa LaGamma, *Kongo: Power and Majesty* (New York: Metropolitan Museum of Art; New Haven: Yale University Press, 2015), p. 17.

6   LaGamma, *Kongo: Power and Majesty*, p. 18.

7   LaGamma, *Kongo: Power and Majesty*, p. 88.

8   David Van Reybrouck, *Congo: The Epic History of a People*, trans. by Sam Garrett (New York: Ecco, 2014), p. 21.

9   Adam Hochschild, *King Leopold's Ghost: A Story of Greed, Terror, and Heroism in Colonial Africa* (Boston: First Mariner Books, 1999), p. 9.

10   Van Reybrouck, *Congo*, p. 20.

11   Ch. Didier Gondola, *The History of Congo* (Westport, CT: Greenwood Press, 2002), p. 30.

12   LaGamma, *Kongo: Power and Majesty*, p. 30.

13   Alisa LaGamma (curator of *Kongo: Power and Majesty*, Metropolitan Museum of Art, New York) in discussion with the author, 2016.

14   An oliphant is a hunter's horn made from an elephant tusk. See *Merriam-Webster*, s.v. "oliphant," accessed March 2, 2018, available at https://www.merriam-webster.com/dictionary/oliphant.

15   LaGamma, *Kongo: Power and Majesty*, p. 21.

16   Peter Schjeldahl, "Power Surge," *New Yorker*, October 12, 2015, available at https://www.newyorker.com/magazine/2015/10/12/power-surge.

17   Hochschild, *King Leopold's Ghost*, p. 73.

18   Gondola, *The History of Congo*, p. 27.

19   Gondola, *The History of Congo*, p. 27.

20   Gondola, *The History of Congo*, p. 27.

21   Gondola, *The History of Congo*, p. 28.

22   Gondola, *The History of Congo*, p. 28.

23   LaGamma, *Kongo: Power and Majesty*, p. 88.

24   Gondola, *The History of Congo*, p. 30.

25   Jason Stearns, *Dancing in the Glory of Monsters: The Collapse of the Congo and the Great War of Africa* (New York: PublicAffairs, 2011), pp. 329–30.

26   LaGamma, *Kongo: Power and Majesty*, p. 88.

27   Van Reybrouck, *Congo*, p. 21.

28   LaGamma, *Kongo: Power and Majesty*, p. 89.

29   LaGamma, *Kongo: Power and Majesty*, p. 129.

30   LaGamma, *Kongo: Power and Majesty*, p. 116.

31   LaGamma, *Kongo: Power and Majesty*, p. 95.

32   Hochschild, *King Leopold's Ghost*, p. 9.

33   Hochschild, *King Leopold's Ghost*, p. 10.

34   Alisa LaGamma (curator of *Kongo: Power and Majesty*, Metropolitan Museum of Art, New York) in discussion with the author, 2016.

35   Hochschild, *King Leopold's Ghost*, p. 15.

Chapter 3

36   Lisa Rein, "Mystery of Virginia's First Slaves Is Unlocked 400 Years Later," *Washington Post*, September 3, 2006.

37   Jesus Garcia et al., *Creating America: A History of the United States* (Evanston, IL: McDougal Littell, 2007), p. 121.

38   "The Arrival of European Traders," The Abolition Project, available at http://abolition.e2bn.org/slavery_42.html.

39   Gondola, *The History of Congo*, p. 45.

40   Van Reybrouck, *Congo*, p. 23.

41   Stearns, *Dancing in the Glory of Monsters*, p. 330.

42   Martin Meredith, *The Fortunes of Africa: A 5,000 Year History of Wealth, Greed, and Endeavor* (New York: PublicAffairs, 2014), p. 103.

43   Hochschild, *King Leopold's Ghost*, p. 11.

44   Van Reybrouck, *Congo*, p. 24.

45   Hochschild, *King Leopold's Ghost*, p. 13.

46   Gondola, *The History of Congo*, p. 32.

47   Richard Gray, *Christianity, the Papacy, and Mission in Africa* (Maryknoll, NY: Orbis, 2012), p. 17. The Catholic Church was deeply divided over the issue of slavery. On the one hand, some of the Catholic clergy were complicit in the slave trade. The mission in Kongo was the largest Catholic mission in Africa in the seventeenth century. Portuguese missionaries created major plantations, which were worked by their enslaved congregations. Professor Sanneh elaborates on page 20 of this citation, "Nearly all the clergy benefited financially from the slave trade. Yet, the prevailing climate of opinion notwithstanding, many members of the clergy launched a vigorous attack on slavery and the slave trade," and in 1686 the Vatican formally condemned the transatlantic slave trade. On page 91 of his book in this citation, Richard Gray asserted, "Potentially this must have been one of the most notable statements on human rights ever to have been published by the papacy. The Catholic Church, however, was not only the church of the poor and the oppressed. . . . It was also the church of the conquistadores. . . . [T]he vested interests in Europe and the Americas ignored this condemnation."

48   Gondola, *The History of Congo*, p. 32; and J. D. Fage and William Tordoff, *A History of Africa* (Abingdon, UK: Routledge, 2002), p. 238.

49   Hochschild, *King Leopold's Ghost*, p. 64.

50   Van Reybrouck, *Congo*, p. 32.

51   Joseph Conrad, "Geography and Some Explorers," *National Geographic*, vol. 45, no. 1–6 (January–June 1924), available at http://www.ric.edu/faculty/rpotter/temp/geog_and_some.html.

52   Hochschild, *King Leopold's Ghost*, p. 118.

53   Gondola, *The History of Congo*, p. 46.

54   Van Reybrouck, *Congo*, p. 39.

55   Hochschild, *King Leopold's Ghost*, p. 37.

56   Neal Ascherson, *The King Incorporated: Leopold II in the Age of Trusts* (London: George Allen and Unwin, 1963), p. 58.

57   Hochschild, *King Leopold's Ghost*, p. 42.

58   Van Reybrouck, *Congo*, p. 39.

59 Hochschild, *King Leopold's Ghost*, p. 87.

60 Richard Mosse, *Infra*, text by Adam Hochschild (New York: Aperture; Washington, DC: Pulitzer Center on Crisis Reporting, 2012).

61 Hochschild, *King Leopold's Ghost*, pp. 120–29.

62 Hochschild, *King Leopold's Ghost*, p. 131.

63 Hochschild, *King Leopold's Ghost*, p. 135.

64 Hochschild, *King Leopold's Ghost*, pp. 136–37.

65 "The Congo profits were used to fund a grandiose policy of public works and urban improvement—in Belgium. The face of Brussels was to be transformed, and large tracts of urban land were acquired for the purpose. On completion, the buildings immediately became the property of the Belgian state. In all, the Belgian nation received property worth more than £2,400,000 from the Congo (equivalent to $3,311,110 based on a March 2018 exchange rate)." See The British Museum, *The Wealth of Africa Congo Free State* (London: British Museum, 2010), available at http://www.britishmuseum.org/pdf/congofreestate_studentsworksheets.pdf; also see Sanderson Beck, "Congo, Angola, and Mozambique 1700–1950," in *Volume 16: Mideast & Africa 1700–1950*, Ethics of Civilization 16 (Santa Barbara, CA: World Peace Communications, 2010), available at http://san.beck.org/16-13 -Congo,Angola,Mozambique.html.

66 Hochschild, *King Leopold's Ghost*, p. 224.

67 Hochschild, *King Leopold's Ghost*, pp. 226 and 233.

68 Hochschild, *King Leopold's Ghost*, pp. 315, 347; also see Isidore Ndaywel è Nziem, *Histoire générale du Congo: De l'héritage ancien à la République Démocratique* (Paris: Duculot, 1998), p. 344.

69 Hochschild, *King Leopold's Ghost*, p. 259.

70 Hochschild, *King Leopold's Ghost*, p. 277.

71 Hochschild, *King Leopold's Ghost*, p. 294.

72 Zephyr Frank and Aldo Musacchio, "The International Natural Rubber Market, 1870–1930," *EH.net Encyclopedia*, ed. Robert Whaples, March 16, 2008, available at https://eh.net/encyclopedia/the-international-natural-rubber -market-1870-1930/; Ingrid Fernandez, "The Upper Amazonian Rubber Boom and Indigenous Rights 1900–1925," in *Proceedings of the Florida Conference of Historians*, vol. 15, March 2008, pp. 51–63, available at http://fch.ju.edu/FCH -2007/Fernandez-The%20Upper%20Amazonian%20Rubber%20Boom%20 and%20Indigenous%20Rights%201900.htm; Charles Mann, "Why We (Still) Can't Live Without Rubber," *National Geographic*, December 1, 2015, available at http://www.nationalgeographic.com/magazine/2016/01/southeast-asia-rubber -boom/; "Death in the Devil's Paradise," *Survival International*, available at https:// www.survivalinternational.org/articles/3282-rubber-boom.

73 Hochschild, *King Leopold's Ghost*, p. 159.

74 Hochschild, *King Leopold's Ghost*, p. 172.

75 Mosse, *Infra*.

76 Van Reybrouck, *Congo*, p. 88.

77   See *Merci Congo*, film produced and directed by Paul Freedman, 2016, http://www. paulfreedman.net/merci-congo/.

78   W. E. B. Du Bois, "The African Roots of War," *The Atlantic*, May 1915.

79   Hochschild, *King Leopold's Ghost*, p. 164.

80   Hochschild, *King Leopold's Ghost*, p. 165.

81   Hochschild, *King Leopold's Ghost*, p. 165.

82   Van Reybrouck, *Congo*, p. 94.

83   Dhruva Jaishankar, "The Big Lie Americans Tell Themselves," *Foreign Policy*, August 9, 2014, available at http://foreignpolicy.com/2014/08/09/the-big-lie -americans-tell-themselves/.

84   Van Reybrouck, *Congo*, pp. 107–9.

85   National Park Service, "Keweenaw Copper at War," available at https://www.nps .gov/articles/keweenaw-copper-at-war.htm.

86   Charles Vickers, ed., *Transactions of the American Institute of Metals* (Buffalo, NY: American Institute of Metals, 1916), vol. 9, p. 439.

87   Van Reybrouck, *Congo*, p. 137.

88   Van Reybrouck, *Congo*, p. 118.

89   Hochschild, *King Leopold's Ghost*, p. 279.

90   Daniel Edelstein, "Copper," US Geological Survey, available at https://minerals .usgs.gov/minerals/pubs/commodity/copper/240798.pdf.

91   Susan Williams, *Spies in the Congo: America's Atomic Mission in World War II* (New York: PublicAffairs, 2016), p. 2.

92   Williams, *Spies in the Congo*, p. 2.

93   Williams, *Spies in the Congo*, p. 11.

94   Williams, *Spies in the Congo*, p. 7.

95   Williams, *Spies in the Congo*, p. 231.

96   Williams, *Spies in the Congo*, p. 248.

97   Williams, *Spies in the Congo*, p. 4.

98   Williams, *Spies in the Congo*, p. 265.

99   IRIN News, "UN Mission Denied Access to Collapsed Uranium Mine," July 21, 2004; Williams, *Spies in the Congo*, p. 277; and see Peter Waggitt, "Radiological Report on an Inter-Agency Mission to the Shinkolobwe Mine Site," International Atomic Energy Agency, Democratic Republic of Congo, October 24 to November 4, 2004, November 16, 2004, Vienna, available at http://www.maliyetu.org /documents/bibliotheque_publication/RADIOLOGICAL_REPORT.pdf.

100 Williams, *Spies in the Congo*, p. 267.

101 Williams, *Spies in the Congo*, p. 233.

102 Georges Nzongola-Ntalaja, *The Congo: From Leopold to Kabila; A People's History* (London: Zed Books, 2002), p. 259.

103 Van Reybrouck, *Congo*, p. 298.

104 Williams, *Spies in the Congo*, pp. 255–56.

105 John Gunther, *Inside Africa* (London: Hamish Hamilton, 1955), p. 662.

106 Hochschild, *King Leopold's Ghost*, p. 301.

107 Hochschild, *King Leopold's Ghost*, p. 302.

108 Williams, *Spies in the Congo*, p. 258.

109 "Telegram from the Embassy in Belgium to the Department of State," is at the Office of the Historian, Department of State, https://history.state.gov /historicaldocuments/frus1958-60v14/d136; and see Bob Feldman, "Columbia University and the Elimination of Patrice Lumumba Revisited—Part 1," *Patch*, July 21, 2017, available at https://patch.com/new-york/upper-west-side-nyc /columbia-university-elimination-patrice-lumumba-revisited-part-1.

110 "Telegram From the Central Intelligence Agency to the Station in the Congo" is at the Office of the Historian, Department of State, https://history.state.gov /historicaldocuments/frus1964-68v23/d14, from Central Intelligence Agency Files, Job 79–00149A, DDO/IMS Files, Box 23, Folder 1, African Division, Senate Select Committee, Volume II. Secret; Rybat; Priority. For COS from Ascham. Drafted by Director of Central Intelligence Allen W. Dulles. A typed notation on the telegram instructed the Cable Secretariat to "limit distribution to Mr. Helms."

111 Lawrence Devlin, *Chief of Station, Congo: A Memoir of 1960–67* (New York: PublicAffairs, 2007), p. 95.

112 Hochschild, *King Leopold's Ghost*, p. 302.

113 David Talbot, *The Devil's Chessboard: Allen Dulles, the CIA, and the Rise of America's Secret Government* (New York: HarperCollins, 2015), quoted in Feldman, "Columbia University and the Elimination of Patrice Lumumba."

114 Hochschild, *King Leopold's Ghost*, p. 302.

115 Mosse, *Infra*.

116 Ian Smillie, *Blood on the Stone: Greed, Corruption and War in the Global Diamond Trade* (London and New York: Anthem Press, 2010), p. 120.

117 Helen Winternitz, *East Along the Equator: A Journey up the Congo and into Zaire* (New York: Atlantic Monthly Press, 1987), p. 270.

118 Hochschild, *King Leopold's Ghost*, p. 303.

119 Van Reybrouck, *Congo*, p. 357.

120 Historian Adam Hochschild states that "his personal peak was estimated at $4 billion." The sources for this are Jimmy Burns and Mark Huband, "How Mobutu Built Up His $4 Billion Fortune," *Financial Times*, May 12, 1997; and Mark Milner, Chris McGreal, and Chris Barrie, "The $4 Billion Rip-off," *The Guardian*, May 13, 1997. Found in Hochschild, *King Leopold's Ghost*, p. 303.

121 Van Reybrouck, *Congo*, pp. 380–81.

122 John H. Davis, *The Guggenheims: An American Epic* (New York: SPI Books, 1994), p. 112.

123 Smillie, *Blood on the Stone*, p. 118.

124 Smillie, *Blood on the Stone*, p. 116.

125 Todd Cleveland, *Stones of Contention: A History of Africa's Diamonds* (Athens, OH: Ohio University Press, 2014), p. 10.

126 Smillie, *Blood on the Stone*, p. 119.

127 Smillie, *Blood on the Stone*, p. 122.

128 Stearns, *Dancing in the Glory of Monsters*, p. 241.

129 Smillie, *Blood on the Stone*, p. 129.

130 Stearns, *Dancing in the Glory of Monsters*, p. 247.

131 Global Witness, *Under-mining Peace: Tin; The Explosive Trade in Cassiterite in Eastern DRC* (Washington, DC: Global Witness Publishing, 2005), available at https://www.globalwitness.org/sites/default/files/pdfs/under-mining%20peace.pdf.

132 The Enough Project, *Getting to Conflict-Free: Assessing Corporate Action on Conflict Minerals*, December 2010, available at https://enoughproject.org/files/corporate _action-1.pdf.

133 Van Reybrouck, *Congo*, p. 457.

134 See "All Data Gold Price in USD/oz," Gold Price, available at https://goldprice.org /spot-gold.html.

135 Stearns, *Dancing in the Glory of Monsters*, p. 300.

136 Stearns, *Dancing in the Glory of Monsters*, pp. 297–98.

137 UN Security Council, *Interim Report of the Group of Experts on the DRC*, S/2010/252, May 24, 2010, para. 77, p. 17, available at http://www.un.org/ga /search/view_doc.asp?symbol=S/2010/252.

138 Holly Dranginis interview with Justine Masika Bihamba, Goma, DRC, July 7, 2015. See "Progress and Challenges on Conflict Minerals," Enough Project, available at https://enoughproject.org/special-topics/progress-and-challenges -conflict-minerals-facts-dodd-frank-1502.

139 Holly Dranginis interview with Lubula Igomokelo, Bukavu, DRC, July 24, 2015. See Holly Dranginis, *Point of Origin. Status Report on the Impact of Dodd-Frank 1502 in Congo*, Enough Project, February 2016, p. 6, available at https:// enoughproject.org/files/DRC_PointofOrigin_022016.pdf.

140 World Gold Council, "Gold Demand Trends, Third Quarter 2014," November 2014, p. 19, available at http://www.gold.org/supply-and-demand/gold-demand -trends.

141 Fidel Bafilemba and Sasha Lezhnev, *Congo's Conflict Gold Rush: Bringing Gold into the Legal Trade in the Democratic Republic of Congo*, Enough Project, April 2015, p. 6, available at https://enoughproject.org/files/April%2029%202015%20 Congo%20Conflict%20Gold%20Rush%20reduced.pdf.

142 Kira Zalan, "Tracing Conflict Gold in the Democratic Republic of the Congo," *Global Post*, June 23, 2017, available at https://www.pri.org/stories/2017-06-23 /tracing-conflict-gold-democratic-republic-congo.

143 Van Reybrouck, *Congo*, p. 119.

144 Van Reybrouck, *Congo*, p. 125.

145 Van Reybrouck, *Congo*, p. 455; UN Security Council, *Plundering of DR Congo Natural Resources: Final Report of the Panel of Experts*, S/2002/1146, October 16, 2002, available at https://reliefweb.int/report/burundi/plundering-dr-congo -natural-resources-finai-report-panel-experts-s20046; Koen Vlassenroot, Sandrine Perrot, and Jeroen Cuvelier, "Doing Business out of War. An Analysis of the UPDF's Presence in the Democratic Republic of Congo," *Journal of Eastern African Studies* 6, no. 1, (April 2012): 2–21, available at http://www.tandfonline.com/doi /pdf/10.1080/17531055.2012.664701.

146 Peter Eichstaedt, *Consuming the Congo: War and Conflict Minerals in the World's Deadliest Place* (Chicago: Chicago Review Press, 2011), pp. 37–39.

147 UN Security Council, *Final Report of the Group of Experts on the Democratic Republic of the Congo*, S/2015/19, pp. 3, 30–31, 100; paras. 138–39, available at http://www.securitycouncilreport.org/atf/cf/%7B65BFCF9B-6D27-4E9C-8CD3 -CF6E4FF96FF9%7D/s_2015_19.pdf.

148 Holly Dranginis, *Interrupting the Silence: Addressing Congo's Sexual Violence Crisis Within the Great Lakes Regional Peace Process*, Enough Project, March 20, 2014, p. 8, available at https://enoughproject.org/files/InterruptingtheSilence _AddressingCongosSexualViolenceCrisiswithintheGreatLakesRegionalPeaceProcess.pdf.

149 Free the Slaves, *Congo's Mining Slaves: Enslavement at South Kivu Mining Sites*, June 2013, p. 18, available at https://www.freetheslaves.net/wp-content /uploads/2015/03/Congos-Mining-Slaves-web-130622.pdf.

150 International Labour Organization International Labour Office, *Minors out of Mining! Partnership for Global Action Against Child Labour in Small-Scale Mining*, International Programme for the Elimination of Child Labour (Geneva, International Labour Office, 2006), p. 14, available at http://www.ilo.org /ipecinfo/product/viewProduct.do?productId=2519. See also Hannah Poole Hahn, Karen Hayes, and Azra Kacapor, *Breaking the Chain: Ending the Supply of Child-Mined Minerals* (Washington, DC: PACT, 2013), p. 10, available at http://www .pactworld.org/sites/default/files/PACT%20Child%20Labor%20Report%20 English%202013.pdf.

151 Enough Team, *From Child Miner to Jewelry Store: The Six Steps of Congo's Conflict Gold*, Enough Project, October 2012, available at http://www.enoughproject.org /files/Conflict-Gold.pdf; World Gold Council, "Gold Demand Trends Full Year 2014," February 12, 2015, p. 1, available at http://www.gold.org/research /gold-demand-trends. World Gold Council figures for 2014 demand indicate that 2,152.9 tonnes of gold demand went to jewelry, 904.6 tonnes went to investment demand, 477.2 tonnes went to central bank net purchases, and 389 tonnes went to technology.

152 The income estimates come from the International Peace Information Service and Sara Geenen. See Steven Spittaels et al., *Analysis of the Interactive Map of Artisanal Mining Areas in Eastern DR Congo: May 2014 Update* (Antwerp: International Peace Information Service, 2014), p. 12, available at http://ipisresearch.be/wp -content/uploads/2014/04/20141031-Promines_analysis.pdf; and Sara Geenen, "'Qui Cherche, Trouve': The Political Economy of Access to Gold Mining and

Trade in South Kivu, DRC," IOB, University of Antwerp, May 2014, p. 173, available at https://www.uantwerpen.be/popup/kalenderonderdeel.aspx?calitem _id=1098&c=LANDP289&n=222966. The debt bondage research comes from Free the Slaves, which notes, "The team leader will borrow money for tools and to pay living expenses until the mine begins to pay off, which doesn't always happen. The miners fall behind in their obligations, which can lead to debt bondage slavery." Free the Slaves, "On the Front Lines of Slavery in Congo," July 14, 2014, available at https://www.freetheslaves.net/on-the-front-lines-of-slavery-in-congo/.

153 Debt bondage is the most persistent form of slavery among those involved in the mining sector. Senior individuals such as the president director general (PDG), who own mining shafts and employ workers, enter into this form of enslavement as they generally invest money to begin production by taking loans at high rates of interest. New miners also become enslaved when they have to borrow money to sustain their daily needs before mining production begins. See Free the Slaves, *Congo's Mining Slaves*, p. 17.

154 Kevin J. Kelley, "EA Fingered in $400m Worth of DR Congo Gold Smuggled to Uganda," *The East African*, February 8, 2014, available at http://www .theeastafrican.co.ke/news/Smuggled--400m-DR-Congo-gold-fuels-war-/2558 -2198074-82g9nc/index.html.

155 Bafilemba and Lezhnev, *Congo's Conflict Gold Rush*, p. 2.

156 The Enough Project, *Breaking the Cycle: Delinking Armed Actors from the Gold Supply Chain in Congo and the Great Lakes Region Through Fiscal Reform and Anti-Money Laundering (AML)*, May 2017, p. 3, available at https://enoughproject.org /wp-content/uploads/2017/05/BreakingTheCycle_April2017_Enough_3.pdf.

157 National Institute of Statistics of Rwanda, *Formal External Trade in Goods: Fourth Quarter 2016*, Kigali, March 2017, available at http://www.statistics.gov.rw /publication/formal-external-trade-goods-statistics-report-q4-2016.

158 Ruben de Koning and the Enough Team, *Striking Gold: How M23 and its Allies Are Infiltrating Congo's Gold Trade*, Enough Project, October 2013, available at http://www.enoughproject.org/files/StrikingGold-M23-and-Allies-Infiltrating -Congo-Gold-Trade.pdf.

159 "Ntaganda Case: The Prosecutor v. Bosco Ntaganda," ICC-01/04-02/06, International Criminal Court, accessed March 2, 2018, available at https://www .icc-cpi.int/drc/ntaganda; Wairagala Wakabi, "Ntaganda's Witnesses Complete Testifying at the ICC," *International Justice Monitor*, February 16, 2018, available at https://www.ijmonitor.org/2018/02/ntagandas-witnesses-complete-testifying-at -the-icc/.

160 PricewaterhouseCoopers (PwC), *Corporate Income Taxes, Mining Royalties and Other Mining Taxes: A Summary of Rates and Rules in Selected Countries*, June 2012, available at https://www.pwc.com/gx/en/energy-utilities-mining/publications/pdf /pwc-gx-mining-taxes-and-royalties.pdf.

161 Bafilemba and Lezhnev, *Congo's Conflict Gold Rush*, p. 1.

162 Virunga National Park, "About Virunga National Park," Virunga National Park, accessed August 2017, available at http://visitvirunga.org/about-virunga/.

163 *Virunga*, written and directed by Orlando von Einsiedal (Grain Media and Violet Films, 2014), available at http://virungamovie.com/.

164 WikiLeaks US State Department Embassy Cables, "Virunga Park Report: Tentative Agreement by Rebel Group to Maintain Conservation Efforts in the Gorilla Sector," December 12, 2008, available at https://wikileaks.org/plusd /cables/08KINSHASA1099_a.html.

165 The Enough Project, Digital Globe, and African Parks, *Poachers Without Borders* (Longmont, CO: Digital Globe, January 28, 2015), p. 1, available at http://www .enoughproject.org/files/PoachersWithoutBorders_28Jan2015.pdf.

166 UN Security Council, *Final Report of the Group of Experts*, S/2016/466, May 23, 2016, para. 169; and *Midterm Report of the Group of Experts on the Democratic Republic of the Congo*, S/2016/1102, December 28, 2016, paras. 90, 93, available http://www.un.org/ga/search/view_doc.asp?symbol=S/2016/1102a.

167 See Ledio Cakaj and Sasha Lezhnev, *Deadly Profits: Illegal Wildlife Trafficking Through Uganda and South Sudan*, Enough Project, July 13, 2017, available at https://enoughproject.org/reports/deadly-profits-illegal-wildlife-trafficking.

168 African Parks and the Institut Congolais pour la Conservation de la Nature, "Poaching Onslaught in Garamba National Park," African Parks, press release, June 12, 2014, available at https://www.african-parks.org/newsroom/press-releases /poaching-onslaught-garamba-national-park.

169 "Garamba," African Parks, available at https://www.african-parks.org/the-parks /garamba.

170 Merrit Kennedy, "Good News for Elephants: China's Price of Ivory Has Plummeted," National Public Radio, March 29, 2017, available at http://www.npr .org/sections/thetwo-way/2017/03/29/521935285/good-news-for-elephants-chinas -price-of-ivory-has-plummeted.

171 Ledio Cakaj, "Tusk Wars: Inside the LRA and the Bloody Business of Ivory," *The Enough Project* (blog), October 2015, available at https://enoughproject.org/blog /tusk-wars-inside-lra-and-bloody-business-ivory.

172 Kennedy, "Good News for Elephants."

173 UN Security Council, *Midterm Report of the Group of Experts*, S/2016/1102, December 28, 2016, p. 18.

174 Jeffrey Gettleman, "Oil Dispute Takes a Page from Congo's Bloody Past," *New York Times*, November 15, 2014, available at https://www.nytimes.com /2014/11/16/world/oil-dispute-takes-a-page-from-congos-bloody-past.html.

175 Gettleman, "Oil Dispute Takes a Page."

176 Marc Santora, "SOCO Oil Company Paid Large Sums to Officer in Congo, Activists Say," *New York Times*, June 9, 2015, available at https://www.nytimes .com/2015/06/10/world/africa/soco-oil-company-paid-large-sums-to-officer-in -congo-activists-say.html.

177 Scott Ramsay, "Interview with Emmanuel de Merode, Director of Virunga National Park," *National Geographic* (blog), May 12, 2017, at https://blog .nationalgeographic.org/2017/05/12/interview-with-emmanuel-de-merode -director-of-virunga-national-park/.

178 Andrew J. Plumptre et al., "Status of Grauer's Gorilla and Chimpanzees in Eastern Democratic Republic of Congo: Historical and Current Distribution and Abundance," unpublished report to Arcus Foundation, USAID, and US Fish and Wildlife Service, April 2016, p. 38, available at http://fscdn.wcs.org/2016/04/04 /inhumeq9_Status_of_Grauers_gorilla_and_eastern_chimpanzee_Report_Final .pdf; and see Stuart Nixon and Holly Dranginis, "The Threat to Grauer's Gorillas," interview by Tom Ashbrook, *On Point*, May 6, 2016, available at http://wbur.org /onpoint/2016/05/06/the-threat-to-grauers-gorillas.

179 Plumptre et al., "Status of Grauer's Gorilla," p. 1.

180 Simon Worrall, "A Prince Battles to Save Gorillas amid Brutal Conflict," *National Geographic*, June 11, 2015, available at https://news.nationalgeographic .com/2015/06/150611-virunga-national-park-emmanuel-de-merode-africa-world/.

181 Ben Anderson, *VICE*, Season 5, episode 22, "Controlling the Narrative & Power to Congo," aired August 18, 2017, on HBO, http://www.imdb.com/title/tt7289614/.

182 This section is adapted from an Enough Project report by Holly Dranginis. See Holly Dranginis, *The Mafia in the Park: A Charcoal Syndicate Is Threatening Virunga, Africa's Oldest National Park*, Enough Project, June 2016, available at https://enoughproject.org/files/report_MafiaInThePark_Dranginis_Enough _June2016.pdf.

183 Holly Dranginis and Fidel Bafilemba interviews with a source who works in Virunga, July 10, 2015; Gilbert Dilis and Daniel Ruiz, Goma, July 2015. See Dranginis, *The Mafia in the Park*, p. 7.

184 Dranginis and Bafilemba interview with source in Virunga, July 10, 2015. See Dranginis, *The Mafia in the Park*, p. 7.

185 Dranginis, *The Mafia in the Park*, p. 7.

186 Dranginis, *The Mafia in the Park*, p. 1.

187 Reliable, up-to-date information on revenues from illegal charcoal requires further research. Estimates gathered during Enough Project research varied. In an interview with an ICCN official, the source estimated the trade was valued at $30+ million per year. In an interview with the Enough Project, another source close to Virunga said the trade is worth $35 million per year. In a confidential 2014 study by MONUSCO Joint Mission Analysis Centre (JMAC) viewed by the Enough Project, MONUSCO reported that ICCN estimated that illegal charcoal production generates around $35 million annually and stated that the claim needs further research. (United States Organization Stabilization Mission in the Democratic Republic of Congo [MONUSCO], "JMAC NTF: FDLR Incorporated? The Movement's Business Model at a Crossroads," July 2014, viewed by the Enough Project.) An April 2015 study published jointly by MONUSCO and the UN Environment Programme (UNEP) and the Office of the Special Envoy of the Secretary-General for the Great Lakes Region (OSESG), said a conservative estimate of the annual net profits to organized crime derived from charcoal is $12–$35 million. (UNEP-MONUSCO-OSESG, *Experts' Background Report on Illegal Exploitation and Trade in Natural Resources Benefitting Organized Criminal Groups and Recommendations on MONUSCO's Role in Fostering Stability and Peace in Eastern DR Congo: Final Report April 15th, 2015*, available at http://postconflict .unep.ch/publications/UNEP_DRCongo_MONUSCO_OSESG_final_report.pdf.)

188 Holly Dranginis and Fidel Bafilemba interview with a Virunga park ranger who requested anonymity, Goma, July 2015. See Dranginis, *The Mafia in the Park*, p. 1.

189 MONUSCO, "JMAC NTF: FDLR Incorporated?"

190 Holly Dranginis and Fidel Bafilemba interview with Jeredy Kambale Malonga, Goma, July 2015. See Dranginis, *The Mafia in the Park*, p. 2.

191 MONUSCO, "JMAC NTF: FDLR Incorporated?" p. 3.

192 Dranginis, *The Mafia in the Park*, p. 9.

193 James West, "Short Tesla Motors Inc.? Robert Fridland and the Coming Cobalt Cliff," *eCobalt*, January 18, 2017, available at http://www.ecobalt.com/news/cobalt -news/short-tesla-motors-inc-robert-fridland-and-the-coming-cobalt-cliff.

194 US Geological Survey, *Cobalt*, Mineral Commodity Summaries, January 2017, available at https://minerals.usgs.gov/minerals/pubs/commodity/cobalt/mcs-2017 -cobal.pdf.

195 Thomas Wilson, "We'll All Be Relying on Congo to Power Our Electric Cars," *Bloomberg*, October 26, 2017, p. 2, available at https://www.bloomberg.com/news /articles/2017-10-26/battery-boom-relies-on-one-african-nation-avoiding-chaos -of-past.

196 Jessica Shankleman et al., "We're Going to Need More Lithium," *Bloomberg Businessweek*, September 7, 2017, available at https://www.bloomberg.com /graphics/2017-lithium-battery-future/.

197 Todd C. Frankel, "The Cobalt Pipeline: Tracing the Path from Deadly Hand-Dug Mines in Congo to Consumers' Phones and Laptops," *Washington Post*, September 30, 2016, available at https://www.washingtonpost.com/graphics/business /batteries/congo-cobalt-mining-for-lithium-ion-battery/.

198 David Stringer, "Race Is On to Mine Metal Powering Electric Vehicles," *Bloomberg Technology*, June 9, 2017, available at https://www.bloomberg.com/news /articles/2017-06-08/cobalt-upstarts-eye-glencore-s-turf-for-244-billion-ev-spoils.

199 Stringer, "Race Is On."

200 Greg Klein, "Cobalt's Congo Conundrum," *Resource Clips*, May 18, 2017, available at http://resourceclips.com/2017/05/03/cobalt%E2%80%99s-congo-conundrum/.

201 Wilson, "We'll All Be Relying on Congo," p. 3.

202 Jim Edwards, "This Child Being Abused in a Cobalt Mine Is Why Apple Is Trying to Fix the Mining Business," *Business Insider*, May 15, 2017, available at http:// www.businessinsider.com/apple-cobalt-mine-child-labor-2017-5.

203 Frankel, "The Cobalt Pipeline."

204 CBS News, "CBS News Finds Children Mining Cobalt for Batteries in the Congo," March 5, 2018, available at https://www.cbsnews.com/news/cobalt -children-mining-democratic-republic-congo-cbs-news-investigation/.

205 CBS News, "CBS Finds Children Mining."

206 Frankel, "The Cobalt Pipeline."

207 Benjamin Faber, Benjamin Krause, and Raúl Sánchez De La Sierra, *Artisanal Mining, Livelihoods, and Child Labor in the Cobalt Supply Chain of the Democratic*

Republic of Congo (Berkeley, CA: Center for Effective Global Action, May 6, 2017), policy report, available at http://cega.berkeley.edu/assets/cega_research _projects/179/CEGA_Report_v2.pdf.

208 Lily Kuo, "The 'Blood Diamond' Magnate Who Is at the Center of Och-Ziff's Bribery Scandal in Africa," Quartz Africa, September 30, 2016, available at https:// qz.com/797182/dan-gertler-the-blood-diamond-magnate-at-the-center-of-och -ziffs-bribery-scandal-in-africa/.

209 William Clowes and Thomas Wilson, "Congo's Gecamines' Accounts Missing $750 million, Group Says," *Bloomberg Markets*, November 3, 2017, available at https://www.bloomberg.com/news/articles/2017-11-03/congo-s-gecamines -accounts-missing-750-million-group-says.

210 Faber, Krause, and De La Sierra, *Artisanal Mining*.

211 Frankel, "The Cobalt Pipeline."

Chapter 4

212 An important Enough Project publication that informed this chapter is Sasha Lezhnev, *A Criminal State: Understanding and Countering Institutionalized Corruption and Violence in the Democratic Republic of Congo*, Enough Project, October 2016, available at https://enoughproject.org/files/A_Criminal_State _Enough_Oct2016_web.pdf; also, Professor Pierre Englebert, H. Russell Smith Professor of International Relations and Professor of African Politics at Pomona College, provided significant input to that Enough Project report.

213 Term coined by Tom Burgis of the *Financial Times*. See Tom Burgis, *The Looting Machine: Warlords, Oligarchs, Corporations, Smugglers, and the Theft of Africa's Wealth* (New York: PublicAffairs, 2015).

214 Michela Wrong, *In the Footsteps of Mr. Kurtz: Living on the Brink of Disaster in Mobutu's Congo* (New York: HarperCollins, 2001), p. 11.

215 Sarah Chayes, *Thieves of State: Why Corruption Threatens Global Security* (New York: W. W. Norton, 2015).

216 Stearns, *Dancing in the Glory of Monsters*, pp. 322 and 331.

Chapter 5

217 Human Rights Watch, *Rwanda/Zaire: Rearming with Impunity: International Support for the Perpetrators of the Rwandan Genocide*, Human Rights Watch Arms Project, vol. 7, no. 4 (London: Human Rights Watch, 1995), p. 1, available at https://www.hrw.org/reports/1995/Rwanda1.htm.

218 Stearns, *Dancing in the Glory of Monsters*, p. 44.

219 Philip Roessler and Harry Verhoeven, *Why Comrades Go to War: Liberation Politics and the Outbreak of Africa's Deadliest Conflict* (Oxford: Oxford University Press, 2016), pp. 10–11.

220 Van Reybrouck, *Congo*, pp. 423–24.

221 Stearns, *Dancing in the Glory of Monsters*, p. 106.

222 Stearns, *Dancing in the Glory of Monsters*, p. 137.

223 UN Office of the High Commissioner for Human Rights, *Democratic Republic of the Congo, 1993–2003: Report of the Mapping Exercise Documenting the Most Serious Violations of Human Rights and International Humanitarian Law Committed Within the Territory of the Democratic Republic of the Congo Between March 1993 and June 2003*, August 2010, p. 279, available at http://www.ohchr.org/Documents /Countries/CD/DRC_MAPPING_REPORT_FINAL_EN.pdf.

224 Stearns, *Dancing in the Glory of Monsters*, p. 79.

225 Van Reybrouck, *Congo*, p. 426.

226 Roessler and Verhoeven, *Why Comrades Go to War*, p. 21.

227 Van Reybrouck, *Congo*, p. 439.

228 Van Reybrouck, *Congo*, pp. 442 and 449.

229 Stearns, *Dancing in the Glory of Monsters*, pp. 250–51.

230 Van Reybrouck, *Congo*, p. 454.

231 Peter Abbott, *Modern African Wars (4): The Congo 1960–2002* (Oxford, UK: Osprey, 2014), pp. 41–42.

232 Stearns, *Dancing in the Glory of Monsters*, p. 295.

233 Ryan Gosling and John Prendergast, "Congo's Conflict Minerals: The Next Blood Diamonds," *Huffington Post*, *The World Post*, available at https://www .huffingtonpost.com/ryan-gosling/congos-conflict-minerals-_b_854023.html.

Chapter 7

234 Dranginis, *Interrupting the Silence*, p. 1.

235 Holly Dranginis, email exchange with authors, November 6, 2017.

236 BBC News, "UN Official Calls DR Congo 'Rape Capital of the World,'" April 28, 2010, available at http://news.bbc.co.uk/1/hi/world/africa/8650112.stm.

237 Justine Masika Bihamba, "The 'Rape Capital of the World'? We Women in Congo Don't See it That Way," *The Guardian*, October 9, 2017, available at https://www .theguardian.com/global-development/2017/oct/09/the-rape-capital-of-the-world -we-women-in-democratic-republic-congo-dont-see-it-that-way.

238 Justine Masika, "The 'Rape Capital of the World'?"

239 US Government Accountability Office, *The Democratic Republic of Congo: Information on the Rate of Sexual Violence in War-torn Eastern DRC and Adjoining Countries*, July 13, 2011, p. 17, available at http://www.gao.gov/products/GAO -11-702; and United Nations Office for Project Services, United Nations Office for Project Services, "Gathering Data to Improve Lives in DR Congo," available at https://reliefweb.int/report/democratic-republic-congo/gathering-data-improve -lives-dr-congo.

240 Dranginis, *Interrupting the Silence*, p. 3.

241 *The Prosecutor v. Jean-Paul Akayesu (Trial Judgment)*, ICTR-96-4-T, International Criminal Tribunal for Rwanda (ICTR), September 2, 1998, available at http:// www.refworld.org/docid/40278fbb4.html; and *Prosecutor v. Dragoljub Kunarac, Radomir Kovac and Zoran Vukovic (Trial Judgment)*, IT-96-23-T & IT-96-23/1-T,

International Criminal Tribunal for the former Yugoslavia (ICTY), February 22, 2001, available at http://www.refworld.org/docid/3ae6b7560.html.

242 Dranginis, *Interrupting the Silence*, p. 5.

243 Dranginis, *Interrupting the Silence*, p. 5.

244 Human Rights First, *Dr. Denis Mukwege: Fighting Sexual Violence in the Democratic Republic of Congo*, Video, October 23, 2013, available at https://www.youtube.com/watch?v=r-OrOE4eq2w#t=74.

245 Megan Bradley, "Sexual and Gender-based Violence in the Democratic Republic of the Congo: Opportunities for Progress as M23 Disarms?" *Brookings Institution*, November 13, 2013, available at http://www.brookings.edu/blogs/africa-in-focus/posts/2013/11/12-sexual-gender-based-violence-congo-bradley#.

246 Géraldine Mattioli-Zeltner, "Justice on Trial: Lessons from the Minova Rape Case in the Democratic Republic of Congo," Human Rights Watch, October 1, 2015, available at https://www.hrw.org/report/2015/10/01/justice-trial/lessons-minova-rape-case-democratic-republic-congo.

247 Mattioli-Zeltner, "Justice on Trial."

248 Fiona Lloyd-Davies, "A Culture of Impunity Still Exists Around Sexual Violence in Conflict," *The Guardian*, June 19, 2017, available at https://www.theguardian.com/global-development-professionals-network/2017/jun/19/culture-impunity-sexual-violence-congo.

249 Van Reybrouck, *Congo*, p. 460.

250 This is a reference to when someone has had enough and decides to do something about it. See John Prendergast and Don Cheadle, *The Enough Moment: Fighting to End Africa's Worst Human Rights Crimes* (New York: Three Rivers Press, 2010).

Chapter 9

251 Nzongola-Ntalaja, *The Congo: From Leopold to Kabila*, p. 3.

252 International Crisis Group, *Boulevard of Broken Dreams: The "Street" and Politics in DR Congo*, Africa Briefing No. 123, October 13, 2016, p. 9, available at https://d2071andvip0wj.cloudfront.net/b123-boulevard-of-broken-dreams-the-street-and-politics-in-dr-congo.pdf.

253 "Congo's War Was Bloody. It May Be About to Start Again," *The Economist*, February 15, 2018, available at https://www.economist.com/news/briefing/21737021-president-joseph-kabila-seventh-year-five-year-term-he-struggling-hold.

254 International Crisis Group, *Boulevard of Broken Dreams*, pp. 10–11.

255 Justine Masika, "The 'Rape Capital of the World'?"

256 Parts of this section thanks to Holly Dranginis, policy analyst for The Sentry, briefings for authors, September 2017.

257 Human Rights Watch, "DR Congo: Deadly Crackdown on Protests," January 24, 2015, available at https://www.hrw.org/news/2015/01/24/dr-congo-deadly-crackdown-protests.

258 See Amnesty International, "DRC: Chilling Crackdown on Dissent Amidst Election Delays," Amnesty International, September 2016, available at https://www.amnesty.org/en/latest/news/2016/09/drc-chilling-crackdown-on-dissent-amidst-election-delays/.

259 Ida Sawyer, "Scores of Arrests During Protests Across DR Congo," Human Rights Watch, *Democratic Republic of Congo in Crisis* (blog), July 31, 2017, available at https://www.hrw.org/blog-feed/democratic-republic-congo-crisis.

260 "Congo, Democratic Republic of (Kinshasa)," Freedom House, available at https://freedomhouse.org/report/freedom-world/2015/congo-democratic-republic-kinshasa.

261 "195 Congolese Civil Society Organizations Welcome Individual Sanctions Imposed by EU and US," Enough Project, available at https://enoughproject.org/blog/195-congolese-civil-society-organizations-welcome-individual-sanctions-imposed-eu-us.

262 *Manifeste du Citoyen Congolais*, "Manifesto of the Congolese Citizen," Paris, August 18, 2017, available at http://www.manifesterdc.com/manifeste/.

Chapter 10

263 Hochschild, *King Leopold's Ghost*, p. 180.

264 Hochschild, *King Leopold's Ghost*, p. 2.

265 George Washington Williams, "An Open Letter to His Serene Majesty Leopold II, King of the Belgians and Sovereign of the Independent State of Congo," BlackPast.org, available at http://www.blackpast.org/george-washington-williams-open-letter-king-leopold-congo-1890; Adelaide Cromwell Hill and Martin Kilson, eds., *Apropos of Africa: Sentiments of American Negro Leaders on Africa from the 1800s to the 1950s* (Abingdon, UK: Routledge, 1969).

266 Pamela Newkirk, *Spectacle: The Astonishing Life of Ota Benga* (New York: HarperCollins, 2015), p. 23.

267 Hochschild, *King Leopold's Ghost*, p. 114.

268 Hochschild, *King Leopold's Ghost*, p. 173.

269 Newkirk, *Spectacle*, p. 95.

270 Hochschild, *King Leopold's Ghost*, p. 315.

271 Marvin D. Markowitz, "The Missions and Political Development in the Congo," *Africa*, vol. 40, no. 3, July 1970, pp. 234, 236–37, available at https://www.jstor.org/stable/1158884?seq=1#page_scan_tab_contents.

272 King Leopold II, Letter to Belgian missionaries about to leave for Congo, 1883, in Ethiotoday, "Do Modern Missionaries Have a Hidden Agenda in Ethiopia(Africa)?" CNN iReport, January 3, 2010, available at http://ireport.cnn.com/docs/DOC-377577.

273 Hochschild, *King Leopold's Ghost*, p. 188.

274 Hochschild, *King Leopold's Ghost*, p. 194.

275 Hochschild, *King Leopold's Ghost*, p. 200.

276 Hochschild, *King Leopold's Ghost*, p. 207.

277 Hochschild, *King Leopold's Ghost*, pp. 209 and 213.

278 Hochschild, *King Leopold's Ghost*, p. 216.

279 Mark Twain, *King Leopold's Soliloquy: A Defense of His Congo Rule* (Boston: P. R. Warren, 1905).

280 Hochschild, *King Leopold's Ghost*, p. 242.

281 Hochschild, *King Leopold's Ghost*, pp. 248–49.

282 Hochschild, *King Leopold's Ghost*, p. 271.

283 Hochschild, *King Leopold's Ghost*, p. 273.

284 Hochschild, *King Leopold's Ghost*, pp. 305–6.

285 UN Security Council, *Final Report of the Panel of Experts on the Illegal Exploitation of Natural Resources and Other Forms of Wealth in the Democratic Republic of Congo*, S/2001/357, April 12, 2001, para. 215, available at http:// http://www.securitycouncilreport.org/atf/cf/%7B65BFCF9B-6D27-4E9C-8CD3-CF6E4FF96FF9%7D/DRC%20S%202001%20357.pdf.

286 Aloys Tegera and Dominic Johnson, *Rules for Sale: Formal and Informal Cross-Border Trade in Eastern DRC* (Goma: Pole Institute, 2007), p. 40, available at http://www.pole-institute.org/sites/default/files/regard19_anglais.pdf.

287 UN Security Council, *Final Report of the Group of Exports on the Democratic Republic of the Congo*, S/2008/773, December 12, 2008, p. 19, available at http://www.un.org/ga/search/view_doc.asp?symbol=S/2008/773.

288 The Enough Project and the Grassroots Reconciliation Group, *A Comprehensive Approach to Congo's Conflict Minerals*, April 2009, p. 3, available at https://enoughproject.org/reports/comprehensive-approach-conflict-minerals-strategy-paper.

289 The Enough Project and the Grassroots Reconciliation Group, *A Comprehensive Approach*.

290 For example, John Prendergast and Sasha Lezhnev, "Opinion: Electronics Companies and Consumers Can Help Stop Congolese Bloodshed," *San Jose Mercury News*, July 28, 2009, available at http://www.mercurynews.com/2009/07/28/opinion-electronics-companies-and-consumers-can-help-stop-congolese-bloodshed/.

291 The episode is available at https://www.cbsnews.com/news/how-gold-pays-for-congos-deadly-war/. Also see Laura Heaton, "Congo Gold Episode of '60 Minutes' Nominated for Emmy," *The Enough Project* (blog), July 16, 2010, available at https://enoughproject.org/blog/congo-gold-episode-60-minutes-nominated-emmy.

292 Sasha Lezhnev, "From Brainstorming to the NYTimes Buzzword List," *The Enough Project* (blog), December 21, 2009, available at https://enoughproject.org/blog/brainstorming-nytimes-buzzword-list.

293 The Enough Project, *Getting to Conflict-Free*.

294 For example, rb137, "Please Help 11th Hour Vote on the New Blood Diamonds," *Daily Kos*, June 23, 2010, available at https://www.dailykos.com/stories/2010/6/23/878780/-#c7.

295 Enough Team, "11 Letters from Congolese Civil Society Groups in Support of the U.S. Conflict Minerals Law," *The Enough Project* (blog), April 4, 2017, available at https://enoughproject.org/blog/seven-letters-congolese-groups-support-us-conflict -minerals-law.

296 Thematic Working Group on Mining and Natural Resources, "An Appeal from the Civil Society Organizations of South Kivu in the Democratic Republic of Congo in Reaction to the Announcement Made by the Security and Exchange Commission (SEC) Regarding the Trump Administration's Decision to Issue an Executive Order Aiming at Suspending the Dodd-Frank Act ('The Obama Law')," February 18, 2017, available at https://www.sec.gov/comments/statement-013117 /cll2-1597728-132417.pdf.

297 Denis Mukwege, "Statement from Dr. Denis Mukwege: European Parliament Vote on Binding Conflict Minerals Legislation 'Is a Victory for Human Rights'," April 18, 2016, available at http://www.panzifoundation.org/blog/2016/4/18/statement -from-dr-denis-mukwege-eu-vote-is-a-victory-for-human-rights.

298 GC Conflict Free Campus Initiative, "Procurement Policy Addresses Conflict Minerals and Electronics," Facebook, June 13, 2016, available at https://www .facebook.com/GCCFCI/posts/1702803553303651.

299 http://cosoc-gl.org/wp-content/uploads/2018/03/Bulletin_MRC-CTC_vf2017121 .pdf.

300 UN Security Council, *Interim Report of the Group of Experts*, S/2010/252, May 24, 2010, para. 77, p.17.

301 IPIS surveyed 2,026 mines. However, 64 percent of gold miners still work at conflict mines. Yannick Weyns, Lotte Hoex, and Ken Matthysen, *Analysis of the Interactive Map of Artisanal Mining Areas in Eastern DR Congo: 2015 Update* (Antwerp: International Peace Information Service, 2016), p. 4, available at http:// ipisresearch.be/wp-content/uploads/2016/10/Mapping-minerals-in-eastern-DR -Congo_v005.pdf.

Chapter 11

302 Nicholas Kristof, "Death by Gadget," *New York Times*, June 26, 2010, available at http://www.nytimes.com/2010/06/27/opinion/27kristof.html.

303 Brian X. Chen, "In E-mail, Steve Jobs Comments on iPhone 4 Minerals," *Wired*, available at https://www.wired.com/2010/06/steve-jobs-iphone4/.

Chapter 12

304 Lezhnev, *A Criminal State*, p. 3.

305 The Enough Project, *Breaking the Cycle*.

306 UN Security Council, *Final Report of the Group of Experts*, S/2016/466, May 23, 2016.

307 Dranginis, *Point of Origin*.

308 UN Security Council, *Midterm Report of the Group of Experts*, S/2016/1102, December 28, 2016, p.16.

309 UN Security Council, *Final Report of the Group of Experts*, S/2016/466, May 23, 2016.

310 UN Security Council, *Final Report of the Group of Experts*, S/2016/466, May 23, 2016, p. 2.

311 For more information on this topic, see recent reports on this issue: The Enough Project, *Breaking the Cycle*; and Bafilemba and Lezhnev, *Congo's Conflict Gold Rush*.

312 Compare full-year gold demand with jewelry gold demand at World Gold Council, "Gold Demand Trends Full Year 2017," February 6, 2018, available at https:// www.gold.org/research/gold-demand-trends/gold-demand-trends-full-year-2017; and also "Distribution of Global Gold Demand by Industry in 2017," Statista, 2018, available at https://www.statista.com/statistics/299609/gold-demand-by -industry-sector-share/.

313 The Enough Project, *Breaking the Cycle*; and Bafilemba and Lezhnev, *Congo's Conflict Gold Rush*.

314 Annie Callaway, *Demand the Supply: Ranking Consumer Electronics and Jewelry Retail Companies on Their Efforts to Develop Conflict-Free Minerals Supply Chains from Congo*, Enough Project, November 2017, p. 19, available at https:// enoughproject.org/reports/demand-the-supply.

315 John Prendergast, "How Congo Defeated the M23 Rebels," *Daily Beast*, November 7, 2013, available at https://www.thedailybeast.com/how-congo-defeated-the-m23-rebels.

316 Aaron Hall and Akshaya Kumar, *Coordinated International Leverage: The Missing Element from Congo's Peace Process*, Enough Project, February 2013, p. 5, available at https://enoughproject.org/files/Coordinated_International_Leverage.pdf.

317 *This Is Congo*, directed by Daniel McCabe (Democratic Republic of the Congo: Vision Entertainment, S2BN Films, Sabotage Films Vienna, Zero Line Films, 2017). See https://www.thisiscongo.com.

318 de Koning and the Enough Team, *Striking Gold*.

Chapter 13

319 Chip Heath and Dan Heath, *Switch: How to Change Things When Change is Hard* (New York: Random House, 2010), pp. 39, 44, and 48

320 Dr. Martin Luther King Jr., "The Three Dimensions of a Complete Life," New Covenant Baptist Church, Chicago, Illinois, April 9, 1967. Brought to our attention during a speech by Samantha Power and available at https://www .drmartinlutherkingjr.com/thethreedimensionsofacompletelife.htm.

Conclusion

321 First cited in John Prendergast, "Hope for an End to World's Deadliest War," CNN, February 22, 2013, available at http://www.cnn.com/2013/02/22/opinion /prendergast-congo-2/index.html.

322 Hochschild, *King Leopold's Ghost*, p. 301.

323 Van Reybrouck, *Congo*, p. 556.

324 "ICT Facts and Figures 2017," International Telecommunications Union, Excel document, available at https://www.itu.int/en/ITU-D/Statistics/Pages/facts /default.aspx.

325 Robert Mattes and Michael Bratton, "Do Africans Still Want Democracy?" Afrobarometer Policy Paper No. 36, November 2016, p. 14, available at http:// afrobarometer.org/sites/default/files/publications/Policy%20papers/ab_r6 _policypaperno36_do_africans_want_democracy.pdf.

326 Karen Rothmyer, "Hiding the Real Africa: Why NGOs Prefer Bad News," *Columbia Journalism Review*, March/April 2011, available at http://archives.cjr.org /reports/hiding_the_real_africa.php.

327 Rothmyer, "Hiding the Real Africa."

Index

Quaranto, Peter, 238

radioactivity in Congo from mining uranium, 36
Raia Mutomboki militia, 271
Ramazani, Emmanuel, 7
Ramsdell, Michael, 263
rape, 2–4, 31, 47, 49, 51, 75, 78, 93, 96, 105–116, 130, 137, 150, 186, 200–202, 235, 246–247, 256–257, 235
    Chouchou Namegabe on, 109–111
    lack of judicial prosecution, 111
    of baby girls, 111, 130–131
Rawls, Caspar, 67
RCD (Rally for Congolese Democracy), 144, 146
Reagan, Ronald, 41
reform efforts in Congo, 211–217
refugees, 297
    camps, 87–89, 150
    aid agencies for, 93
Resolve (group), 266
Restrictions of Hazardous Substances (European regulation), 48
Rhodes, Derick, 250–251
RIM supply chain reforms, 237
rivers as resource, 296
Robinson, Mary, 246
Rodgers, Aaron, 243
Roessler, Philip, 90
Roosevelt, Franklin D., 34
Roosevelt, Theodore, 32, 226, 229
rubber, terror, 20, 28, 30–32, 228–229, 274
Rwanda Revenue Authority (RRA), 144
Rwanda, xiii
    diamond interests in Congo, 44
    genocide in, 62, 71, 87–92, 107, 134
    gold mining in Congo, 50–52
    invasion of Congo, 44–47, 50–51, 88–90, 137–139, 144, 151
    massacre of Hutu militias, 47
    mineral exploitation in Congo by, 47, 48–49, 235
    smuggling income, 48, 262

Salah, Salim, 51
Sanneh, Lamin, 24
Save Darfur campaign, 265–266
Save the Children (organization), 139
scale, importance of, 281–285
Sentry, The, 49, 51, 105, 259
Sese Seko, Mobutu, xiii, 40–42, 60, 79, 133, 212
    coup by, 41
    diamond revenues to, 44
    fall, 44

homes owned by, 41
    kleptocracy by, 78
    nationalization of uranium mine, 41
    overthrown, 89
    parties thrown by, 42
    support for Rwandan Hutu, 88
    US financial support of, 41
sexual and gender-based violence (SGBV), 47–49, 51, 103, 105–132
    decline in Congo, 110
Shabunda, Congo, 4
Shannon, Lisa, 249–250
Sheppard, William, 226
    photographs by, 227
Shinkolobwe mine, Congo, 34–36, 37, 37, 39
Sierra Leone, 263, 268
Signet Jewelers, conflict gold and, 261
slave trade, transatlantic, xii, 5–6, 16–17, 20
    contributing to breakdown of Kongo Kingdom, 17, 23
smelting/smelters, 14, 33, 234–237, 243, 251, 253–254
Smillie, Ian, 43
Smith, Gayle, 266
social media in Congo, 213
Société Internationale Forestière at Minière du Congo (Forminière), 43
SOCO oil company, drilling in Virunga, Congo, 56
SOS Africa (group), 146
South Africa, apartheid, 217, 232, 265, 268
South Sudan, 281–283
    kleptocracy in, 282
    Lost Boys of, 282–283
Soviet Union, 37–41
Spain, Kongo diplomats in, 15
Spectacle (book), 273
Spies in the Congo (book), 35
STAND (student anti-genocide organization), 240
Stanley Henry Morton, 27
Stearns, Jason, 49, 79, 89, 91
stereotypes of Congo by Europe and US, 272–273
    countering, 273–280
stereotypes of Kongo by Europe, 16
stones, xii
    exploitation of, 6, 21
Strong Roots Congo (NGO), 60
student movements, in US against conflict minerals, 232–244
Sudan, 91
suffering of Congolese, 4, 9–10
Sullivan, David, presentation to Apple, 252

World War II, 6, 20, 33–36, 275
    industrial diamonds during, 43
World's Fair (1958), Belgium, 273
Wright, Robin, 243

Yaka uprising, 28
Yemen, 283–285
    civil war in, 283–284
    direct trade in, 284
Yole!Africa Cultural Center, 71–75
    civic engagement by, 74
    funding, 74

Youth movements, 212–214
YouTube, 250

Zaire, xiii, 5
    name change back to Congo, 90
    renamed from Congo, 41
    US financial support of, 41
Zimbabwe, 89–92
    diamond interests in Congo, 44
zinc, 296
Zinn, Howard, vii

About the Contributors

FIDEL BAFILEMBA is a Congolese field researcher who coordinates a civil society network called GATT-RN.

JOHN PRENDERGAST is a *New York Times* bestselling author who founded and runs both the Enough Project and The Sentry.

RYAN GOSLING is an actor and filmmaker.

CHOUCHOU NAMEGABE is a Congolese journalist.

SORAYA AZIZ SOULEYMANE is a Congolese development specialist.

DAVE EGGERS is a writer and co-founder of the International Congress of Youth Voices.

SAM ILUS is a Congolese artist.

SASHA LEZHNEV is a Congo analyst.

ANNIE CALLAWAY is a human rights advocate.

DR. NAMEGABE MURHABAZI is a Congolese children's rights advocate.

Final Thought from John

In April 2018, Ryan and I accompanied my wife, Sia Sanneh, a staff member of the Equal Justice Initiative (EJI), to EJI's headquarters in Montgomery, Alabama. There we had the honor of attending the official opening of the National Memorial for Peace and Justice, a poignant reminder of the history of racial terror here in the United States. We had the opportunity to listen to the extraordinary Bryan Stevenson, the founder of EJI, which created the memorial and the accompanying Legacy Museum, which traces America's history of enslavement to mass incarceration. Bryan's inspiring words throughout that week outlined a number of themes that also happen to precisely explain why we decided to do this book.

First, there is the critical lesson we all learn in school that we need to understand the mistakes of history in order to not repeat them. Beyond that, there is simply no way to begin healing unless historical wounds are acknowledged and addressed. We need to better understand and more honestly acknowledge the truth behind our shared history. We must understand abusive and unjust historical patterns in order to break them. To build a better future, we should seek to more fully understand the "structural sins" of the past. And finally, acting on a true understanding of history will allow us to liberate ourselves from centuries of bigotry and exploitation.

It is my fervent hope that an honest accounting of the "structural sins" inherent in the relationship the United States and Europe have had and continue to have with Congo—exploitation entrenched over five centuries—will lead to more understanding of Congo's current struggles and greater acknowledgment of the degree to which the progress of the West has come at the expense of Congo's people and resources. And that understanding and acknowledgment will in turn lead to real action to reverse the negative patterns of the past.

This book, its accompanying website, and the activities we will undertake are just small contributions to this mammoth task. But having come to know the Congolese in this book and beyond, whose lead we follow, I am filled with hope.

John Prendergast
Washington, DC
August 2018